STRATEGY FOR DEFEAT

Vietnam in Retrospect

Admiral U.S.G. Sharp

STRATEGY FOR DEFEAT
Vietnam in Retrospect

Admiral U. S. Grant Sharp, U. S. Navy (Retired)

PRESIDIO PRESS

This edition printed in 1998

Published by Presidio Press
505 B San Marin Drive, Suite 300
Novato, CA 94945

Library of Congress Cataloging in Publication Data

Sharp, Ulysses S. Grant, 1906–
  Strategy for defeat.
  Includes bibliographical references and index.
  1. Vietnamese Conflict, 1961—1975—Untied States. 2. United
States—History—1945. I. Title.
DS558.S46   959.704'33'73   78-17607
ISBN 0-89141-672-2 (paperback)

Printed in the United States of America

To my children and grandchildren

ILLUSTRATIONS

x

INTRODUCTION

Debate about the effective use of our air and sea power during recent international crises convinces me that this account of my experience during the Vietnam War is as relevant today as it was when initially published. The tragic misuse of air and naval power in the Vietnam War, where the United States had a decisive military advantage, resulted in an unnecessarily protracted and costly war. The indecisive prosecution of the war fragmented the cohesiveness of our society and undermined the public's respect for their government and military. We blundered into a strategy for defeat.

The 1991 Gulf War was waged with the lessons of Vietnam obviously in mind. President George Bush clearly articulated Gulf War military objectives and grand strategy. He empowered military commanders to develop a strategy for victory. Forceful and determined presidential leadership avoided any chance of a stalemate and entanglement in fruitless negotiations. The president rushed large military forces to the theater of war and insisted on their early use against enemy forces. Overwhelming air power applied quickly achieved objectives with minimal losses. As a result, a blazing tempo of operations imposed a rate of destructive punishment that shattered the enemy's cohesion and military capacity, ending in defeat of Iraq's forces and liberation of Kuwait.

While there were many important differences between the Gulf and Vietnam Wars, decisive differences were in the policies and methods adopted for controlling their conduct. Determined commitment, delegation of authority, speed of decision making, speed of force buildup, and speed of combat power applied against Iraq governed the conduct of the Gulf War. In contrast, irresolute commitment, centralization of authority, hesitant decision making, prolonged force buildup, and self-imposed constraints on the application of combat power against North Vietnam characterized the direction of the Vietnam War. *Strategy For Defeat* illustrates the consequences of flawed policies and methods that controlled the use of air and naval power during the Vietnam War.

My desire is that we never forget the lessons of this defeat. These timeless lessons apply to future uses of air power. My account will interest a whole new generation of media, politicians, policy makers, analysts, historians, scholars, military, and most importantly the public. For many in this new generation our Vietnam defeat is only a dim memory. Yet many in this new generation may soon be thrust into shaping, influencing, questioning or supporting our military objectives and strategy. I hope my experiences as related here will help this generation to avoid the critical mistakes of the Vietnam War.

The media is a major force in determining the level of popular support engendered for military operations. Popular support is essential to the American way of war. Well-informed media have an obligation to appreciate and report the sound aspects of military strategy while recognizing and exposing serious deficiencies. The media can find insights here that will help them discriminate between those courses of action that exploit our military advantages and those that fail to fully use our strengths.

The president and his closest civilian advisors have the ultimate authority for determining military strategy in our form of government. They bear a heavy responsibility to inform themselves about the possible uses and misuses of military force and the nature of the foe we contemplate engaging. These civilian authorities determine the process by which military advice is sought on objectives and strategies. They commit the nation's resources necessary to engage in conflict. Elected civilian authorities have their will and determination to prosecute a successful conflict challenged at every turn and from every corner. I hope my experiences as related here will help elected authorities in guiding our military efforts wisely.

A large group of individuals, in and out of government, influence military policy in many ways. They are the national security policy makers currently serving in the executive and legislative branches, as well as military analysts, historians, teachers and students of national security affairs.

I describe how people from this group influenced choices made about our strategy during the Vietnam War.

The military will find from my experiences strong motivation to convey required courses of action clearly to their civilian superiors. They also will see the importance of specifying the level of commitment that could become necessary to secure success when adopting a particular strategy. From my account, insights can be gleaned about the pitfalls arising out of disagreements and misunderstanding over intended strategy and tactics between the military and their civilian superiors.

Citizens will find information in my narrative that make them better able to judge how well their armed forces are commanded by the civilian authorities they elect to fulfill this awesome duty. The public can relate the lessons described here to debates about the future use of air and naval power.

FOREWORD

For of all sad words of tongue or pen,
The saddest are these: "It might have been!"

This book, though indispensable to future historians, will prove to be agonizing reading to all those who believe that Vietnam was a war that could—and should—have been won. And to those with other points of view, a study of Admiral Sharp's frustrating experiences will surely provide basic documentation and historical enlightenment and some balance to the prevalent shibboleths—all too often accepted uncritically—that Vietnam was inherently wicked and unwinnable.

This chilling narrative of how to lose a war must have particular poignancy to anyone who saw at first hand the courage and sacrifice of so many of the men who fought in Vietnam—most of them unhonored and unsung now in their own country.

In the fall of 1965 the 1st Cavalry Division (Air Mobile) was hastily thrown into what its troopers called "on-the-job-fighting." They were rushed into the Vietnamese highlands as one of the first of many U. S. units to build dikes against the tide of Communist aggression from the north. In its initial battles some of the division's units suffered heavily in killed and wounded. I shall never forget an after-action talk I had with the commander of one of the outfits involved back at the division's base camp. He had been severely affected—as all good commanders are—by the loss of his men. He had led them bravely in action; now he had just buried the dead and was facing the melancholy task of writing the letters of bereavement to their families. But, already as we talked, the indecisiveness and vacillation of our Washington leadership and the alienation of many media representatives in Vietnam were beginning to be apparent.

"What if we don't win this war?" I asked.

The colonel's eyes filled with tears. "I could never face my men or the families of the dead again," he said. "I would have to turn in my suit."

But in those days I never really believed we would have to think about the unthinkable—defeat.

The unthinkable has now become past history, though its consequences go on and on, and we shall not be able to assuage them completely during the lifetime of this generation.

If we are not to be condemned to repeat the past, we had best learn from it. This is Admiral Sharp's purpose—that and to put the woefully distorted record straight.

This is a textbook of how *not* to win a war—a recipe for defeat. It deals primarily with one aspect of the Vietnam War—the view from the headquarters of the war's top operational commander, the Commander in Chief Pacific, at Hawaii. Sharp presents war as he saw it, through official despatches, briefings, contacts and conversations. This *is* the record; little is left to memory. The author deals primarily with the bombing of North Vietnam—perhaps the most flagrant misuse of air power in its brief history—and with the attempts of the services to shut off the source of Viet Cong supplies at the source by mining and/or blockading the North Vietnamese coast. He deals only inferentially with the ground warfare in the south. His book makes it clear that Washington—not the military on the scene—lost the Vietnam War.

Gradually the truth will out. This volume is a good companion piece to *A Soldier Reports*, the memoirs of Gen. William C. Westmoreland, the U. S. commander in the south, and to Peter Braestrup's *The Big Story*, a meticulously detailed exposé of the distortions, inaccuracy and bias of the media before, during and after the Tet offensive of 1968.

These books and other much-needed correctives to the widely accepted perceptions of Vietnam make it clear that the blame for the lost war rests, *not* upon the men in uniform, but upon the civilian policy makers in Washington—those who evolved and developed the policies of gradualism, flexible response, off-again-on-again bombing, negotiated victory, and, ultimately, one-arm-behind-the-back restraint, and scuttle-and-run.

I have never believed—nor does Admiral Sharp believe—that air power alone is the single key to victory in conventional war. It did not win World War II, though victory probably could not have been won without it. It failed to strangle Chinese lines of supply in the famous "Operation Strangle" in Korea. And we lost the war in Vietnam despite the unprecedented tonnage of bombs dropped on the north.

But one must look beyond the panoply of statistics, as Admiral Sharp has done, or—as he writes—we shall "bury yesterday's mistakes under today's obsessions."

To put it tersely, again in the author's words, our Vietnam policies, forged in Washington, forced our military men to "the most asinine way to fight a war that could possibly be imagined." In effect, the failure to employ properly the tremendously superior U. S. air and sea power in Vietnam caused thousands of unnecessary U. S. and South Vietnamese casualties on the ground in South Vietnam, indefinitely prolonged the fighting, and resulted ultimately in the loss of the war. And our political ploys with Hanoi— to "negotiate victory"—repeated the same basic political and psychological negotiating mistakes we had made in Korea, despite emphatic and reiterated warnings.

For these results—for this first defeat in American history—the historical blame must be placed squarely where it belongs—*not* primarily upon our military leaders whose continuous and protracted frustrations burst forth from these pages—but upon the very top civilian policy makers in Washington, specifically the Commander in Chief. President Lyndon B. Johnson fashioned what

Sharp tersely describes as a "strategy of equivocation." He blew hot and cold; he could not make up his mind. He tried to apply the strategy of domestic policies—consensus and compromise—to battlefields where fire power alone was the arbiter. He built his policies, too, on a number of completely mistaken assumptions. In short, he took counsel of his fears and never fully enlisted—as any great war leader must always do—the country's strengths, either physically or psychologically.

But his right-hand man in this "strategy of equivocation," indeed, an architect of it, was the then Secretary of Defense Robert S. McNamara, and the "whiz kids" and arrogant academicians who surrounded him.

These faceless civilians—nearly all of them theorists, few of them with pragmatic backgrounds, virtually all of them military amateurs—were brilliant statisticians, theoretical analysts, computer experts, but they tended to scorn the experience factor, and they had scant use for what they believed to be the limitations of the military mind. These second- or third-level political appointees exercised great authority with no responsibility (save to the bar of history), and they used it ruthlessly to override, subvert, compromise, distort or destroy opposing points of view.

These are the men who, with "flagrant arrogance or naive wishful-thinking," fashioned the policies of defeat in Vietnam; some of them—unfortunately—have returned to positions of influence and power in Washington today.

Yet to allocate blame where it belongs is not enough and is certainly not the sole or primary purpose of this important volume. We must learn from the past; the truth may save us tomorrow; we must never repeat the stupidities of yesterday.

This book deserves wide reading as a source of history and a lesson in political science. It may even help to prevent the decline and fall—after so brief a record—of the United States of America.

Hanson W. Baldwin
Roxbury, Connecticut
March, 1978

PREFACE

I offer this book to the American public as my personal exposition of one of the more dramatic phenomena in American history, the debacle of our involvement in the Vietnam conflict. My desire to do so stems from two sources: first, my belief that lessons learned derive primarily from mistakes scrupulously analyzed; and, second, my professional role during four of the most crucial years of this tragically extended war.

Here, then, is my uncensored account not merely of the Vietnam War, but also of the effects of that war on the promise of peace for all Americans.

Here, more importantly, is my account of why America — for the first time — lost a war.

I became Commander in Chief Pacific on 30 June 1964, just before our first engagement with the North Vietnamese, and continued in that command until 31 July 1968. As such, I was in overall charge of all operations in the Pacific, covering an area extending from the west coast of the United States to the Indian Ocean, and including the Vietnam area. While I exercised overall supervision over our military actions in South Vietnam, the strategy and tactics of the ground war were left in the capable hands of the officers on the scene in South Vietnam, specifically the Commander U. S. Military Assistance Command Vietnam—first Gen. William C. Westmoreland, U. S. Army, and then Gen. Creighton W. Abrams, U. S. Army. However, the air war over North Vietnam was under my close, personal direction, exercising operational control through Commander in Chief U. S. Pacific Fleet, Commander in Chief Pacific Air Forces, and Commander U. S. Military Assistance Command Vietnam.

This book will concern itself in general with the overall strategy of the war, from my viewpoint, and in particular with the conduct of the air war over North Vietnam. I have consciously chosen not to discuss in any significant detail the strategic or tactical direction of the ground forces in South Vietnam since it is generally understood and accepted that ground forces are crucial to the defeat of an enemy in the rugged jungle terrains of Southeast Asia. I believe, however, that it is *not* generally understood that the conduct of the air war had a tremendous influence on the outcome of this conflict and was an especially revealing example of near-flagrant misuse of air power. This needs setting straight in the record books.

Throughout the text I quote extensively from official dispatches between my headquarters and the Joint Chiefs of Staff. These messages were recorded in a series of "oral history" interviews I gave to the U.S. Naval Institute and were cleared by the Department of Defense for declassification in connection with the publication of those interviews. The Department of Defense publication "United States—Vietnam Relations 1945–1967" (referred to hereafter by its infamous pseudonym, the Pentagon Papers) is also a major source of chronology and pertinent facts. This twelve-volume document contains an enormous amount of information on decision making at the Washington level, and it combined well with my own oral history recordings to sharpen my memory of many events in which I participated vis-à-vis the subject at hand.

The reader will note, moreover, that this book is not a personal memoir and I have in general avoided dealing in personalities. With few exceptions, my concern herein is to discuss and critique from my perspective the *decisions* that were made, without digressing into an assessment of the personal character traits of the people who made them.

Looking to the past, this study of the strategy and tactics of the war should provide an important complement to any comprehensive history of our total involvement. Critics of the war frequently describe our use of air power—specifically the bombing—as a failure. Our air power did not fail us; it was the decision makers. And if I am unsurprisingly critical of those decision makers, I offer no apology. My conscience and professional record both stand clear. Just as I believe unequivocally that the civilian authority is supreme under our Constitution, so I hold it reasonable that, once committed, the political leadership should seek and, in the main, heed the advice of the military professionals in the conduct of military operations.

Looking to the future, the taxpayer today sees much of his tax dollar going to support military air power, and he may well ask, "Why should we spend more money on air power? It didn't get the job done in Vietnam." My purpose is primarily to tell those who will listen how air power could have done the job if only it had been used properly, and also to justify, thereby, its future utility.

The United States made a major effort in this protracted conflict to achieve its stated objective—an independent, non-Communist South Vietnam. We failed. An in-depth analysis of that failure is essential to ensure that those mistakes are not repeated. I hope this narrative will be an important contribution to such an investigation.

U. S. Grant Sharp
Admiral, U. S. Navy (Ret.)

ACKNOWLEDGMENTS

I am deeply indebted to many friends and associates who assisted me in taking the manuscript of this book through several revisions before it finally went to the publisher. To begin with, it was Gen. Wallace M. Greene, Jr., U. S. Marine Corps (Ret.), who some time ago urged me to write about my experiences as Commander in Chief Pacific during four of the most crucial years of the Vietnam War. The noted journalist, Hanson Baldwin, reviewed an early draft, gave me much sound advice and encouragement, and graciously offered to write the foreword. Comments from such a seasoned and respected military writer add a special quality for which I am most grateful.

Subsequently, Dr. James D. Atkinson, Professor of International Relations at Georgetown University, reviewed the manuscript, as did Ted Sell, former military correspondent for the *Los Angeles Times* with a considerable background in Vietnamese affairs. Both provided most useful suggestions on style and substance. I also received a valuable added perspective on the air war in my discussions with Vice Adm. James B. Stockdale, U. S. Navy, as well as his generous permission to quote his remarks at two pertinent points in the text.

I am most indebted also to Capt. Robin L. Quigley, U. S. Navy (Ret.), who worked hundreds of hours with me as we produced the last three revisions of the text. Her great gift for clarity and forceful-ness of expression, and her ability to smooth out my sometimes disjointed presentation, combined to make the manuscript salable. It has been a pleasure to have the assistance of this brilliant and tal-ented woman, who has come to hold a special place in our family.

There is, of course, no measure to the contribution made by my loving wife Pat, who, during the years that this book was develop-ing, patiently put up with the mess that an amateur author creates. She kept our home functioning smoothly in the calm and efficient manner that has made our forty-eight years of married life a constant pleasure.

The great fund of data that I used in preparing the book was available to me in general through the able performance of the officer and enlisted personnel who served on my staff at Pacific Command Headquarters, most notably because of the superb competence and foresight of Capt. Rembrandt C. Robinson, U. S. Navy, my Execu-tive Assistant. Tragically, in both a professional and personal sense, this top-flight naval officer, by then a Rear Admiral, lost his life in a helicopter accident in the Gulf of Tonkin in 1972.

Finally, I am grateful in the broadest context to the millions of Americans who fought for their country in this misunderstood war. To them belongs my ultimate and humble acknowledgment for what they gave to all of us.

CHAPTER 1

VIETNAM: THE VISION AND THE TRAGEDY

I N FEBRUARY 1965, after a long and tortuous prelude, President Lyndon B. Johnson committed U.S. armed forces to combat to save South Vietnam from being overrun by Communist aggression from North Vietnam. Our motives, as I understand them, were altruistic. We wanted the South Vietnamese to be able to determine their own form of government without interference from North Vietnam. At the peak of the fighting we had 550,000 American troops in South Vietnam; in the aggregate we lost 55,000 of our fighting men and spent about 150 billion dollars. We disengaged in 1973 with a single objective won—the release of our POWs. Having supplied South Vietnam well with military equipment prior to the Paris agreement of January 1973, Congress subsequently cut military aid so drastically that the South Vietnamese had insufficient supplies, fuel, and ammunition. In early 1975, President Nguyen Van Thieu ordered a partial withdrawal to consolidate his defense perimeter. The retreat became a rout, and South Vietnam was overrun.

For the first time in United States history we had become engaged in a conflict in which we failed to gain a satisfactory settlement.

1

How did we fail? We had superior forces; why didn't we win?

The world was amazed that North Vietnam was able to hold off the United States for so many years and to make progress with their aggression in South Vietnam. This despite the fact that the United States poured division after division of good American fighting men into South Vietnam and assembled a mighty air armada. We seemed unable to bring Hanoi to the conference table to negotiate a satisfactory termination to this conflict.

There have been all kinds of explanations for this phenomenon. Some said it was the fierce dedication of the North Vietnamese people. Some blamed it on our inability to fight effectively in Communist-infested jungles. Partial answers, at best. In a sense, of course, the North Vietnamese people were dedicated. In an autocratic dictatorship the ordinary soldier is either "dedicated" to the cause or is liquidated by political commissars! And, contrary to popular belief, our troops did fight well in the jungles. My explanation rests in a simple but grave tragedy: we were never allowed to move decisively with our tremendous air and naval power.

Once the decision was made to participate in this war and engage Americans in the military conflict, I believe we should have taken the steps necessary to end the war successfully in the shortest possible time. It was folly to commit Americans to combat and then force them to fight without utilizing the means we so richly possessed to win an early victory. It is my firm belief, however, that we did exactly that by not using our air and naval power to its full effectiveness. Instead, we lapsed into a concept of gradualism. Slowly, very slowly, we increased the pressure on North Vietnam in a series of nibbles that permitted them to build up their defenses and to anticipate every move we made. Meanwhile we poured more and more army soldiers and marines into South Vietnam to fight a ground war without giving them the full support of our powerful air force and naval air arms. This policy resulted only in a long and drawn-out war with far too many killed and wounded unnecessarily.

We could have brought the Vietnam War to a successful conclusion in short order, early in the game, once the decision had been made by the civilian leadership to engage with U. S. forces. All we needed to do was assemble the necessary force and then use it the way it was designed to be used. (I do *not* include atomic weapons in my definition of necessary force. In my view, there was never a need for employing nuclear devices in Southeast Asia, and I never recommended such.) In fact, we assembled the necessary force quite rapidly. By mid-1965 we had strong air power available. By 1966 we had the full measure of air power to do the job, and our ground forces were strong enough that in combination with such air power properly applied we could have forced Hanoi to give up its efforts to take over South Vietnam. But authority to use our air power to this end was simply not forthcoming.

From the very beginning I recommended to the Joint Chiefs of Staff (JCS) that we take military action to resolve this conflict as quickly as possible. I wanted to hit the enemy where it hurt—in the heartland of North Vietnam. We should have done this *before* the enemy was given the chance to deploy an effective air defense system. The JCS strongly supported my recommendations and did everything in their power to get on with the war, but the roadblocks were unbelievable. They will become apparent in the ensuing chapters.

More than eighty-five percent of the sinews of war arriving in North Vietnam came in by sea through the port of Haiphong. Ships flying the Soviet flag—or the flags of Soviet satellites such as East Germany and Poland—regularly poured material of war into that seaport, and cargoes were unloaded twenty-four hours a day. Every available pier space was occupied, and the anchorages were crowded.

Repeatedly my messages, which the JCS supported, urged the aerial mining of the harbors of North Vietnam, but we were never able to get authorization. At long last, in 1972, President Nixon authorized the mining of those harbors. They were mined in a one-day operation and were closed to all shipping until *we* swept the mines in 1973, after the so-called truce. The mine-laying operation cost the United States less than a million dollars. Not a single person on either side was lost. Why didn't we do this in 1965? Or in 1967? Or in 1969?

I recommended early on, and unremittingly, that we use air power to destroy the overland supply routes from China to Hanoi, but this was not permitted until much later in the war, and then only in such a limited manner as to be ineffective.

The element of surprise has always been an extremely important factor in successful military operations, but we were very infrequently able to utilize it in the air war against North Vietnam. Since we were forced to move target selections from the southern part of North Vietnam up toward the heartland in small steps over a protracted period, the enemy could predict with reasonable accuracy when the important targets would be hit. They could make all preparations to receive our pilots with the maximum amount of defense power. As a result, about seventy percent of our POWs were captured while on missions over North Vietnam.

Why were we not permitted to fight this war to win? In my view, it was partly because political and diplomatic circles in Washington were disproportionately concerned with the possibility of Communist Chinese and Soviet intervention. In addition to the apparent specter of the mythical "hordes" of Chinese coming down from the north, or a supposed "confrontation" with the Soviet Union that would result in a much wider war, the leadership in these circles was also conspicuously sensitive to so-called world opinion. More debilitating, however, was what appeared to be the political leadership's naive hope that a major involvement could somehow be avoided by using a "carrot and stick" sort of diplomacy as a means of initiating negotiations with the North Vietnamese. I shall have more to say about this delusion. For now, it is enough to say that while such concerns and hopes may be understandable in a reasonable balance, they are inexcusable in the obsessive form, and in fact effectively throttled the military's ability to conclude successfully the commitment into which that leadership had drawn us.

And, for that matter, why were we drawn into this commitment in the first place? Leaving to others the already well-trodden ground of moral, ethical, and foreign policy issues inherent in that question, I do say there was a logical (which does not necessarily equate to justifiable) sequence of events that led us into this unfortunate war, and I consider their review essential to the context of my discussion about the crucial years of military involvement.

CHAPTER 2

How Did The United States Get Involved?

THE INVOLVEMENT OF the United States in Southeast Asia can be traced back to 1954 when the Geneva agreements were signed. The U. S. position was that these agreements—or disagreements—enhanced the opportunity for Communist exploitation of Southeast Asia. We were determined to contain that exploitation if possible by collective action with our Free World allies. A review of the chronology of events reveals the logic of our deepening commitment.

During World War II, the United States pursued a somewhat ambiguous policy toward Indochina. Although we appeared to support France's position that all her colonial possessions (to include Indochina) should be returned to her after the war, we were also deeply committed to the Atlantic Charter, which supported national self-determination for all countries. In particular, President Roosevelt pushed hard for eventual independence for Indochina, believing that it should be turned over to a trusteeship rather than being returned to France. He was thwarted, however, by the military parameters of the situation. Since the United States had concentrated its forces against Japan rather than in the Southeast Asia theater, it had accepted the fact that the British would have military cognizance in that area. But in September 1945, French military forces began replacing the British in former French colonies and protectorates in Southeast Asia, and by April of 1946, when the official Allied occupation of Indochina was terminated, they had succeeded (not without the use of considerable force to subdue opposition from Vietnamese guerrilla forces) in reestablishing full French control over the area. The United States was forced to acknowledge the fact of this *fait accompli* and the problems of U. S. policy toward Vietnam were subsequently dealt with in the context of our relationship with France.

By this time, open defiance of French rule in Vietnam was being actively pursued by the Viet Minh (a Communist-oriented Vietnamese resistance movement, initially against the Japanese). Their leader, Ho Chi Minh, had been trained and was obviously being supported to a large degree by the Russians. Our concerns about what this trend might portend were considerably heightened with the collapse of the Chinese Nationalists in 1949, and by the end of that year, U. S. policy was firmly directed toward blocking further Communist expansion in Asia. Although we considered the preferable course to be one of encouraging the Asians themselves to develop collective security, in collaboration with major European allies, we were willing, if necessary, to step in directly and make bilateral agreements to achieve our goal. (It was this policy that led the United States to join with South Korea in opposing the Communist powers in the Korean War of 1950-53.)

In early 1950, while still engaged in trying to either suppress or negotiate an end to Viet Minh resistance, the French formally ratified independence for Vietnam. The Vietnamese leader at that time was the former emperor, Bao Dai. Having abdicated the throne in 1945 in favor of the Viet Minh Provisional Government of the Democratic Republic of Vietnam (DRVN), Bao Dai had spent the better part of four years in exile by the time he returned to rule in 1949. Despite his success in negotiating Vietnam's independence from France, he was a passive and ineffective head of state. The French, in granting independence, had in fact yielded very little control, and the internal affairs of the country were soon more chaotic than ever. The Vietnamese army was dependent on French leadership—the Bao Dai regime virtually impotent. There seemed to be no viable alternatives at the time (except for the unacceptable one of eventual Communist domination), and it was apparent that the French alone held the key to containing communism in Indochina. So, although the United States would have preferred to see a more truly independent democratic-nationalist government in operation, we were forced into accepting strong French supervision of Bao Dai's government of South Vietnam.

In response to a French request, the U. S. Secretary of State, Dean Acheson, announced in May 1950 that we would give economic aid and military equipment to the Associated States of Indochina (Vietnam, Cambodia and Laos) and to France in order to assist them in restoring stability and permitting these states to pursue their peaceful and democratic development. President Truman approved ten million dollars of aid in urgently needed military assistance items for Indochina, and a Military Assistance Advisory Group (MAAG) was set up in Saigon to oversee the project.

During the Eisenhower administration, we became even more committed to an anti-Communist policy in Southeast Asia, and State Department policies were geared to preventing the loss of Indochina. China was openly warned not to intervene, and the French were exhorted to use maximum military effort to expel the Communist insurgents.

By late 1953, however, the French appeared to be in danger of succumbing in their battle with the Viet Minh, and an intense debate was generated within our government on the desirability and feasibility of military intervention by U. S. forces. The Department of Defense (to include the JCS) rejected an initial proposal to confine our intervention to air and naval forces only on the theory that such a limited commitment would never turn the tide of Viet Minh advances. On the other hand, President Eisenhower was apparently unwilling to intervene with U. S. forces of any size or nature without congressional approval, which was unlikely unless there was active allied participation. Consequently, when French requests for direct U. S. military assistance at Dien Bien Phu* brought the matter to a head, the Eisenhower administration took the position that we would only respond as part of a combined force of a number of our European and Far Eastern allies. Support for such united action was not forthcoming, however, except in Thailand and the Philippines. The British, for example, were not only hesitant to become involved, but were in downright opposition to taking direct military action at this time. In the end, President Eisenhower remained convinced that unilateral action on our part would be a mistake, and the French were left to face the final tragedy of defeat at Dien Bien Phu on their own.

The Geneva Conference, which convened on 26 April 1954, was called by the United States, the Soviet Union, France, and Great Britain ostensibly to seek a solution to the Korean War, but also—and more importantly—to find a compromise settlement for the Indochina conflict. No agreement was reached on the Korean problem, and the Indochina war became the major issue for discussion early on. Delegates from nine states were in attendance: France, Great Britain, the United States, the Soviet Union, the People's Republic of China, Cambodia, Laos, Bao Dai's Government of South Vietnam. (India sent an observer later.)

The Viet Minh took a strong position at Geneva, arguing that they spoke for all of the Indochinese people. Their aim was to achieve French withdrawal, leaving the way open for them to im-

---

*Dien Bien Phu was a remote outpost and airfield on an access route to Laos, about 160 miles west of Hanoi and near the North Vietnam-Laos border. French General Henri Navarre chose this site to engage the Viet Minh under General Vo Nguyen Giap, believing the Viet Minh would eventually run out of supplies while the French could be resupplied by air. However, Giap did maintain his supply line by using porters, and furthermore, he broke the French supply line by interdicting the French airstrip with Chinese-supplied artillery. Forty thousand Viet Minh opposed about 20,000 French in a battle that started on 13 March 1954. The Viet Minh gradually closed in on the encircled French forces and overwhelmed them on 7 May.

pose their will on the vulnerable non-Communist population. Their specific objectives were partition at the thirteenth parallel (giving them about two-thirds of Vietnam), complete withdrawal of opposition forces from the north, and nationwide elections to be held six months after an armistice. Interestingly enough, they were frustrated in their desires by the conciliatory mood of Moscow and Peking, who appeared determined to dissuade U. S. intervention by any diplomatic means available.

The conference finally ended on 21 July 1954 with the partitioning of Vietnam at the seventeenth parallel, which gave the government of South Vietnam about half the total territory. Elections, to be internationally rather than locally controlled, were postponed for two years. More than likely the Communist states involved—the Soviet Union, Communist China, and North Vietnam—held the private view that a stable situation in South Vietnam was highly problematic and that North Vietnam would eventually gain control of the entire country. Under the terms of the Geneva Accords, France became the guarantor of South Vietnam's sovereignty, unity, and territorial integrity, and was designated to supervise and guarantee the all-Vietnam elections to be held two years after the accords were signed.

United States policy toward Indochina began to change as the Geneva Conference closed. This revision was spurred by the belief that Geneva had been a major setback for Free World security interests in the Far East, giving the Communists a new foothold in Southeast Asia and enhancing Peking's prestige, while restricting the movements of the Free World in that area.

The first step toward countering this situation was the formation of the Southeast Asia Treaty Organization (SEATO). Secretary Dulles hoped that SEATO would form a strong anti-Communist shield to prevent further Communist expansion in Southeast Asia, but the SEATO treaty was not as strong as he would have liked. Article IV of the treaty, which is the mechanism for collective action in case of an enemy threat, did not pledge automatic response with force. Instead, each signatory promised to "act to meet the common danger in accordance with its constitutional processes." Overall, however, the obligation assumed in the SEATO treaty emphasized how important the United States government now considered Southeast Asia to be.

The post-Geneva period saw France embroiled in internal political difficulties as well as significant colonial problems in Algeria. Consequently, her policies toward South Vietnam were becoming more and more ineffectual and disinterested. This strained our patience to the point where, by late September 1954, we began to bypass France and negotiate our offers of assistance directly with South Vienamese Premier Ngo Dinh Diem, his government, and his armed forces.

The French were obviously disgruntled at this turn of events (as indeed were some members of our own government), and diplomatic relations between France and this country grew more uncomfortable. As a consequence, the JCS reversed their earlier stand in opposition to our assuming responsibility for training the army of South Vietnam, and now took the position that if political considerations did dictate such U. S. involvement, then the training-mission assignment to MAAG Saigon should specifically guard against French interference.

In November of 1954, Gen. J. Lawton Collins, U. S. Army, was sent to South Vietnam with broad authority to coordinate all U. S. programs. His directions were to get things moving, with French support, and by December he and French General Paul Ely had come to an understanding. The French were to grant full autonomy to the army of South Vietnam by July of the following year. The United States would assume primary training responsibility through MAAG Saigon, but under General Ely's overall authority, and both French and U. S. instructors would be phased out as the Vietnamese army became more efficient. Washington approved the agreement, but the French objected at first, particularly to the phase-out of the French trainers. After an exchange of views, however, they finally agreed to the understanding in February of 1955.

Meanwhile, Premier Ngo Dinh Diem had been gradually taking over control of the government from the titular head of state, Bao Dai. By now Diem had become virtually a dictator, but his administration was coming under strong fire. Though he had managed to keep in line both the army leaders and the several armed factions which roamed the country, he was by no means assured of long-term political success. To make matters worse, Bao Dai (who by now was living in exile in France), in retaliation for Diem's growing strength, was actively seeking to supplant him. Diem, for his part, was increasingly reactive to both the French and Bao Dai. The French were openly hostile to Diem. They considered him incapable of unifying South Vietnam and advised that he be replaced, but at the time there was no one on the scene who could realistically challenge his position. So he remained in power.

In March and April of 1955 Diem successfully engaged the South Vietnamese army in turning aside a direct challenge to his authority by the armed sects (politico-religious groups called the Cao Dai, Hoa Hao, and Binh Xuyen, anti-Communist in orientation and basically feudalistic). Encouraged by Diem's victory in this instance, the United States declared its support for him as opposed to Bao Dai. The French saw this as mandating their ultimate complete withdrawal from South Vietnam, and although temporary compromise was eventually struck, the end of joint U. S.-French policy in Vietnam had effectively been reached.

In October of that year, Diem won an overwhelming victory by a popular referendum in which the voters were given the choice between him and Bao Dai. The South Vietnamese Republic was born, and, some six months later, on 26 April 1956, the French high command in Saigon was finally disestablished.

The Geneva Accords had called for consultations between North and South Vietnam in preparation for the national elections to be held in July of 1956, and had stated explicitly that those elections must be free and under international supervision. President Diem had consistently maintained that he would not participate in the elections, since he considered that they could not be free in North Vietnam. He was quite correct—there was no way to hold free elections in North Vietnam under the Communist dictatorship. The deadline for the elections passed without international action and, therefore, the seventeenth parallel, with its demilitarized zone on either side, became an international boundary de facto.

As provided for in the Geneva Accords, 900,000 civilians moved voluntarily from North Vietnam to South Vietnam, and more than 100,000 Viet Minh soldiers and civilians in the south were permitted to relocate to the north. In both cases, these groups had considerable impact on events in their adopted homelands despite their minority status. For example, the refugees from the north were living proof that there was oppression and terror in North Vietnam from which to flee, and they provided convincing evidence for Diem's argument that free elections there would be impossible. In addition, the idea of hundreds of thousands of people fleeing their homes and fortunes to escape Communist tyranny captured the sympathies of the American people, who responded with an out-pouring of U. S. aid, both governmental and private, thereby cementing our decision to support Diem.

The Geneva settlement had called for an International Control Commission (ICC) to supervise and control the terms of the agreement. This body, manned by Poland, India, and Canada, was supposed to ensure that the strength of the armed forces of both North and South Vietnam was fixed at the level existing in 1954, that further foreign influences were excluded, and that neither country allowed its territory to be used for renewal of aggression. It became evident very soon that the ICC was powerless. The Communist members refused to join in any investigation that might uncover activities adverse to them. The Indian members were highly sympathetic to the Communists. Only the Canadians would take an unbiased stand on any matter, and they were rendered virtually powerless by the obstructionist tactics of the other two member nations.

Under Diem's leadership, South Vietnam had become well established as a sovereign state by 1955. He had installed a government that was as representative as any in that part of the world, had drafted a new constitution, and had extended South Vietnamese government control to regions that had been under the Viet Minh or under rule of one of the sects for a decade. With American help he started to establish a modern army and formed rural security forces to police the countryside. In accomplishing all of this, he surprised the Vietnamese in the north, who had expected his imminent downfall.

Unfortunately, Diem's political concepts severely hampered his effectiveness as a democratic leader. Despite the fact that he was a staunch Roman Catholic and had been exposed extensively to Western philosophies by both travel and education, he remained committed to the old, mandarin ways and to Vietnam's past. As a result, the political structure of his government was rigidly organized, overcentralized and dominated by Diem family members. In the long run, his personality combined with his political shortcomings to alienate the peasantry and, indeed, most of the rest of Vietnamese society, until, by late 1960, his regime rested chiefly on its own bureaucracy.

The history of the armed resistance against Diem, which has been pieced together fairly accurately from studies of defectors, prisoners of war, and captured documents, can be traced through three general periods. The first, from 1954 through 1957, was marked by random dissidence in the countryside, which Diem succeeded in quelling. The second period began with South Vietnam seeming to enjoy the first peace it had known for over a decade. By mid-1957, however, incidents of violence attributed to the Viet Cong were noted and grew in intensity through 1959. The Viet Cong (a derogatory contraction of a term meaning Vietnamese Communist) were Communist guerrilla groups active in South Vietnam, principally composed of South Vietnamese but including some migrants from the north. They cooperated with, but were not part of, the North Vietnamese army units which later operated in South Vietnam. And finally, the third period was characterized by full-scale military activity. In early 1959 Diem responded to the increasingly serious attacks by committing the army of South Vietnam to fight the dissidents. In short order the Viet Cong showed themselves able to field units of battalion size against regular army formations, and by 1960 they could operate in sufficient strength to seize provincial capitals and hold them for periods of time up to twenty-four hours. They were also able to cut off entire districts from communications with government-controlled towns.

The Viet Cong were not alone in their effort. Captured documents and prisoner interrogations show that in 1957 and 1958 some activity was being generated by the Communists from Hanoi. For example, the party was apparently taking pains to construct an underground apparatus in South Vietnam, which used assassinations and kidnappings, but avoided military operations. Then in May of

1959 the Communist party of North Vietnam adopted a resolution identifying the United States as an enemy of peace and as the main obstacle to the realization of the hopes of all the Vietnamese people. This resolution called for a strong North Vietnam as a base for helping the sympathetic South Vietnamese to overthrow Diem and eject the United States. We know from studying testimony of high-ranking captives that the South Vietnamese Communists regarded this resolution as the point of departure for North Vietnamese intervention in the south. There is also evidence that in forming their strategy, Hanoi obtained concurrence from Moscow at each critical juncture for each new aggressive course of action. It is quite clear that the objective of the North Vietnamese, as well as that of the Soviets and Chinese, was Communist control of South Vietnam.

The South Vietnamese army was at a distinct disadvantage at this time since the departure of the French Expeditionary Corps in 1955 had, unfortunately, left it virtually devoid of officer leadership, a role that had been almost exclusively filled by the French. The United States was therefore faced with the very challenging problem of training an army that had no middle- or high-level leadership. Also, although the early effort had been to mold the South Vietnamese forces into shape to combat aggression from the north, concentrating by and large on conventional tactics, the changing picture now dictated that an anti-guerrilla capability should be developed within the regular force structure. In March of 1960, the JCS took steps to accomplish this, and in May the MAAG was authorized to place U. S. advisers in the South Vietnamese army echelons down to the battalion level. The following month additional U. S. Army Special Forces arrived in South Vietnam. They worked quickly, and during the summer a number of Vietnamese Ranger Battalions were activated for counter-guerrilla operations.

When President John F. Kennedy took office, the prospect of an eventual crisis in South Vietnam was evident. Our Ambassador in Saigon, Elbridge Durbow, had even suggested that we might have to consider replacing Diem at some time in the future. Nonetheless, the new President moved within ten days to authorize a forty-one million dollar increase in aid to South Vietnam to underwrite both a force-level increase and improvements in the civil guard. In return for this assistance, Diem was asked to institute a number of reforms, all of which appeared to make good sense. (For example, it was vital that he straighten out the command arrangements for the Vietnamese army, under which *forty-two* different officials were *directly* responsible to Diem and shared operational command. These forty-two officials included thirty-three province chiefs, three regional commanders, and the Chief of Staff of the army!)

In March of 1961, Ambassador Durbow was routinely transferred to another post and Frederick E. Nolting became U. S. Ambassador to the Republic of Vietnam.

Negotiations over the changes the United States wanted in South Vietnam were both difficult and protracted. The essential reforms proposed, including those to which Diem had seemed to agree, were never really put into effect; although Diem promised action on some of the points and finally even issued some decrees, none of them was followed up. Eventually it became obvious that pressuring Diem would serve no purpose, and a campaign to win his confidence was embarked upon as a more productive approach.

The situation in Laos at this time was affecting our diplomatic relations and political thoughts in the South Vietnamese affair. The U. S.-backed and pro-American faction in that country, under Phoumi Nosavan, was losing to the Communist-neutralist faction which was supported by the Soviet Union and North Vietnam. Commitment of U. S. forces to Laos was even being considered. Since I was then serving as Deputy Chief of Naval Operations for Plans and Policy in Washington, an assignment that required me to attend JCS sessions, I can vividly recall the many arguments that went on about Laos and the determination of some JCS members that we not get our forces involved on the ground there. In any event, the use of U. S. forces in Laos at that time was rejected, and on 2 May 1961, a cease-fire was declared. President Kennedy took a compromise position and decided to support the coalition government, even though the odds were low that the coalition leader, Souvanna Phouma, would stay in power. As a consequence of this "middle-of-the-road" decision, however, there was increasing concern in the government that other Southeast Asian leaders would doubt the sincerity of the U. S. commitment to the area. It seemed necessary to do something that would restore their confidence and demonstrate to the international community that the United States was resolved not to withdraw from that part of the world. It is obvious, then, that even at this stage our concerns about Laos were an integral part of the development of our policy toward South Vietnam.

Another factor that affected our attitude toward South Vietnam was the impact of the Bay of Pigs disaster, which took place on 20 April 1961. Adding to President Kennedy's concern over the situation in Laos, it made him more anxious than ever to present a strong program to save South Vietnam. On that very day, in fact, he asked Deputy Secretary of Defense Roswell L. Gilpatric to outline such a program. The first draft contained significant input from Brig. Gen. Edward Lansdale, U. S. Air Force, who was then Assistant to the Secretary of Defense for Special Operations. General Lansdale had become famous for his work in the Philippines, advising on the successful campaign against the Huk insurgents, and in 1955 and 1956 he had been a key figure in installing and establishing Diem as President of South Vietnam.

After much coordination between the Departments of Defense and State, the Gilpatric program recommended a two division increase in the South Vietnamese army, with deployment of 3,600 U. S. troops to South Vietnam to train the new divisions and another 400 special U. S. troops to help speed up overall counterinsurgency training. Secretary Gilpatric had also originally recommended that a special task force be set up in Washington to recommend what steps to take in South Vietnam, but before his report finally worked its way through the various agencies in Washington, the whole task force idea had been downgraded to an interagency working group to be headed by George Ball, who was then Undersecretary of State. Notwithstanding the recommendations in the Gilpatric report, President Kennedy signed a letter to President Diem on 8 May which promised strong U. S. support, but did not offer to finance an expansion of South Vietnamese forces or to station American troops in South Vietnam. When the letter was delivered by Vice President Lyndon B. Johnson the following week, President Diem brought up his worries about U. S. policy in Laos. In response, and as a gesture of U. S. commitment, Vice President Johnson, obviously acting on oral instructions from the President, did allude to the possibility of stationing American troops in South Vietnam and of a bilateral treaty between the U. S. and South Vietnam. Diem was apparently not interested in either.

The following month, however, Diem responded to an invitation President Kennedy had extended through the Vice President by sending an aide to Washington with a letter outlining Saigon's "essential military needs." Those needs included a large increase in U. S. financial and material support for South Vietnamese forces—large enough to raise the strength of their army from 170,000 to 270,000 men—and selected elements of the American armed forces to establish training centers for the South Vietnamese and to serve as a symbol of American commitment to South Vietnam. After some study, the United States finally agreed to support an increase of only 30,000, rather than the 100,000 requested. Interestingly enough, no answer was given to the request for elements of American armed forces.

In September of 1961, Viet Cong attacks increased sharply, and there were indications of some weakening in Diem's military position. At the end of the month, Diem forwarded a request through our Ambassador for a treaty that would commit the United States to defend South Vietnam. In response, and out of concern for the deteriorating situation, President Kennedy sent Gen. Maxwell D. Taylor, U. S. Army (Retired), and Dr. Walt Rostow (who were then members of the White House staff) to South Vietnam to survey the situation.

General Taylor and Dr. Rostow reported that the problem revolved around a lack of faith that the United States would in fact remain South Vietnam's firm ally (arising from our policies in Laos), and a feeling of uncertainty as to whether or not the unpopular and inefficient Diem government could actually cope with the Viet Cong threat. In their view, the first issue could be overcome by a U. S.

military commitment in-country. As for the second difficulty, they speculated that perhaps some American personnel interposed at each echelon of the South Vietnamese government and army would produce a "can-do" spirit and a desire for governmental reform at all levels.

General Taylor further concluded that the Communist strategy of taking over Southeast Asia by guerrilla warfare was well on its way to success in South Vietnam. He recommended more U. S. support for the paramilitary groups and more U. S. units, specifically helicopter companies, which would give the South Vietnamese army mobility. He also indicated that the Military Assistance Advisory Group should be reorganized and increased in size. He further recommended that limited U. S. forces be introduced into South Vietnam to provide a military presence, which would demonstrate our interest in resisting a Communist takeover. These forces would also provide an emergency reserve to back up the South Vietnamese military in a heightened crisis and would conduct such combat operations as were necessary for the self-defense and security of the area in which they were stationed. It was Taylor's view that South Vietnam was in trouble and major U. S. interests were at stake. Prompt and energetic action—military, economic, and political—could bolster the Diem regime and lead to victory without a U. S. takeover of the war. He held, as well, that if the United States was forced to take direct military action, a bombing program against the north was a more appropriate course of action than the introduction of large numbers of ground troops.

Following this visit and the report of its findings, the President received a memorandum dated 8 November from Secretary of Defense Robert S. McNamara, on behalf of himself and the JCS, stating that they were inclined to recommend the Taylor program, but only on the understanding that more troops could be sent as needed and that the U. S. would be willing to attack North Vietnam. The memorandum said that the fall of South Vietnam would have extremely serious strategic implications worldwide, that chances were probably against preventing such a fall without U. S. troop commitment, but that even with major troop deployment the U. S.

objectives would still be at the mercy of external forces—Diem, Laos, and U. S. domestic political problems—and thus success could not be guaranteed. Secretary McNamara recommended against deployment of the limited forces suggested by General Taylor unless we were willing to commit ourselves fully to saving South Vietnam. The full text of this important memorandum may be found in Appendix A.

On 11 November the Secretaries of State and Defense submitted a joint memorandum to the President on the general subject of our policy towards South Vietnam. This memorandum recommended that we promptly deploy support troops and equipment (including helicopters, transport aircraft, some maritime equipment, trainers, special intelligence and air reconnaissance groups, and any other men and material needed to improve logistics) and that we defer studying the possibility of deploying major ground combat forces to a later date. It concluded that the United States should commit itself to the clear objective of preventing the fall of South Vietnam to communism and that it should be prepared to send troops and to strike at the source of aggression in North Vietnam.

During this time, the U. S. Ambassador to South Vietnam was operating under the directed position that additional aid was contingent upon President Diem's instituting the necessary governmental reform measures the United States had recommended. However, some of President Kennedy's advisers were suggesting that there was not much point in bargaining with Diem since he would never follow through on any of his promises. One such adviser was John Kenneth Galbraith, then Ambassador to India, who counseled obliquely in favor of an anti-Diem military coup as potentially the most productive turn of events.[1]

By early 1962 a new strategy for containment of the Communist insurgency in South Vietnam had been devised. It was called the Strategic Hamlet Program. The principal U. S. and South Vietnamese participants apparently all agreed that this represented the optimum unifying concept for the country. The objective of providing security to rural Vietnam, and thereby developing support among the peasants for the central government, was to be accomplished in phases: clearing insurgents from an area, protecting the rural populace, establishing a rural hamlet government, and, finally, building up the economic status of the hamlets.

President Diem, however, apparently sought to use the Strategic Hamlet Program as a means of maintaining his personal direction of the counterinsurgent effort, and he resisted sharing responsibility (and, thereby, leadership) in the project with either U. S. or his own senior military personnel. The essential difference between his perception and that of the U. S. advisers as to how the program should function, combined with our lack of experience in attempting such a long-term pacification strategy and active resistance by much of the peasant population to the central government's directing so drastic a change in their way of life, resulted in the dismal failure of the program.

Actually, U. S. policymakers were not aware early on of how poorly things were going with the Strategic Hamlet Program. Optimism dominated official thinking, even to the extent of creating a formal plan and a budget for the phased withdrawal of U. S. forces. In fact, at a Secretary of Defense conference in Honolulu on 23 July 1962, Secretary McNamara, with guidance from the President, put this planning into motion. He noted that tremendous progress had been made in South Vietnam, and directed that a comprehensive, long-range program be developed for building up South Vietnam's military capability and for phasing out the U. S. role. In early 1963 he further directed that the pace of the phase-out planning be speeded up. Although the situation in South Vietnam continued to deteriorate drastically, the White House nonetheless publicly promised in October to effect a 1,000-man withdrawal in December of that year—a promise they were forced to keep. Subsequently, the ever-worsening situation in South Vietnam was finally faced up to and any further planning for a U. S. phase-out was dropped.

In the meantime, on 8 May 1963, the Diem regime had violently suppressed a Buddhist religious protest over the favoritism being shown toward the Catholic church and the accompanying discrimination against the Buddhists. Until then the Buddhists had not been active politically, but after this badly handled incident, they began to speak up. In fact, they became a voice for the widespread popular resentment of Diem's arbitrary and often oppressive rule. A crisis in American policy was obviously generated, since we had consistently supported Diem as the only national leader capable of unifying his people. When the Buddhist protests revealed this not to be the case, the United States embarked on a program to convince Diem that he must correct the situation. Ambassador Nolting's diplomatic persuasions over the ensuing months were unproductive, however, and Diem remained adamant in his personal and political philosophies. When Nolting finally left Saigon in mid-August (he was to be replaced by Henry Cabot Lodge in September), he had only succeeded in extracting a vague promise from Diem that he would try to improve the climate of relations with the Buddhists. Less than a week later, even that was sharply repudiated by Ngo Dinh Nhu, Diem's brother, who initiated a series of midnight raids on Buddhist pagodas throughout South Vietnam which resulted in the wounding of about thirty monks, the arrest of over 1,400 Buddhists, and the closing of the pagodas. The new Ambassador Lodge proceeded to Saigon immediately and informed Diem that the United States would not stand for any further such incidents.

Soon thereafter, on 23 August 1963, a group of South Vietnamese generals made contact with a U. S. representative to advise that a coup against Diem was in the offing. Ambassador Lodge was informed and, after consultation with Washington, notified the generals that the U. S. could no longer support a regime that included Nhu, but the decision on Diem was entirely up to them. For whatever reasons, however, the planned coup was apparently aborted, at least for the time being.

In Washington the Diem regime's difficulties with the Buddhists and the coup issue raised many questions. The general situation was discussed at several National Security Council meetings, and at one point there was controversy over the particular problem of whether or not the Buddhist religious troubles were so serious that large numbers of Buddhists serving in the South Vietnamese army might defect to the Communists. Two men were appointed to go to South Vietnam to find the answer to this question: the Defense Department sent Maj. Gen. Victor Krulak, U. S. Marine Corps, who was on duty with the JCS, and the State Department sent a Vietnam expert, Joseph Mendenhall. There is a considerable amount of dispute on both the purposes and the conclusions of their mission. According to the Pentagon Papers, this visit was to bring back a judgment as to whether there was any hope of victory—a much broader question than the one the men were purportedly sent to answer. The Pentagon Papers go on to say that Krulak and Mendenhall came back with diametrically opposed views, so much so that President Kennedy asked them, "You two did visit the same country, didn't you?"

General Krulak has stated that the Pentagon Papers are in error. To begin with, he says, the question he and Mendenhall were sent to investigate was in fact the narrower one, that is, whether we could expect mass defections from the South Vietnamese army to the Communist side. Further, Krulak asserts that he traveled throughout the South Vietnam countryside collecting information and found absolutely no evidence of such prospective defections, while Mendenhall simply visited three cities as a basis for his pessimistic conclusion. Back in Washington they did present their opposing views to the President, and he did then ask if they had been in the same country. As Krulak relates it, the situation was embarrassing, and there was a moment of strained silence. Finally, he said, "Mr. President, I think I can answer your question—I went to the countryside, my State Department colleague went to the cities; but the war is in the countryside."

A short time later, the President directed Secretary McNamara and General Taylor (who by then was serving as Chairman of the JCS*) to go to South Vietnam to assess the problem. Accompanied by a team of civilian and military assistants, they arrived in South Vietnam on 26 September and returned to Washington on 2 October. During their visit they received extensive briefings from the

---

*In October 1962 President Kennedy decided that he wanted his own man as Chairman of the Joint Chiefs of Staff. Accordingly, Gen. Maxwell D. Taylor, who had been serving as Military Advisor to the President, was ordered into that position, replacing Gen. Lyman L. Lemnitzer, U. S. Army.

Commander, U. S. Military Assistance Command (COMUS-MACV) and his staff, as well as from embassy personnel, and returned with mounds of detailed data. They reported to the President that the south was winning the war, that it would be successfully concluded in three of the four military geographical regions (called corps tactical zones) by the end of 1964, and in the fourth region, the delta, by 1965, by which time the American advisers could then be withdrawn. However, they did note that political tensions were starting to have an adverse effect on the conduct of the war and recommended that Ambassador Lodge be instructed to continue a policy of aloofness from the Diem regime. As is usually the case on short visits such as this one, McNamara and Taylor were largely dependent on in-country personnel for the accuracy of the data and the general impressions they brought home. In this particular case it subsequently became apparent that COMUSMACV and others who briefed the visitors were, unfortunately, far too optimistic about the progress of the military program and the probable impact of the deteriorating political situation.

In the aftermath of the McNamara/Taylor mission, U. S. embassy personnel in Saigon were once again approached by the South Vietnamese generals with word that they were preparing to move against Diem. Washington advised Ambassador Lodge that while the United States was definitely not encouraging a coup, he should nonetheless maintain contact with the generals so as to monitor their plans. By this time Lodge was convinced that Diem was unlikely to respond to our pressures, and although Washington had directed that he consider ways of delaying or preventing a coup if he doubted its prospect for success, it was his opinion that by now the matter was out of our hands. The generals had taken the initiative and could only be stopped at this point by our denouncing them to Diem. While we pondered our diplomatic dilemma, the generals acted out their plan.

The coup was begun on 1 November, shortly after Ambassador Lodge and Adm. Harry D. Felt, U. S. Navy, (who was then Commander in Chief Pacific) had paid a courtesy call on President Diem. Led by General Duong Van Minh (known as "Big Minh," the most respected of the senior generals) and his co-conspirators Generals

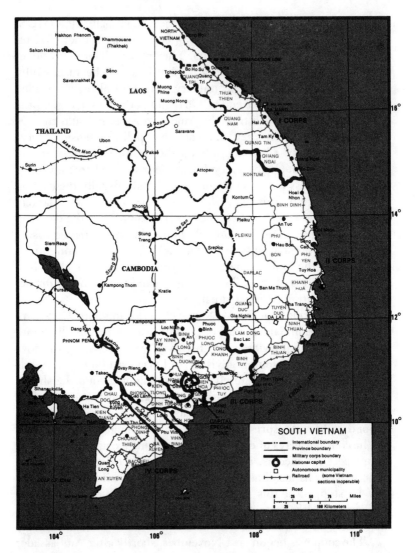

SOUTH VIETNAM CORPS TACTICAL ZONES. South Vietnam was divided into military regions called Corps Tactical Zones. Each region was the responsibility of a South Vietnamese Army Corps. The Capital Special Zone was created in 1964.

Tran Van Don, Le Van Kim, and Tran Thien Khiem, the coup forces moved with swift effectiveness, and by late afternoon only the palace guards remained to defend the Diem brothers. At 4:30 P.M. President Diem contacted Lodge, who was generally equivocating vis-à-vis the U. S. position in this affair, although he did indicate our concern for Diem's physical safety. Finally, after refusing safe conduct offers from the generals, the Diem brothers escaped the palace that evening by means of a secret passageway and hid out in a Saigon suburb. Unfortunately, their escape route was uncovered when the palace fell the next morning, their whereabouts discovered and, before Ambassador Lodge could intercede on their behalf, they were murdered.

Despite the fact that we were appalled by the brutality of the coup, the United States recognized the newly formed Saigon government on 8 November 1963, since it was a necessary step in maintaining diplomatic relations. Very soon, however, it became undeniably evident that the lack of expertise in the new government and the faltering economy of the country were combining with the generally deteriorating military situation (including the Strategic Hamlet Program) to force a serious reappraisal of our objectives and intentions in South Vietnam.

By the end of 1963, although the U. S. policy of resisting further advances by Communist countries into Southeast Asia was well developed, and a free South Vietnam was considered the key to blocking Communist aggression, the survival of freedom in South Vietnam was by no means assured. And our commitment to this end had resulted in progressively deeper involvement.

CHAPTER 3

THE SITUATION IN SOUTH
VIETNAM DETERIORATES

AT THE END of September 1963, I arrived in Honolulu to relieve Adm. John H. Sides, U. S. Navy, as Commander in Chief Pacific Fleet. In this position, I would be one of the three Component Commanders operating under the Commander in Chief Pacific (CINCPAC). The other Component Commanders were Gen. Jacob E. Smart, Commander in Chief Pacific Air Forces, and Gen. James F. Collins, Commander in Chief, U. S. Army Pacific. Both of these generals also had their headquarters in Honolulu.

On 20 November 1963, at President Kennedy's direction, a conference was convened in Honolulu for a full-scale review of all aspects of the situation in South Vietnam. Plans and policies in the political, military, economic, and information fields were to be reassessed in view of the recent change of South Vietnamese government. About forty-five U. S. officials—military and civilian—attended this conference, including the Secretary of State, Secretary of Defense, Special Assistant to the President for National Security Affairs, Chairman of the JCS, Director of the CIA, CINCPAC, the

Ambassador to South Vietnam and his whole country team,* including the Commander, U. S. Military Assistance Command Vietnam (COMUSMACV), Gen. Paul D. Harkins, U. S. Army.

During the conference, Ambassador Lodge assessed the prospects for South Vietnam as hopeful. He thought the new government had some promise, that South Vietnamese military leadership appeared to be united and determined to step up the war effort, that our plans for eventual military withdrawal from South Vietnam should be maintained, and that the announced 1,000-man withdrawal was having a salutary effect. He also indicated that excellent working relations between U. S. officials and members of the South Vietnamese government had been established. General Harkins noted that Viet Cong attacks had temporarily increased immediately following the coup, but he agreed with Lodge's overall assessment and said that military operational statistics generally showed a more or less favorable balance. All in all, the briefings and assessments at the conference gave an encouraging outlook for the principal objective of joint U. S./South Vietnamese policy in South Vietnam—the successful prosecution of the war against the Viet Cong. In light of all of this, and despite the guarded assessment of the military situation, it was agreed that the accelerated plan for withdrawal should be maintained. CINCPAC proposed a fairly expansive military assistance program, but Secretary McNamara suggested that it be cut back. He did say, however, that he would stand prepared to provide at some future time such funds as might be required to support the South Vietnamese government.

The Honolulu conference had just concluded when President Kennedy was assassinated and the United States lost a strong, purposeful leader. Instantly, a freeze went into effect on the direction and momentum of U. S./Vietnam policy, to last until President Johnson's desires were known. It soon became apparent that he

---

*Country team is diplomatic terminology referring to a diplomatic group consisting of the Ambassador, his key embassy officials, and the chiefs of other U. S. government agencies in a foreign country.

would avoid change of any kind during that early, critical period of his presidency.

On 26 November, the White House issued a National Security Action Memorandum (NSAM)* dealing with South Vietnam. This document reaffirmed and continued the Kennedy administration policies, maintained military assistance at essentially the same level as had been granted to Diem, and reiterated plans for troop withdrawal. It proposed no new programs or increase in U. S. assistance. The war remained basically a South Vietnamese affair to win or lose.

During December conflicting intelligence estimates of the situation in South Vietnam began to come in, and by the end of the year it was clear that the unsettled atmosphere following the November coup had proven costly in the countryside. Many strategic hamlets were overrun or were revealed to have been Communist-controlled all along. Death and losses inflicted by the Viet Cong increased sharply. Many local paramilitary units simply melted away into the population. It was now unclear whether the new government would be able to heal the country's internal wounds and provide the leadership required to reverse the course of the struggle.

In late December, Secretary McNamara visited Saigon for an assessment of the situation. His ensuing trip report to the President noted that it was, in fact, "very disturbing." Current trends, unless reversed in the next two or three months, would most likely lead to a Communist-controlled state. While he indicated concern over the indecisive character of the new South Vietnamese government, he went on to complain that the U. S. country team was a problem as well in that it lacked leadership and was poorly informed. One of the most serious deficiencies was a grave reporting weakness on the U. S. side. Our undue dependence upon the distorted South Vietnamese reporting system had kept us unaware of how badly the

---

[1]A NSAM is a policy statement originated in the National Security Council and issued, after approval by the President. It is disseminated to all government agencies that have cognizance of the subject matter involved for either action or information purposes.

situation in the countryside had been deteriorating since July, and he recommended, therefore, that our staffs be expanded enough to provide a reliable, independent appraisal of the status of operations. McNamara concluded with the observation that despite his tone, the Ambassador, COMUSMACV, and General Minh were not discouraged and looked forward to significant improvements in January.

Shortly after President Johnson took office, he received a letter from Sen. Mike Mansfield of Montana, Senate Democratic Majority Leader, proposing that South Vietnam be partitioned between the Government of South Vietnam and the Viet Cong, and that the United States withdraw. Secretary McNamara wrote a strong memorandum countering the position of Senator Mansfield, arguing that division of the present territory would inevitably mean a new government in Saigon that would in short order be Communist dominated, and predicting that the consequences of this would be extremely serious, both for the rest of Southeast Asia and for the U. S. position in that and other key areas of the world.

On 30 January 1964, there was another coup—a power struggle, largely bloodless, between military groups in South Vietnam—and the ruling Minh government was ousted. General Nguyen Khanh emerged as Premier.

In Washington, government officials were still unsure about the actual state of affairs in South Vietnam and remained convinced that an improved reporting system would do much to solve the problem. So in early February, yet another fact-finding mission, this time a special CIA group, was sent off to South Vietnam. A series of reports were produced and transmitted to the Secretary of Defense and the Secretary of State, all concluding that the situation was serious and steadily worsening. Viet Cong gains in the past several months were noted, as were the steadily increasing quantity and improving quality of Viet Cong arms. The reports further indicated that the Strategic Hamlet Program was at a virtual standstill, and that the tide of insurgency in all four corps areas appeared to be going against the South Vietnamese. Gen. Paul Harkins (who at that time was still COMUSMACV) immediately took issue with the tone of the CIA group's broad findings. He said he had had no knowledge of their reports prior to publication, but did not agree with the degree of deterioration noted.

On 6 March, the Secretary of Defense convened another major conference at CINCPAC headquarters in Honolulu to reassess the situation. The consensus was that the military picture was definitely discouraging. Many of the participants were of the opinion that the insurgency could be expected to go on beyond 1965. After this conference Secretary McNamara and General Taylor continued on to South Vietnam. Following their return, the Secretary submitted a formal report to the President in which he stated that the situation was unquestionably worse. The South Vietnamese military position generally was weakening, desertion rates in the South Vietnamese armed forces were increasing, and the Viet Cong position was improving, apparently with more and more North Vietnamese support. McNamara concluded that greater U. S. support was therefore needed, and he recommended measures involving a limited increase in personnel, a significant increase in the military assistance program budget, and additional economic aid to bolster the South Vietnamese government.

As a result of the McNamara/Taylor trip, another National Security Action Memorandum concerning South Vietnam was issued, NSAM #288. Dated 17 March 1964, it reviewed U. S. objectives and appraised the situation, discussing various alternative courses of action. This document was a declaration of government policy vis-à-vis South Vietnam that remained on the record throughout the war. It read in part:

> We seek an independent, non-Communist South Vietnam. We do not require that it serve as a Western base or as a member of a Western alliance. South Vietnam must be free, however, to accept outside assistance as required to maintain its security. This assistance should be able to take the form not only of economic and social measures, but also police and military help to root out and control insurgent elements.
>
> Unless we can achieve this objective in South Vietnam, almost all of Southeast Asia will probably fall under Com-

munist dominance (all of Vietnam, Laos, and Cambodia), accommodate to Communism so as to remove effective U. S. and anti-Communist influence (Burma), or fall under the domination of forces not now explicitly Communist, but likely then to become so (Indonesia taking over Malaysia). Thailand might hold out for a period without help, but would be under grave pressure. Even the Philippines would become shaky, and the threat to India on the west, Australia and New Zealand to the south, and Taiwan, Korea, and Japan to the north and east would be greatly increased.

All of these consequences would probably have been true even if the U. S. had not, since 1954, and especially since 1961, become so heavily engaged in South Vietnam. However, that fact accentuates the impact of a Communist South Vietnam not only in Asia, but in the rest of the world where the South Vietnam conflict is regarded as a test case of U. S. capacity to help a nation to meet the Communists' "war of liberation."

Thus purely in terms of foreign policy, the stakes are high.[1]

Although the objectives given in NSAM #288 encompassed a wide field and were strongly stated, the specific implementing programs it recommended were comparatively limited. For example, among the alternatives that had been considered but rejected for the time being were putting overt military pressure on North Vietnam, evacuating U. S. dependents, furnishing a U. S. combat unit to secure the Saigon area, and proposing a full takeover of command in South Vietnam by the United States. One specific plan recommended for implementation was civil and military mobilization to put South Vietnam on a war footing. In this connection, the armed forces, both regular and paramilitary, were to be strengthened by at least 50,000 men, and the civil administrative corps was to be increased by an additional 7,500 people in the near term, with an ultimate target of at least 40,000 for service in the hamlets, villages and provincial centers. The document also called for providing the South Vietnamese air force with twenty-five A-1H aircraft in exchange for their less capable T-28s. The A-1H, a single-engine, propeller-driven Douglas attack aircraft, which had been used for a long time by the U. S. navy, was a fine attack aircraft and carried a large load of weapons. The South Vietnamese army was also to be provided with additional armored personnel carriers and river boats.

There were, of course, factions in the government that did not consider that the programs specified in NSAM #288 were responsive to the situation. The JCS, for example, viewed the Vietnam problem primarily in its military dimensions and believed that the political and logistic source of Viet Cong strength in the north should be neutralized by an air campaign against war-supporting installations. In that context they advised the Secretary of Defense that they considered the overall NSAM program to be inadequate militarily and that much more aggressive policies were necessary, mainly against North Vietnam but also against the Cambodian sanctuaries of Viet Cong forces.

This JCS criticism highlighted a basic problem in U. S. policy throughout the whole Vietnam War period. Policy objectives were stated in very comprehensive terms, but definitive programs and actions adequate to secure those objectives were not generated. This situation appears to me to have stemmed in part from an excessive reluctance on the part of the civilian leadership in the Department of Defense, and indeed in the White House as well, to accept the decisive, precisely drawn military actions recommended by the JCS and other cognizant military commanders in response to those broadly stated policy objectives. There seemed to be a desire to keep the actual means to stated ends both consciously limited and purposely indirect. This was undoubtedly caused to some degree by the ever-present fear of overt involvement on the part of Communist China or the Soviet Union, but beyond that one has the feeling that the civilian leadership considered that if they deliberately kept the outlines of our specific commitments somewhat fuzzy or vague they could work some clever ploy to cause the North Vietnamese to disengage from their support of the insurgents in the south. In any event, the U. S. would simply not employ all of its military might, or even a substantial portion of it, in a way that would ensure winning a battle that was viewed by our government as critical to the fate of all Southeast Asia.

Any analysis of the effectiveness of NSAM #288 must, of course, take into consideration the domestic political climate at the time of its issuance. Certainly the President and other senior government officials were well aware that no base of either congressional or popular support existed for direct, offensively oriented intervention by American forces in this far-away conflict. At best, support could probably only come in response to a policy designed primarily to assist South Vietnam in winning its own war. In essence, the dynamics of NSAM #288 rested largely on the pragmatism of politics rather than military expediency.

CHAPTER 4

THE TONKIN GULF
INCIDENTS

THE SENIOR U. S. leadership in Saigon underwent a major change in mid-1964. The President directed that General Taylor, Chairman of the JCS, be retired from active military duty for the second time to become Ambassador to South Vietnam. Gen. Earle G. Wheeler, who was Army Chief of Staff at the time, replaced him as Chairman. A respected career diplomat, U. Alexis Johnson, was appointed deputy to Ambassador Taylor with the rank of Ambassador. General Harkins departed Vietnam and Gen. William C. Westmoreland, U. S. Army, who had been serving as his deputy since 27 January 1964, assumed command of the U. S. Military Assistance Command Vietnam.

In the latter part of June, I was relieved as Commander in Chief Pacific Fleet by Adm. Thomas H. Moorer, and I succeeded Admiral Felt as Commander in Chief Pacific. Thus began my four years of close personal involvement, under the direct authority of the JCS, with the course of events in Southeast Asia. Since my relationship with the JCS during this period was certainly a decisive element in my overall role as Commander in Chief Pacific, it seems worthwhile to describe how the JCS operate and to mention my previous personal acquaintance with many of the members.

The regular members of the JCS include the Chiefs of Staff of the Army and the Air Force, the Chief of Naval Operations and the Chairman. The Commandant of the Marine Corps participates as a member when matters affecting the Marine Corps are under consideration. Normally, JCS meetings are held twice a week and are also attended by the Director of the Joint Staff and the Secretary of the Joint Staff, who keeps a record of the proceedings. In addition, certain designated three-star officers from each of the services, referred to as Operations Deputies, are in attendance and are authorized to act for their Chief of Staff in his absence. The Operations Deputies and the Director of the Joint Staff also hold separate, frequent meetings at which they act on routine matters for their chiefs.

I served as Navy Operations Deputy from 1960 to 1963, and came to know many of the officers with whom I was to be so closely associated in my tenure as CINCPAC. For example, General Taylor had been the Chairman during that time, and General Wheeler had been both Director of the Joint Staff and, subsequently, Army Chief of Staff. Also, Gen. Harold K. Johnson, who was Army Chief of Staff when I became CINCPAC, had been my army counterpart as Operations Deputy. And finally, Gen. Curtis E. LeMay, Air Force Chief of Staff, and Adm. David L. McDonald, Chief of Naval Operations, had held those posts during part of my tour as Navy Operations Deputy. I therefore had the great advantage of having worked with many of the military professionals with whom I would be dealing as CINCPAC. This was particularly germane since the distances involved dictated that most of our business would be conducted by means of written messages, as opposed to personal contact, and knowing each other well often meant that we were one step ahead by being able to read between the lines of official communications.

On 5 July General Taylor came through Honolulu on his way to Saigon, and I had a chance to talk to him at some length. He advised me that he had been given unusually broad authority in pursuing his new ambassadorial duties and showed me the letter from President Johnson which outlined these prerogatives:

> As you take charge of the American effort in South Vietnam I want you to have this formal expression not only of my confidence, but of my desire that you have and exercise full responsibility for the effort of the United States Government in South Vietnam. In general terms this authority is parallel to that set forth in President Kennedy's letter of May 29, 1961, to all American Ambassadors; specifically, I wish it clearly understood that this overall responsibility includes the whole military effort in South Vietnam and authorizes the degree of command and control that you consider appropriate.
>
> I recognize that in the conduct of the day-to-day business of the Military Assistance Command Vietnam you will wish to work out arrangements which do not burden you or impede the exercise of your overall direction.
>
> At your convenience I should be glad to know of the arrangements which you propose for meeting the terms of this instruction so that appropriate supporting action can be taken in the Defense Department and elsewhere as necessary.
>
> This letter rescinds all conflicting instructions to U. S. Officers in Vietnam.
>
> Sincerely,
>
> Lyndon B. Johnson

This letter could, of course, have been construed to eliminate CINCPAC in the command chain from South Vietnam, but Ambassador Taylor assured me that I had no reason for concern and indicated that although he intended to maintain overall policy control, he did not propose to interfere in the day-to-day business of the military effort. He was certainly true to his word, and the arrangements were quite satisfactory from my viewpoint. I should add that the comprehensive authority over military operations given to

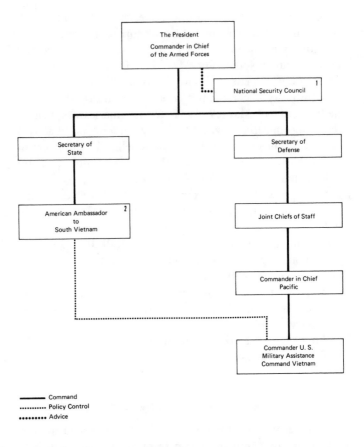

COMMAND STRUCTURE FOR POLITICO–MILITARY
DECISION MAKING VIS–A–VIS VIETNAM

[1]The National Security Council includes: the President, Vice-President, and the Secretaries of State and Defense. The Director of the Central Intelligence Agency and the Chairman, Joint Chiefs of Staff meet with the Council in the role of Advisors. The Council advises the President with respect to the integration of domestic, foreign, and military policies relating to the national security.

[2]The Ambassador to South Vietnam exercised policy control over all U. S. operations in South Vietnam.

Ambassador Taylor worked in this particular case because he was a broad-gauge thinker, a skillful diplomat and an experienced military leader of the first order. He fully understood the great difficulty that would be caused if he interfered with the details of military operations. We were fortunate that such was the case and that we were not dealing with a career foreign-service officer whose only military experience might well have been a one-year course at the National War College. In this connection, I would hope that the broad authority granted to Ambassador Taylor does not set a precedent, for it carries the potential of being extremely disadvantageous to the efficient prosecution of military operations.

On 27 July the United States announced it was sending an additional 5,000 men to South Vietnam, bringing the military mission there to a total of 21,000. It should be remembered that this was still an advisory mission and our personnel were not participating in military action at this point. I had just departed on my first western Pacific trip as CINCPAC, and my itinerary included Saigon, where I met with General Westmoreland and was briefed on the situation. We called on Ambassador Taylor to talk over conditions in general, and subsequently called on General Khanh and Maj. Gen. Nguyen Van Thieu.

On a different subject, I had proposed to the JCS in early July that we order an intelligence gathering patrol (called DeSoto patrols) in the Gulf of Tonkin to investigate coastal activity in North Vietnam. JCS approval came on 22 July, with the specification that we begin not later than the thirty-first. The destroyer *Maddox* was assigned to this duty, picked up the necessary equipment and personnel, and was ready to go on schedule. Navy ships had conducted such intelligence gathering missions many times in all areas of the world for years—there was nothing unusual about it—and always under strict orders to operate only in international waters. This particular mission was directed to observe junk traffic and naval activity, and to collect both hydrographic data and information concerning North Vietnamese electronic installations. The objective was to update our overall intelligence picture in case we had to operate against North Vietnam.

On 2 August, while on her mission in the Gulf of Tonkin, the *Maddox* was attacked by three North Vietnamese patrol boats. I was airborne on my return trip from Saigon at the time, just about to land at Wake Island, and when I arrived in Honolulu I was queried on the incident by the press. Among other things, I remember saying, "Our ships are always going to go where they need to be and if they shoot at us we are going to shoot back."

An important backdrop to the events which took place immediately preceding and during the attack on *Maddox* was the fact that during the spring and summer of 1964 the South Vietnamese were being organized and trained for harassing missions against the North Vietnamese coastal region. The concept was to use South Vietnamese crews to man fast patrol craft that were capable of mortar fire and carried frogmen with weapons and explosive equipment to blow up installations on the beach. Another important objective was to intercept and destroy North Vietnamese junks and fishing craft, which were being used to ferry arms and equipment to the Viet Cong in the south. As it so happened, one of these early missions was carried out on 31 July. It consisted of landings on the islands of Hon Me and Hon Ngu off the North Vietnamese coast at nineteen degrees north latitude. The significant thing to note is that *Maddox* was about 120 miles to the south at the time.

Maddox had started her patrol on the afternoon of the thirty-first and had proceeded up the coast of North Vietnam that day and the next. She had been directed to stay at least eight miles off the coast of North Vietnam (since they had declared a five-mile territorial waters zone), and not to approach islands in the Gulf of Tonkin closer than four miles (thus ensuring she would be outside the internationally recognized three-mile territorial waters limit).

On the morning of 2 August, *Maddox* reported having some intelligence information that indicated possible action from North Vietnam. She was directed to continue her patrol. She then reported sighting a large number of junks near her patrol area and subsequently, some patrol craft that generally paralleled her course but stayed out of range. Later that afternoon, while it was still daylight, three patrol craft approached her at high speed. At that point *Maddox* had reached the northern extreme of her patrol and was headed south. She increased speed and continued her southerly course toward the mouth of the Gulf of Tonkin. Since the three North Vietnamese patrol boats were approaching her at high speed and in a threatening manner, *Maddox* fired three warning shots. Then, when they continued their approach, she took them under destructive fire. The aircraft carrier USS *Ticonderoga*, which was responsible for supporting *Maddox*, was at that time in the southern area of the Gulf of Tonkin. When *Maddox* reported the patrol craft approaching, *Ticonderoga* launched aircraft with orders not to fire unless the patrol craft took hostile action. By the time the aircraft arrived over *Maddox*, the patrol craft had already engaged (one boat had launched torpedoes which missed by about 200 yards, another boat passed astern and hit *Maddox* once with machine gun fire), so our planes attacked with rockets and gunfire. Between the aircraft hits and gunfire from *Maddox*, all three patrol craft were either sunk or badly damaged.

It has been suggested that the South Vietnamese harassment operation on the islands of Hon Me and Hon Ngu was directly related to the attacks on *Maddox*. It is true, of course, that the North Vietnamese were especially alert, because some of their radar stations had recently been shelled by the South Vietnamese patrol craft. (As an interesting aside, such periods of special alert always mean that the maximum amount of enemy electronic equipment will be operating, so it is a fine time to pick up information on what they have and how it operates.) The important facts, however, are that the *Maddox* went up the coast in daylight, she was easily seen from the beach, and she was, in addition, being tracked by North Vietnamese radar from the time she went north of the DMZ (a demilitarized zone between North and South Vietnam established in the Geneva Accords of 1954*) and thereafter for as long as she was

---

*The Geneva Accords of 1954 established "A Provisional Military Demarcation Line and Demilitarized Zone." The demarcation line was fixed on a map attached to the agreement. The Ben Hai River was the line in the mid and eastern part of the zone, while in the west it was marked by a series of prominent topographical points. The line was generally just south of the

within range. There is no doubt that the North Vietnamese knew what and where *Maddox* was, and also that she was always in international waters. Furthermore, *Maddox* had been told to keep clear of the South Vietnamese patrol boat actions, and her schedule was arranged so that the two operations would not be in the same area together. It was my view at the time, and remains so, that while the North Vietnamese may have been agitated by the South Vietnamese harassment operation, they had absolutely no reason to attack a U. S. ship, even close to their coast, much less far out in international waters. The United States simply cannot tolerate such an attack by any country—our warships must be free to sail in international waters anywhere and anytime.

The following day, our State Department sent a formal diplomatic protest to the Hanoi government emphasizing the unprovoked nature of the North Vietnamese attack and offering the following warning: "U. S. Government expects that the authorities of the regime of North Vietnam will be under no misapprehension as to the grave consequences which would inevitably result from any further unprovoked offensive military actions against U. S. forces."

That same day, I submitted for JCS approval my plan to increase the security of the DeSoto patrols but to continue with their approved schedule, which still had two days to run. The JCS approved my request to resume the patrols at a distance of at least eleven nautical miles from the North Vietnamese coast. This time *Maddox* was to be joined by another destroyer, the USS *Turner Joy*.

As an additional precaution, Adm. Tom Moorer, who was Commander in Chief Pacific Fleet, and I decided to order the aircraft carrier USS *Constellation* to leave Hong Kong, where she was on a recreation visit, and proceed south at best speed to join the *Ticonderoga* in the Gulf of Tonkin. The carrier USS *Kearsarge* and her

---

seventeenth parallel. A demilitarized zone was established on both sides of the demarcation line to a width not to exceed five kilometers from the line. The actual width along the length of the zone varied from three to five kilometers (the total width thus varying between six and ten kilometers, averaging about six miles).

anti-submarine warfare task force was also dispatched to the area immediately.

The *Maddox* and the *Turner Joy* together formed a task group commanded by Capt. J. J. Herrick, U. S. Navy. The ships entered the Gulf of Tonkin on 3 August and had an uneventful day of patrolling. The following day, however, intelligence sources once again indicated that the North Vietnamese were preparing for action. That evening, shortly after dark, the destroyers were proceeding on an easterly course at a speed of about twenty knots when Captain Herrick observed on the surface search radar at least five objects (contacts) about thirty-six miles distant. He evaluated these contacts as probable torpedo boats. *Maddox* and *Turner Joy* quickly changed course to the south and increased speed to avoid what appeared to be an imminent attack. About an hour later both ships' radars still held the contacts—now only about fourteen miles to the east. At that time the two ships were approximately sixty miles from the North Vietnamese coast. When it became evident from the maneuvers of the approaching enemy craft that they were pressing in for an attack position (now only 6,000 yards from *Maddox*), both U. S. ships opened fire and observed numerous hits on the enemy boats. Radar tracking indicated that the contacts turned away. Then torpedo noises were heard on *Maddox*'s sonar, and personnel aboard the *Turner Joy* reported sighting a torpedo wake passing abeam about 300 feet to port. The *Turner Joy*'s captain and other crew members said they saw a thick column of black smoke from one of the enemy craft at which the destroyers had fired. The action went on until about midnight and ended when radar contact on the last enemy boat was lost. Estimates were that at least two enemy craft had been sunk and possibly two more damaged. Neither of the destroyers received any damage.

As soon as the attack was reported terminated, I recommended to the JCS that authority be granted for immediate punitive air strikes against North Vietnam. Two hours later we received a reply: we were to plan strikes for first light the following day. Meanwhile, however, Admiral Moorer and I got a report from Captain Herrick saying that, although the *Turner Joy* now claimed to have positively sunk three boats, the entire action left many doubts in his mind, except for the attempt to ambush our destroyers at the beginning. He suggested thorough reconnaissance in daylight by aircraft and a complete evaluation before any further action.

In the interim, I was in telephone contact with General Wheeler, Chairman of the JCS, and Secretary McNamara. The Secretary was trying to confirm in his own mind that an attack on our ships had actually occurred, and we, of course, were trying to do exactly the same by correlating all reports coming in. After a few hours, Admiral Moorer and I decided that there was enough information available to indicate that an attack had, in fact, occurred. Accordingly, I called McNamara and informed him of our evaluation, indicating that, while reports from the ships were not conclusive by themselves, the weight of evidence (including some radio intercept intelligence) supported our conclusion.

Many telephone consultations with Washington followed. We finally received an order from the JCS to strike North Vietnamese patrol-craft bases the next day—specifically to conduct a one-time attack against five patrol-boat bases at various locations in North Vietnam, against any patrol boats sighted, and also against the fuel installations at Vinh.

The strikes were delayed until the afternoon of 5 August because the *Constellation* was unable to get within range until that time, but we eventually got word from both attack carrier task groups that they had launched aircraft on schedule. They reported that fuel-oil tanks were burning profusely at Vinh and that patrol boats had been attacked in various ports with some destroyed, others damaged. Generally speaking, it was a successful action, with reported destruction of eight boats and damage to twenty-one, and an estimated ninety percent of the fuel installation at Vinh destroyed. Two U. S. navy aircraft were lost.

The Secretary of Defense immediately announced the reinforcement of Pacific forces, indicating that we were sending interceptor and fighter-bomber aircraft to South Vietnam, to Thailand and to other locations in the Pacific, that we were dispatching an attack carrier group to the western Pacific and an Anti-Submarine Warfare (ASW) group to the South China Sea, and that all army and marine forces in the Pacific area had been alerted.

That same day, 5 August, President Johnson sent a message to Congress on the Tonkin Gulf incidents and asked for passage of a joint resolution in support of U. S. Southeast Asian policy. The resolution had been prepared by the administration and was introduced on its behalf by the Chairman of the Foreign Relations Committee of the Senate (Sen. J. William Fulbright) and the Chairman of the Foreign Affairs Committee of the House (Rep. Thomas E. Morgan). Both the House and the Senate called top administration officials to testify, including Secretary McNamara. On the seventh, the Southeast Asia Resolution, commonly called the Tonkin Gulf Resolution, was passed by both houses by an almost unanimous vote. The President now had the legislative rung on the ladder of support he hoped to build for his overall Vietnam policy. This crucial document, which proved so controversial in the years of our Southeast Asia involvement, reads as follows:

The Southeast Asia Resolution

Whereas naval units of the Communist regime in Vietnam, in violation of the principles of the Charter of the United Nations and of international law, have deliberately and repeatedly attacked United States naval vessels lawfully present in international waters, and have thereby created a serious threat to international peace; and

Whereas these attacks are part of a deliberate and systematic campaign of aggression that the Communist regime in North Vietnam has been waging against its neighbors and the nations joined with them in the collective defense of their freedom; and

Whereas the United States is assisting the peoples of Southeast Asia to protect their freedom and has no territorial, military or political ambitions in that area, but desires only that these peoples should be left in peace to work out their own destinies in their own way: Now, therefore, be it

Resolved by the Senate and House of Representatives of the United States of America in Congress assembled, That the Congress approve and support the determination of the President, as Commander in Chief, to take all necessary measures to repel any armed attack against the forces of the United States and to prevent further aggression.

Sec. 2. The United States regards as vital to its national interest and to world peace the maintenance of international peace and security in Southeast Asia. Consonant with the Constitution of the United States and the Charter of the United Nations and in accordance with its obligations under the Southeast Asia Collective Defense Treaty, the United States is, therefore, prepared, as the President determines, to take all necessary steps, including the use of armed force, to assist any member or protocol state of the Southeast Asia Collective Defense Treaty requesting assistance in defense of its freedom.

Sec. 3. This resolution shall expire when the President shall determine that the peace and security of the area is reasonably assured by international conditions created by action of the United Nations or otherwise, except that it may be terminated earlier by concurrent resolution of the Congress.

By swift reprisal action and the passage of the congressional resolution in the Gulf of Tonkin incidents, the United States had called to public view its commitment to South Vietman and Southeast Asia in general, as embodied in NSAM #288. Hanoi could not have failed to understand the message. And, significantly, the American public apparently not only understood but accepted the message, since domestic criticism was essentially nil. However, some of us, Ambassador Taylor included, were concerned that we follow through with appropriate action to underscore this boldly demonstrated resolve. My view, as expressed in a message to the JCS, was that "pressures against the other side once instituted should not be relaxed by any actions or lack of them which would destroy the benefits of the rewarding steps previously taken."[1]

Much discussion of strategy began to take place in and between the embassy at Saigon, the State and Defense Departments, the JCS, and my headquarters. I told the JCS that I thought our recent action against North Vietnam and the augmentation of our forces in the western Pacific should indicate to the Communists that we were in fact going to assist the South Vietnamese and that the North Vietnamese would be well advised to reconsider their present course of action. I recommended that we continue to increase our readiness posture by deploying troops, ships, aircraft, and logistics resources in such manner as to give us maximum flexiblity and freedom of action to respond to future situations as we desired. In addition, I thought we should proceed with further action against North Vietnam—increasing the covert operations and maintaining the De-Soto patrols—and all these actions should be pursued with vigor and determination. I also suggested that since we were now moving aircraft squadrons into South Vietnam we needed to consider how to assure the security of these forces. The South Vietnamese troops were not yet well-trained or disciplined enough to depend on for ground security; therefore, our best move might be to deploy our own combat forces to protect our own people.

The on-going strategy discussions were impacted at this time by a paper on the general subject of insurgency, which State Department Counselor Walt Rostow had authored some months earlier. His thesis was that insurgency supported by external power must be dealt with through measures to neutralize the *sources* of support.

Briefly, Rostow postulated that by applying limited, graduated military actions, as well as political and economic pressures, on a nation providing external support for insurgency, we should be able to cause that nation to decide to reduce greatly, or eliminate altogether, its support for the insurgency. The objective was to affect the enemy's evaluation of his own interests by a number of factors including: (1) loss and fear of further loss of military and economic facilities, (2) fear of involvement in a much larger conflict, (3) fear of increased dependence upon, and loss of independent action to, a major Communist country, and (4) fear of internal political upheaval and loss of power. The military actions that might cause the foregoing could include naval blockade and the destruction of specific targets by aerial bombardment or naval gunfire, supported by such passive actions as aerial reconnaissance, harassment of civil aviation and maritime commerce, and a show of military force at sea or near land borders.

Although some criticism of Rostow's thesis was voiced in both the State and Defense Departments, his approach was given considerable attention in weighing our future decisions with regard to pressures against North Vietnam.

In the meantime, not much was actually being done in the way of applying pressure against North Vietnam. The limited actions which had been approved included resumption of the offshore U. S. navy patrols and covert South Vietnamese coastal operations, minor air and ground operations in the Laotian corridor, and a preparedness to respond to any further attacks on a tit-for-tat basis.

In South Vietnam the situation was not good during this period. The government was weak, and the South Vietnamese had more than they could handle between the Viet Cong and the North Vietnamese. By late summer it had become evident that the Viet Cong posed an immediate threat to Saigon. They were active in critical provinces around the capital city, and one of our major problems became keeping the Saigon environs secure. The Viet Cong were also becoming well armed, receiving quantities of the Soviet AK-47 assault rifle, mortars and good machine guns, to the point that they had achieved a firepower margin of about five to one over the South Vietnamese forces.

On 1 November 1964, the Viet Cong staged a mortar strike on the important air base at Bien Hoa, about twenty miles northeast of Saigon. This attack killed five Americans, wounded seventy-six, and destroyed five B-57 aircraft while damaging eight others. Our stated policy at that time was to retaliate against North Vietnam for any such incident in South Vietnam, but the White House, ostensibly concerned about further escalation and uncertain as to how the Communist Chinese would respond, made a critical—and portentous—decision to make no retaliatory move. (Since this was the eve of presidential elections here at home, the assumption that domestic political concerns were also involved is probably reasonable.) The President's decision was taken against the advice of Ambassador Taylor and against a strong recommendation by the JCS.

The JCS had proposed a twenty-four-to-thirty-six-hour period of air strikes in Laos and low-level air reconnaissance south of the nineteenth parallel in North Vietnam—this to provide cover as U. S. security forces were introduced to protect our installations in South Vietnam and as U. S. dependents were evacuated from Saigon. These actions would be followed, in the JCS plan, by B-52 strikes for the next three days against the airfield at Phuc Yen (near Hanoi) where North Vietnamese fighter aircraft were based, as well as by strikes against other airfields and major fuel facilities in the Hanoi/Haiphong area. Subsequent strikes would be on infiltration routes and transportation-related targets in North Vietnam, augmented by progressive tactical aircraft and B-52 action against various other military and industrial targets in the north.

It is interesting to contemplate what the effect of these JCS-proposed strikes might have been. At that time the air defenses in North Vietnam were minimal, so our attacks would have been virtually unopposed. In addition, they would have been initiated with the element of surprise so essential to maximum success in military operations. These factors would have combined to produce small losses of either aircraft or men. In my opinion, such attacks would have had a major effect upon North Vietnam and might well have been the very thing needed to stop North Vietnamese aggression in the south and to bring Southeast Asia back to a peaceful, stabilized situation. At this critical juncture, some eleven years before its end, we might have prevented the costly and drawn-out war that followed.

CHAPTER 5

U. S. Involvement: Should It Deepen?

IN LIEU OF the decisive retaliatory action that it should have precipitated, the attack on the air base at Bien Hoa drew only the mildest of reactions in Washington: an inter-agency working group of the National Security Council (NSC) was established to study potential courses of further U. S. action in South Vietnam. This group, chaired by William Bundy, Assistant Secretary of State for Far Eastern Affairs, was asked by the newly reelected President to conduct a thorough review of our Vietnam policy and to present him with a fresh set of alternatives and recommendations. One of the most important tasks was to examine U. S. interests and objectives in South Vietnam. There was considerable discussion over the possibility that we might want to back off from the clear statements of those objectives, which had been outlined in NSAM #288 and supported in the Tonkin Gulf Resolution. Various fall-back positions, to include the extreme of withdrawal from the area, were considered. Ultimately, it was decided that the broad objectives of NSAM #288 should hold, but that the group should append to its study an assessment of possible fall-back positions vis-à-vis change in our interests and objectives should South Vietnam fall.

The NSC working group then turned to an examination of the various options available for specific action programs that might be taken in support of U. S. interests and objectives. As a general background to these deliberations, it is worthwhile to consider the alignments within the administration at that time. The military— and that included COMUSMACV, CINCPAC, and the JCS— supported a strong campaign designed to interdict infiltration routes, to destroy the overall capacity of the north to support the insurgency, and to undermine North Vietnam's will to continue supporting the Viet Cong. With the exception of George Ball, the Under Secretary of State, who favored negotiations as the *only* course, the civilian side of the house wanted to see a campaign of gradually increasing military pressures that would, they hoped, act as both "carrot and stick" to induce North Vietnam to settle the war on our terms.

The continuing dialogue between my headquarters and the JCS during this period clearly reflected the military's view that we needed to hit hard and right away. My general recommendations were punctuated with specific insistence that the minimum action we should take now would be to attack lines of communications (LOCs) in North Vietnam, including targets associated with infiltration into the south. We had designated a series of those targets, ranging from the DMZ right on up to Hanoi. We recommended aerial mining of various ports in North Vietnam (including Haiphong, of course) and, along with the mining, a naval blockade. We also wanted to systematically step up the air attacks, making them stronger and increasingly severe as time went on, eventually striking all of the military and industrial targets in North Vietnam. In addition, we pointed out that it might be necessary to control shipping into Cambodia, because the North Vietnamese would quite likely resort to moving supplies from North Vietnam to their forces in the south via Cambodia. (Later in the war, they did exactly that.)

On the other hand, the view of the civilian element in the State and Defense Departments, as succinctly characterized in the Pentagon Papers, held that "carefully calculated doses of force could bring about predictable and desirable responses from Hanoi. The threat implicit in minimum but slowly increasing amounts of force . . . would, it was hoped by some, ultimately bring Hanoi to the [negotiating] table on terms favorable to the United States."[1]

In my view, the concept of carefully calculated doses of force completely—and dangerously—ignored the iron will of the Communist philosophy in pursuit of its goals. The JCS obviously shared this view and, on four different occasions during the deliberations of the NSC working group, submitted formal proposals for direct military action using doses of force large enough to stand a realistic chance of impacting that iron will.

It is important to note that the aspect of a negotiated settlement was basic to the analysis of the NSC working group. The perception appeared to be that, no matter what we did otherwise, negotiations would, in the end, be the key to resolving the Vietnam conflict. However, an enemy who has the upper hand militarily and on whom you have inflicted no real military pressure is generally not inclined to negotiate the end to a conflict in consideration of your terms: he thinks he is winning the conflict, on his terms. In this context, the United States had little or no bargaining power to force negotiations because, since the Tonkin Gulf reprisals, we had not taken any military measures that would cause pain in North Vietnam. The working group apparently had some understanding of this fact and at least contemplated a number of actions that could give us some bargaining leverage with North Vietnam, even to include taking the major step of introducing combat ground forces into the northern provinces of South Vietnam. What is important to remember is that at this early stage of our involvement many civilians in the Pentagon and the State Department were already considering ways to negotiate ourselves out of Southeast Asia, *despite* the fact that we were in the weakest possible position for negotiation with the Communists.

The NSC working group studied on through November, focusing eventually on three courses of action which appeared to be the most viable. The first would be to continue such military and naval actions as were currently under way or authorized, to include taking prompt reprisal action against the north for any further attacks on U. S. forces. Under this course of action we would resist entering into negotiations unless North Vietnam agreed in advance to our conditions. The second possible course of action would be to augment current military actions with systematic, sustained military pressures, to include a strong air campaign that would continue during negotiations should they be forthcoming. The third (and weakest) course of action proposed only the most modest campaign against the north, designed solely to bring North Vietnam to the negotiating table—apparently more out of good will than desire to avoid further military pressure. Under this course of action, we would suspend even this modest campaign if the north agreed to negotiate, with the threat of resumption should negotiations break down.

The working group finally submitted its findings and proposals to the National Security Council during the last week in November. Ambassador Taylor, in Washington at the time, brought the members up to date on the picture in Vietnam—which was not encouraging—and made it clear that strong action against the north was needed to bring about a change for the better. After considerable deliberation it was decided to recommend to the President a two-phase course of action, which was essentially a compromise between the civilian and military views. Phase One was merely an extension of presently authorized military actions, with some increased air activity by the United States against North Vietnamese infiltration routes through Laos (the Ho Chi Minh Trail), and tit-for-tat reprisals against the north for Viet Cong attacks on U. S. forces or for other major incidents in South Vietnam. During this period, the South Vietnamese government would be informed of our desire for its reform. Phase Two directed a campaign of gradually escalating air strikes against the north, which would begin only after the desired South Vietnam governmental reforms were well under way. On 1 December, this proposal was presented to the President, who approved the first phase but, although he appeared to accept it in principle, withheld final approval of the second phase as a step to be taken only if absolutely necessary.

Operation Barrel Roll, a limited program of armed reconnaissance by U. S. aircraft in the Laotian panhandle, initiated Phase One action on 14 December. The JCS had anticipated that we would increase the number of sorties flown on a weekly basis, but right at the beginning Secretary McNamara set the level of only two missions of four aircraft each, and there it stayed through the end of January. Also denied was the JCS proposal to use direct U. S. air and naval action in support of covert South Vietnamese operations along the coast, which were still being conducted at this time.

Then on 24 December, the Viet Cong bombed a U. S. officers' housing area in Saigon, killing two Americans. COMUSMACV, CINCPAC, the JCS, and Ambassador Taylor all called for an immediate reprisal strike of the kind authorized under Phase One. Without offering any rationale, the administration decided against such action. Thus, the tit-for-tat reprisals called for in the first phase were already being ignored. The reason can only be assumed to be that the policymakers in Washington were concerned out of all proportion about the domestic and international political repercussions that might follow any U. S. military action.

Earlier in the month, Gen. Nguyen Khanh had spearheaded a move on the part of the senior South Vietnamese military to usurp power from the civilian regime of Premier Tran Van Huong. Their spokesman, Air Commodore Nguyen Cao Ky, indicated that they only intended to mediate between the government and the Buddhists in order to achieve national unity. (The Buddhists had been demonstrating again and threatening to provoke civil disorders in protest against Huong.) The U. S. government reacted strongly to this turmoil in Saigon, and Ambassador Taylor was directed to inform both Huong and the generals that further U. S. assistance was contingent on a strengthened and stable government of South Vietnam. As a result, General Khanh and Premier Huong did attempt to come to mutually acceptable terms with respect to the governing power, but it was short-lived. Soon after it was announced on 17 January that there would be an increase in military draft calls—a step long advocated by the U. S. country team—student and Buddhist riots broke out in Hue and Dalat, and ten days later the generals again withdrew their support for the Huong government. General Khanh resumed power "to resolve the political situation." From our perspective, the situation was anything but resolved.

The continuing South Vietnamese government crisis quite naturally heightened public consciousness and concern about our involvement there. Newspapers and periodicals began to be quite vocal in questioning U. S. objectives in that part of the world, and it is interesting to note that even at this early date the *New York Times* had already taken a strong stance in opposition to the administration. Not surprisingly, congressmen on all sides joined the debate, and speeches on the subject abounded.

In early January, Assistant Secretary of State William Bundy had sent a memorandum to Secretary Rusk recommending action. He took note of the continued deterioration of the military situation in South Vietnam, as well as the low state of morale, and concluded that, even in the face of the on-going South Vietnamese political crisis, the United States should probably proceed with Phase Two of the NSC proposal by initiating the escalating air strikes against the north. By the end of the month, the JCS had forwarded a memorandum to the Secretary of Defense on the subject of reprisals which made the point that continued lack of U. S. response to major enemy provocations risked inviting more such actions. They urged that "the next significant provocation be met with positive, timely, and appropriate response" (undertaken preferably within twenty-four hours) against selected targets in North Vietnam, and noted that plans had been made for such possible reprisal actions under the code name "Flaming Dart."

On 6 February, Soviet Premier Alexei N. Kosygin arrived in Hanoi for a state visit, for the obvious purpose of demonstrating Soviet support for the North Vietnamese cause. His visit was dramatically underscored by the Viet Cong attack the next day on the U. S. base at Pleiku. The strike was well-coordinated and resulted in damage to the U. S. advisers' barracks and the helicopter base nearby.

In this instance, there was no hesitancy in the President's response. The decision to strike back was taken at a meeting of the National Security Council that very evening, with Senate Majority Leader Mike Mansfield and House Speaker John McCormack in attendance.

The first reprisal strike, Flaming Dart I, was launched early the following day, but it was not a very effective attack. First of all, as an example of what was to become an unfortunate pattern throughout the war, the civilian decision makers selected the weakest of the attack options available; that is, the combination of targets selected and amount of force employed that would have the least impact on the enemy. In addition, when the order to strike was given only one attack aircraft carrier, the USS *Ranger*, was near at hand at Yankee Station (a designated area of naval operations in the Tonkin Gulf off North Vietnam), and there was some delay before the other two carriers that had been in the area could return to take up a strike position. By then, poor weather conditions had become a factor, which generally lessened the overall impact of our action.

The following day, Secretary McNamara asked the JCS for recommendations on an initial plan for military air actions against North Vietnam, which would extend over a period of eight weeks. The Secretary restricted the planning to targets along a major highway (Route 7) south of the nineteenth parallel and directed that the plan employ both South Vietnamese and U. S. forces. Such constraints obviously inhibited the JCS from conceiving a plan that fully suited their views. For example, General McConnell, Air Force Chief of Staff, considered that the heavier air strike recommendations made by the JCS in late 1964 were preferable to the restrained actions now being contemplated. General Wheeler, the Chairman, wanted an air campaign against North Vietnam's transportation system, and concurred with General Johnson, Army Chief of Staff, in his belief that three U. S. ground divisions would be needed in Southeast Asia.

As part of their plan, the JCS recommended deploying about 325 additional aircraft to the western Pacific in preparation for any escalation that might be forthcoming. These numbers included thirty B-52s to Guam and deployment of nine more U. S. Air Force Tactical Fighter Squadrons and a fourth aircraft carrier.

The plan also set forth an assessment of the escalatory risks as seen by the JCS. As subsequent events evolved, it turned out to be very accurate—almost a forecast of the future:

The Joint Chiefs of Staff believe that the DRV [North Vietnam], Communist China and the Soviet Union will make every effort through propaganda and diplomatic moves to halt the U. S. attacks. The DRV also will take all actions to defend itself and open overt aggression in South Vietnam and Laos by the DRV might occur. In addition, the mere initiation of the new U. S. policy almost certainly would not lead Hanoi to restrain the Viet Cong, Hanoi would probably elect to maintain the very intense levels of activity of the past few days. However, if the United States persevered in the face of threats and international pressures and as the degree of damage inflicted on North Vietnam increased, the chances of a reduction in Viet Cong activity would rise.

They further believe that the Chinese Communists would be reluctant to become directly involved in the fighting in Southeast Asia; however, as the number and severity of U. S. attacks against the DRV increase they probably would feel an increased compulsion to take some dramatic action to counter the impact of U. S. pressures. There is a fair chance that Peiping would introduce limited numbers of Chinese ground forces as "volunteers" into North Vietnam and/or Northern Laos intending to raise the specter of further escalation to underline its commitment to assist the North Vietnamese and to challenge the Soviets to extend corresponding support. They also believe that the probable Soviet response to these U. S. courses of action would consist both of a vigorous diplomatic and propaganda effort to bring the United States to the conference table and the provision of military support to North Vietnam. While the extent and nature of the latter are difficult to predict, it almost certainly would include anti-aircraft artillery and radars in order to provide a more effective defense against the U. S. air attacks. North Vietnam would probably press for surface-to-air missiles. The chances are about even that the Soviets would agree to provide some SA-2 defenses but they would do so in ways calculated to minimize the initial risks to them. By providing the necessary Soviet personnel in the guise of technicians, the USSR could preserve the option of ignoring any Soviet casualties. In the event the DRV and Communist Chinese openly undertake aggressive actions, the United States and its allies can deal with them adequately.[2]

In the long run, some of the force deployments recommended in the JCS plan were approved, but the plan's air-strike proposal was not, primarily because the administration was not ready to commit itself to a multi-week program of military actions, preferring to continue making decisions on a case-by-case or, at most, a weekly basis.

On 10 February the Viet Cong again struck at U. S. forces with an attack on some of our barracks at Qui Nhon. In retaliation a combined U. S./South Vietnamese response, designated Flaming Dart II, was launched. It was, however, a small strike against rather insignificant targets in the southern part of North Vietnam and generally ineffective as a reprisal action.

Early in the month, the President had sent his Special Assistant for National Security Affairs, McGeorge Bundy, to South Vietnam for intensive discussions with the U. S. mission in Saigon on possible policy alternatives vis-à-vis Vietnam. He was accompanied by the Assistant Secretary of Defense for International Security Affairs, John T. McNaughton, White House Aide Chester Cooper, and the Chairman of the Vietnam Coordinating Group in the State Department, Leonard Unger. Their memorandum of report to the President contained summary conclusions that were of great importance to the changing U. S. policy:

> The situation in Vietnam is deteriorating and without new U. S. action defeat appears inevitable—probably not in a matter of weeks or perhaps even months, but within the next year or so. There is still time to turn it around, but not much.
>
> The stakes in Vietnam are extremely high. The American investment is very large and American responsibility is a fact of life which is palpable in the atmosphere of Asia and even elsewhere. The international prestige of the

United States and a substantial part of our influence are directly at risk in Vietnam. There is no way of unloading the burden on the Vietnamese themselves and there is no way of negotiating ourselves out of Vietnam which offers any serious promise at present. It is possible that at some future time a neutral non-Communist force may emerge, perhaps under Buddhist leadership, but no such force currently exists and any negoitated U. S. withdrawal today would mean surrender on the installment plan.

The policy of graduated and continuing reprisal . . . is the most promising course available in my judgment. That judgment is shared by all who accompanied me from Washington and I think by all members of the country team.

The events of the last 24 hours [a Viet Cong attack on U. S. base at Pleiku on 7 February] have produced a practicable point of departure for this policy of reprisal and for the removal of U. S. dependents. They may also have catalyzed the formation of a new Vietnamese government. If so, the situation may be at a turning point.

There is much that can and should be done to support and to supplement our present effort while adding sustained reprisals. But I want to stress one important general conclusion, which again is shared by all members of my party: The U. S. Mission is composed of oustanding men, the U. S. policy within Vietnam is mainly right and well directed. None of the special solutions or criticisms put forward with zeal by individual reformers in government or in the press is of major importance and many of them are flatly wrong. No man is perfect and not every tactical step of recent months has been perfectly chosen, but when you described the Americans in Vietnam as your first team you were right.[3]

After the McGeorge Bundy group departed Saigon, Ambassador Taylor went on record with his own views concerning a future reprisal program. His concept differed from Bundy's in a most pertinent sense: Bundy considered the main objective to be influencing the course of the struggle in the *south*, while Taylor considered the priority to be influencing the *north* to cease the intervention by applying enough pressure to give the North Vietnamese doubts about their chances of ultimate success.

Commenting on Ambassador Taylor's reprisal and negotiating concepts, I officially called attention to the need to make the reprisal program a very forceful one, if North Vietnam was to be persuaded to accede to a cessation on U. S. terms. My message to the JCS read, in part, as follows:

> While it may be politically desirable to speak publicly in terms of a "graduated reprisal" program, I would hope that we are thinking, and will act, in terms of a "graduated pressures" philosophy which has more of a connotation of steady, relentless movement toward our objective of convincing Hanoi and Peiping of the prohibitive cost to them of their program of subversion, insurgency and aggression in Southeast Asia.

> If a firm decision is made to embark upon a graduated pressures program, the recommendation contained in Taylor's message to undertake discussions with the South Vietnamese reference joint U. S./GVN [South Vietnamese] military actions is most necessary. Failure to develop firm arrangements concerning roles and responsibilities could result in over reliance on the U. S. contribution to the war effort, and perhaps GVN resorting to rash military actions from which we would have to bail them out.

> There is no question of the desirability of concurrently educating the GVN, as also proposed in Ambassador Taylor's message, toward formulation of war objectives, demands and negotiating procedures to be employed against the DRV [North Vietnam]. I believe that such an educational process, combined with a graduated military pressures program will further contribute to GVN stability.

> We must be certain that we are dealing from a posture of strength before we sit down at the bargaining table. Successful direct increasing military pressures against North

Vietnam must be complemented by a reversal of the trend toward VC success within South Vietnam. We must also exhibit complete confidence in our ability to win in Vietnam and so indicate by our willingness to rely on our military superiority if need be.

We must not be driven to premature discussions with the DRV in our eagerness to find a solution to the Southeast Asian problem. We should continue our military pressures, making our general objectives publicly known, while awaiting some sign that the DRV is ready to negotiate towards achievement of those objectives. . . .

Finally, any political program which is designed to formulate terms and procedures for reaching agreement on cessation of a graduated military pressures program will be successful in proportion to the effectiveness of the military pressures program itself.[4]

Thus we moved, haltingly, toward a deeper political commitment in South Vietnam. At the same time, however, the policy objectives which had been enunciated rather firmly in NSAM #288 and in the Tonkin Gulf Resolution were being emasculated by implementing courses of action that were mostly weak and vacillating. Military proposals were being watered down or ignored. Meanwhile U. S. military personnel were being subjected to increasingly frequent harassing attacks, and our retaliatory responses were either ineffective or denied outright.

CHAPTER 6

ROLLING THUNDER: ON THE BEGINNING

T HE THIRTEENTH OF February, 1965, President Johnson approved the inauguration of an air warfare campaign against North Vietnam, an action we hoped might prove a decisive step in the right direction. Under strict limitations and controlled very closely by the President, these air operations were to be called "Rolling Thunder," a name that stayed with us throughout the war.

As a rather unpropitious beginning, the JCS directive to CINCPAC on Rolling Thunder 1 indicated the first strike was to take place on 20 February as a one-day reprisal attack by U. S. and South Vietnamese forces against the Quang Khe naval base and the Vu Con barracks, with two other barracks and a small airfield as weather alternates. All these targets were in the southern part of North Vietnam and were relatively minor. Before we could even initiate action, however, Rolling Thunder 1 was cancelled, as were the next three planned attacks in the series, because of the ongoing political unrest in Saigon. Part of the problem was that the total attention of the South Vietnamese armed forces was focused on the possibility of another coup attempt. They were thus unavailable to join with U. S. forces in the air strikes, which had been a mandatory stipulation. In any event, the first Rolling Thunder operation to finally get off the ground was Rolling Thunder 5, a single strike on 2 March by 104 U. S. air force and 19 South Vietnamese air force planes against one ammunition depot and the small naval base at Quang Khe.

All of us at CINCPAC were disturbed by the assignment of insignificant targets and the long delays between strikes. Ambassador Taylor echoed our impatience, and in a message to Washington on 8 March, he hit at what he considered to be the underlying cause of the problem:

> I am concerned from the standpoint of our overall posture vis-à-vis Hanoi and the Communist bloc that current feverish diplomatic activity, particularly by the British and French, tends to undercut our ability to convey a meaningful signal to Hanoi of our determination to stick it out here and progressively turn the screws on the DRV [North Vietnam]—it appears to me evident that to date DRV leaders believe air strikes at present levels on their territory are meaningless and that we are more susceptible to international pressure for negotiations than are they. Their estimate may be based in part on activities of our friends to which we seem to be an active party.
>
> In my view current developments strongly suggest that we follow simultaneously two courses of action. First, attempt to apply brakes to the British and others in their headlong dash to the conference table until there is clear evidence that Hanoi (and Peking) are prepared to leave their neighbors alone. And, two, step up the tempo and intensity of our air strikes in the southern part of DRV in order to convince Hanoi authorities they face the prospect of progressively severe punishment. I fear that to date Rolling Thunder in their eyes has merely been a few isolated thunder claps. . . .
>
> It seems to me that we may be in for a tough period ahead, but I would hope we will continue to do whatever is

required and that we try to keep fundamental objectives
vis-à-vis Hanoi clear and simple.[1]

None of us were reassured by the still minimal effort expended
in Rolling Thunder 6. After initial delays, it was eventually
launched on 15 March as a joint South Vietnamese/U. S. operation
against weapons and radar installations on Tiger Island (a small
island twenty miles off the North Vietnamese coast on which were
located some artillery units that had been sending in sighting reports
and firing on South Vietnamese patrol craft en route to raids on
North Vietnam) and against the ammunition depot near Phu Qui in
the southern part of North Vietnam. A combined force of 100 U. S.
air force and navy planes struck the latter.

In the meantime, the President had sent Army Chief of Staff
General Johnson to Saigon in early March to see what was required
to move ahead with stabilizing and controlling the situation in the
south. On his return, Johnson submitted a twenty-one point program to the JCS and the Secretary of Defense. His recommendations reflected the views of General Westmoreland and, on the
subject of air power in South Vietnam, were in line with my earlier
statement that "the single most important thing we can do to improve the security situation in South Vietnam is to make full use of
our air power."

As for the air campaign against North Vietnam, General
Johnson put forth two specific proposals:

1. Increase the scope and tempo of U. S. air strikes against
   North Vietnam. This action could tend to broaden and
   escalate the war. However, it could accomplish the
   U. S. objective of causing Hanoi to cease its support
   and direction of the Viet Cong aggression. To date, the
   tempo of punitive air strikes has been inadequate to
   convey a clear sense of U. S. purpose to North
   Vietnam.

2. Remove self-imposed restrictions on the conduct of air
   strikes against North Vietnam which have severely reduced their effectiveness and made it impossible to ap-

proach the goal of 4 missions per week. Restrictions which should be lifted are:

   a. Requirement that a U. S. strike be conducted concurrently with a [South] Vietnamese Air Force strike.

   b. Requirement that U. S. aircraft strike the primary target only.

   c. Ban on use of classified munitions.

   d. Narrow geographical limitations imposed on target selection.

   e. Requirement to obtain specific approval from Washington before striking alternate targets when required by adverse weather conditions or other local conditions.[2]

The President ultimately approved most of what General Johnson had recommended, but was cautious in opening up limited new initiatives in the air campaign. Depots, lines of communications, and air defense facilities were to be emphasized as future targets, and the awkward requirement for concurrent U. S./South Vietnamese air strikes was removed. Furthermore, the restriction that aircraft could not opt for a secondary target if the primary target was obscured, and instead had to drop their bombs in the ocean (an absolutely nonsensical limitation), was lifted. It was also agreed that some flexibility would be provided for such contingencies as weather delays.

I should note here that the weather over North Vietnam during certain periods of the year is a serious hindrance to air operations. During the winter monsoon, which starts about the first of December and lasts until mid-May, the cloud cover over North Vietnam is usually quite low, the average ceiling being perhaps in the neighborhood of 6,000 feet with solid overcast above. To get to the target under such conditions, a visual bomber must come down through the overcast and fly at an altitude of 4,000 to 6,000 feet, and at that altitude an aircraft is very vulnerable to ground fire. About mid-May the weather begins to shift, and by the middle of June it is generally good, with overcast occurring a much smaller percentage of the time. It is important, therefore, in any discussion of the air strikes on North Vietnam during a particular time frame, to keep in mind what weather period was involved.

Rolling Thunder 7 (authorized for 19–25 March) eliminated the requirement that we strike only on a specifically designated day and left the precise timing to field commanders, within a one-week time frame. Five so-called primary targets and weather alternates were authorized, as were one U. S. and two South Vietnamese armed reconnaissance missions. The mission of armed reconnaissance aircraft is to fly over certain portions, or "route segments" as they are called, of the transportation system—roads, railroads or waterways—with authority to strike any trucks or other conveyances that are discovered. If these aircraft are present over critical parts of the various highways a large percentage of the time, day and night, they can hinder traffic and make transportation very difficult. However, one mission in a week, as authorized by Rolling Thunder 7, was completely insignificant. The North Vietnamese probably didn't even know the planes were there! In any event, we were making progress, slow though it was.

In mid-March, in an attempt to get more logical targets authorized, I had prepared an attack plan against lines of communication targets to counter enemy infiltration. I utilized the findings of a study group established in my headquarters the previous month. This was a very limited attack plan, and not intended as a substitute for the strong plans that both the JCS and I had recommended earlier. It was merely an attempt to get our current small-scale operations moving in a way that would give them some effectiveness. As outlined in a long message to the JCS, the plan provided for bridge and ferry destruction and highway blockage on major long-haul road and rail routes. The program was to cut the full road network, including all feeder and bypass routes, which became the four main entry channels into Laos and South Vietnam. The targets were selected so as to be difficult to bypass. We considered that cutting the roads would create a broad series of new targets such as backed-up convoys, off-loaded material, dumps, and personnel staging areas. The program also provided for concurrent disruption of the sea routes to South Vietnam by strikes against suspected coastal

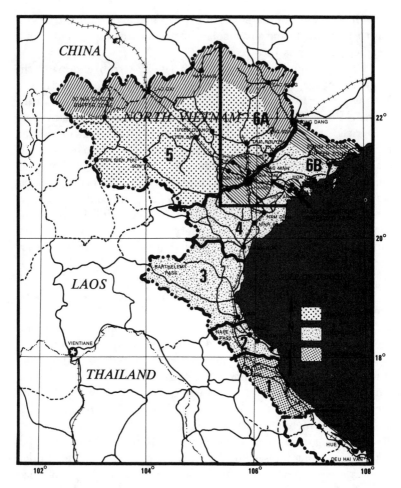

NORTH VIETNAM ARMED RECONNAISSANCE ROUTE PACKAGE AREAS. CINCPAC divided North Vietnam into six areas to facilitate command and control of air operations. They were called Armed Reconnaissance Route Package Areas. CINCPACFLT was assigned coordination control of Areas 2, 3, 4 and 6B; CINCPACAF, Areas 5 and 6A. Area 1 was assigned to CINCPACFLT until April 1966 when it was transferred to COMUSMACV. Each command planning flights into another command's assigned area was expected to advise and coordinate to avoid interference with scheduled flights.

staging points. Coupled with these strikes, the plan recommended wide-ranging armed reconnaissance missions to hamper repairs and to harass and attrite coastal staging facilities. In military parlance, this was an interdiction plan. We were proposing to seriously impede enemy traffic by bombing bridges, roads and railroads. We were also hoping, by submission of this plan, to achieve greater flexibility in target selection.

About the time my message reached the JCS, they were deeply involved with the issue of a proposed large-scale U. S. troop deployment to South Vietnam, and with reaching an acceptable consensus on how the evolving bombing campaign should take shape. Secretary McNamara had directed the JCS to work up a twelve-week program of air attacks against the north. As usual, however, the prescribed parameters within which the program had to be developed constrained the chiefs from putting forth a proposal they considered adequate or forceful enough to do the job. Air Force Chief of Staff General McConnell wanted a shorter, hard-hitting twenty-eight-day program, which would destroy all targets on the chiefs' so-called 94 Target List. He proposed to start the air strikes in the southern part of North Vietnam and move them northward at two- to six-day intervals until Hanoi itself was attacked. Although he supported future appropriate deployment of ground forces in South Vietnam, his view was that such action must be taken "in concert with [an] overall plan to eliminate the source of insurgency."

Rolling Thunder 8, conducted during the period of 26 March to 1 April, authorized nine radar site targets and three armed reconnaissance missions. The South Vietnamese air force was also authorized to strike one barracks. Obviously the targets selected in this instance were still insignificant and did nothing to put any increased pressure on North Vietnam.

Meantime the Viet Cong brazenly continued their harassment tactics and, on 29 March, exploded a bomb outside the U. S. embassy in Saigon, killing and wounding many Americans and South Vietnamese. If ever swift reprisal was warranted, now was the time. I promptly urged the JCS to recommend a forceful reply to this outrage in the form of a heavy bombing attack on a significant target or targets in North Vietnam. Although this would have given the North Vietnamese a message they could understand, a strong response was ruled out. Instead, these terrorist tactics were met with timidity in Washington, and the President merely issued a statement to the effect that the United States had no intention of conducting any further specific reprisal raids against North Vietnam in reply to the bombing of the embassy. Thus, an opportunity to demonstrate American resolve and to rally the American people was lost; indeed, a fatal lack of will surfaced at the highest level of our government, and our enemies were not slow to grasp it.

Two days later the President further obscured his real intentions on this whole issue when he responded equivocatingly to press inquiries concerning any dramatic new developments that the Viet Cong attack might have precipitated, saying, "I know of no far-reaching strategy that is being suggested or promulgated." In fact he was at that time on the verge of approving a proposal that could not be characterized as anything other than a far-reaching strategy change—namely, the concept of U. S. troops engaged in offensive ground operations against Asian insurgents in South Vietnam.

In this context, a presidential policy review was undertaken on 1 April to look at the whole gamut of military and non-military actions that might be undertaken in South and North Vietnam. The situation in South Vietnam was difficult to evaluate clearly. General Westmoreland was worried about South Vietnam's ability to counter a summer offensive by the Viet Cong. Ambassador Taylor, who was in Washington at the time, believed that the psychological atmosphere in Saigon had become more favorable and could continue on that upward turn if we exerted increasing pressure on North Vietnam. He expressed some reservation, however, over the fact that the South Vietnamese government was still incapable of providing purposeful leadership. In any case, the main thrust of the policy review centered on the prospect of major deployments of U. S. and third country (i.e., Australia, New Zealand, or Korea) ground combat forces to South Vietnam.

The presidential decision came out as NSAM #328 on 6 April 1965. It read, in part, as follows:

The President approved the deployment of two additional Marine Battalions and one Marine Air Squadron and associated headquarters and support elements.

The President approved a change in mission for all Marine Battalions deployed to Vietnam to permit their more active use under conditions to be established and approved by the Secretary of Defense in consultation with the Secretary of State.

The President approved the urgent exploration with the Korean, Australian and New Zealand governments of the possibility of rapid deployment of significant combat elements from their armed forces in parallel with the additional Marine deployment.

Subject to continuing review, the President approved the following general framework of continuing action against North Vietnam and Laos:

We should continue roughly the present slowly ascending tempo of Rolling Thunder operations, being prepared to add strikes in response to a higher rate of Viet Cong operations or conceivably to slow the pace in the unlikely event the Viet Cong slacked off sharply for what appeared to be more than a temporary operational lull.

The target system should continue to avoid the effective ground combat intercept range of MIG aircraft in North Vietnam. We should continue to vary the types of targets, stepping up attacks on lines of communication in the near future and possibly moving in a few weeks to attack some rail lines north and northeast of Hanoi.

Leaflet operations should be expanded to obtain maximum practical psychological effect on the North Vietnamese population.

Blockade or aerial mining of North Vietnamese ports needs further study and should be considered for future operations. It would have major political complications, especially in relation to the Soviets and other third countries, but also offers many advantages.

Air operations in Laos, particularly route blocking operations in the panhandle area, should be stepped up to the maximum remunerative rate.[3]

Despite the fact that the President wished to minimize the significant impact his decision to engage our ground forces offensively would clearly have on our long-standing policy vis-à-vis the South Vietnam conflict, at least one top administration official did not hesitate to express his concern about the possible ramifications. John A. McCone, the brilliant and respected Director of Central Intelligence, had developed his thesis with particularly incisive logic in a memorandum circulated earlier, on 2 April, to no one but Secretary Rusk, Secretary McNamara, McGeorge Bundy, and Ambassador Taylor. The following extracts highlight his concern:

I feel that the latter decision [to change the mission of our ground forces in South Vietnam] is correct only if our air strikes against the North are sufficiently heavy and damaging really to hurt the North Vietnamese. The paper we examined yesterday does not anticipate the type of air operation against the North necessary to force the North Vietnamese to reappraise their policy. On the contrary it states, "We should continue roughly the present slowly ascending tempo of Rolling Thunder operations . . . " and later outlining the types of targets states: "The target systems should continue to avoid the effective GCI [ground-controlled interception] range of the MIGs" and these conditions indicate restraints which will not be persuasive to the North Vietnamese and would probably be read as evidence of a U. S. desire to temporize.

I have reported that the strikes to date have not caused a change in the North Vietnamese policy of directing Viet Cong insurgency, infiltrating cadres and supplying material. If anything, the strikes to date have hardened their attitude.

I have now had a chance to examine the twelve-week program referred to by General Wheeler, and it is my personal opinion that this program is not sufficiently severe or damaging to the North Vietnamese to cause them to compromise their present policy.

On the other hand, we must look with care to our position under a program of slowly ascending tempo of air strikes. With the passage of each day and week we can expect increasing pressure to stop the bombing. This will come from various elements of the American public, from the press, the United Nations and world opinion. Therefore, time will run against us in this operation and I think the North Vietnamese are counting on this.

I think what we are doing is starting on a track which involves ground operations which in all probability will have limited effectiveness against guerrillas, although admittedly will restrain some Viet Cong advances. However, we can expect requirements for an ever-increasing commitment of U. S. personnel without materially improving the chances of victory. I support and agree with this decision but I must point out that in my judgment forcing submission of the Viet Cong can only be brought about by a decision in Hanoi. Since the contemplated actions against the North are modest in scale, they will not impose unacceptable damage on it nor will they threaten the DRV's vital interests, hence, they will not present them with a situation with which they cannot live, though such actions will cause the DRV pain and inconvenience.

I believe our proposed track offers great danger of simply encouraging Chinese Communist and Soviet support of the DRV and Viet Cong cause if for no other reason than the risk for both will be minimum. I envision that the reaction of the North Vietnamese and Chinese Communists will be to deliberately, carefully, and probably gradually, build up the Viet Cong capabilities by covert infiltration of North Vietnamese and possibly Chinese cadres and thus bringing an ever-increasing pressure on our forces. In effect, we will find ourselves mired down in combat in the jungle in a military effort that we cannot win and from which we will have extreme difficulty extracting ourselves.

Therefore, it is my judgment that if we are to change the mission of the ground forces we must also change the ground rules of the strikes against North Vietnam. We must hit them harder and more frequently and inflict greater damage. Instead of avoiding the MIGs we must go in and take them out. A bridge here and there will not do the job. We must strike their airfields, their petroleum resources, power stations, and their military compounds. This, in my opinion, must be done promptly and with minimum restraint.

If we are unwilling to take this kind of a decision now, we must not take the actions concerning the mission of our ground forces for the reasons I have mentioned above.[4]

McCone had taken a very clear and strong position, and had set down an amazingly correct prophecy of what would eventually, in fact, occur. Further, his views coincided precisely with the views expressed by me and by the JCS. It is a shame that this most lucid document did not have a greater influence on the conduct of the war and received such limited distribution within the administration. Having sometime previously informed the President of his desire to retire, John McCone was succeeded as Director of the CIA on 28 April 1965 by Vice Adm. William F. (Red) Raborn, U. S. Navy (Retired). Subsequently, Vice Admiral Raborn was asked to prepare his own comments on McCone's views. Those comments were forwarded to Secretaries Rusk and McNamara on 6 May and read, in part, as follows:

Our limited bombing of the North and our present ground force buildup in the South are not likely to exert sufficient pressure on the enemy to cause him to meet our present terms in the foreseeable future. I note very recent evidence which suggests that our military pressures are becoming somewhat more damaging to the enemy within South Vietnam, but I am inclined to doubt that this damage is increasing at a rate which will bring him quickly to the conference table.

The DRV is, in my view, unlikely to engage in meaningful discussions at any time in coming months until U. S. air attacks have begun to damage or destroy its principal economic and military targets.

Insofar as possible we should try to manage any program of expanded bombings in ways which (1) would leave the DRV an opportunity to explore negotiations without complete loss of face, (2) would not preclude any Soviet pressures on Hanoi to keep the war from expanding, and (3) would not suddenly produce extreme moral pressures against us. In this connection the timing and circumstances in which bombings were extended northward could be of critical importance, particularly in light of the fact that there have been some indications of differing views between Moscow, Peiping and Hanoi. For example, it would probably be advantageous to expand the bombings after, not before, some major new Viet Cong move; . . . and after, not before, any current possibilities of serious negotiations have been fully tested. And such bombing should not be so regular so as to leave no interval for the Communists to make concessions with some grace. Indeed, we should keep in mind the possibility of a pause at some appropriate time which could serve to test the Communist intentions and to exploit differences on their side.[5]

This was a much softer position than the one taken by McCone. Although it was a correct appraisal of the effects of the Rolling Thunder operations as they were then being conducted, Admiral Raborn's recommendations for the conduct of the air war in the future invoked all the political limitations that the Johnson administration had used to date to make the air war ineffective.

At that time much effort was being devoted to public explanation of our actions in Vietnam, but a climate of criticism persisted. The net result was to force the President into making a major public statement expressing our desire to negotiate, which he did on 7 April in a speech at Johns Hopkins University. He began by indicating our willingness to start negotiations without posing any preconditions. He then went on to offer the possibility of a billion-dollar American investment in a regional Mekong River basin development effort in which North Vietnam might also participate, and announced that he had appointed Eugene R. Black, a prominent banker, to head up that effort.

The President's speech was well received with respect to international public opinion, but the peace bloc was not satisfied and Hanoi's reaction was predictable. On the following day, North Vietnamese Premier Pham Van Dong responded with a four-point plan, which he indicated was the only acceptable road to a peaceful settlement of the war. In fact it amounted to nothing more than a plan calling for the surrender of the United States. Briefly, the four points were:

1. The United States must withdraw from South Vietnam all troops, military personnel and weapons, must dismantle all U. S. military bases there, and cancel its military alliance with South Vietnam. The United States must stop acts of war against North Vietnam.
2. While Vietnam is still divided, there need be no foreign military bases or troops in either territory.
3. Internal affairs in South Vietnam must be settled in accordance with the Communist Viet Cong NFLSV (National Front for the Liberation of South Vietnam) program without foreign interference.
4. Reunification of Vietnam must be settled by Vietnamese people without foreign interference.

Two days later North Vietnam proclaimed that "the United States was using the peace label to conceal its aggression and that the Southeast Asia development proposal was simply a 'carrot' offered both to offset the 'stick' of aggression and to seek to allay domestic and international criticism of U. S. policy in Vietnam."[6] Clearly the President's appeal had been turned aside with flagrant disdain.

In the meantime, an air interdiction campaign against lines of communications in North Vietnam, south of latitude twenty degrees, had been initiated on 2 April with Rolling Thunder 9. The Dong Phuon and Thanh Hoa bridges were the most important targets in this program, which also included a few armed reconnaissance strikes. In Rolling Thunder 10, the number of authorized armed reconnaissance sorties rose slightly to not more than twenty-four per twenty-four-hour period, and this level held through Rolling Thunder 12. We were still operating at less than optimum effectiveness, however, and certainly well below our capability. (We could have flown ten times as many sorties as were permitted.)

Ironically, we picked up a piece of fateful intelligence information during this time frame. On 5 April, a strategic reconnaissance mission photograph revealed the first surface-to-air missile (SAM) site (being prepared to receive the Soviet-supplied type SA-2 missile) under construction fifteen miles southeast of Hanoi. While we dawdled, moving forward with mincing steps in the inconsequential southern part of North Vietnam, a hot reception was being prepared for us when we finally did move up into the heartland of the enemy's home territory.

By the middle of April 1965 a considerable difference of opinion had developed between Washington and Saigon. In a series of messages, the Secretary of Defense expressed his desire to move ahead quickly with the introduction of U. S. and third-country ground forces and their employment in a combat role. Ambassador Taylor became increasingly distressed by what he perceived to be an insistence on moving in a direction and at a pace which exceeded the actions authorized earlier in NSAM #328. As a result, Secretary McNamara convened a conference in Honolulu on 20 April attended by General Wheeler, Chairman of the JCS; General Westmoreland, COMUSMACV; myself, CINCPAC; Ambassador Taylor from Saigon; William Bundy from the State Department; and John T. McNaughton, Assistant Secretary of Defense for International Security Affairs.

At this meeting it became clear that Secretary McNamara intended to downgrade the air war against North Vietnam and to emphasize the air and ground war in South Vietnam. He insisted that the requirement for air power in South Vietnam must get the

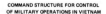

COMMAND STRUCTURE FOR CONTROL
OF MILITARY OPERATIONS IN VIETNAM

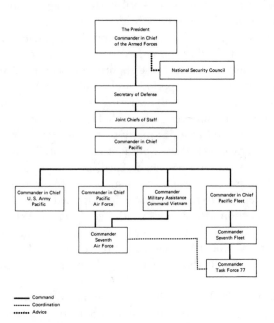

Air operations *against North Vietnam* were controlled by CINCPAC through his subordinates, the Commander in Chief Pacific Fleet (CINCPACFLT) and the Commander in Chief Pacific Air Force (CINCPACAF). CINCPACFLT issued operational directives to Commander Task Force 77, keeping Commander Seventh Fleet informed. CINCPACAF issued operational directives to Commander Seventh Air Force, who was based in Saigon.

Air operations *in South Vietnam* were directed by Commander U. S. Military Assistance Command Vietnam (COMUSMACV) through Commander Seventh Air Force. Thus Commander Seventh Air Force reported to two superiors and had two different groups of aircraft under him. The air force aircraft based in South Vietnam were used primarily in South Vietnam, while those aircraft based in Thailand were used in North Vietnam and Laos.

Navy air operations in North Vietnam and Laos were coordinated with air force operations by a Commander Task Force 77 Coordinating Group, which was based with Commander Seventh Air Force in Saigon.

The organization for air operations was criticized at times, usually by people who did not understand it, and occasionally by people who had a parochial axe to grind. The organization satisfied diverse operational requirements and performed to my satisfaction.

first call on our air assets. It was his decision that anytime there was not enough air power in South Vietnam to take care of requirements, more would be brought in; but until it was in place, air assets programmed for attacks in the north would be diverted to satisfy the needs in the south.

A précis of the pertinent points that Secretary McNamara made in his report of the meeting includes the following:

1. North Vietnam cannot be expected to capitulate or to come to a position acceptable to us in less than six months. This is because the conferees believe that a settlement will come as much, or more, from a Viet Cong failure in the south as from inflicting pain on North Vietnam, and that it will take more than six months, perhaps a year or two, to demonstrate Viet Cong failure in the south.

2. With respect to strikes against the north, the conferees all agree that the present tempo is about right, that sufficient increasing pressure is provided by repetition and continuation. All envision a strike program continuing at least six months, perhaps a year or more, avoiding the Hanoi/ Haiphong/Phuc Yen areas during that period. There might be fewer fixed targets, or more restrikes, or more armed reconnaissance missions. All believe that the strike program is essential to our campaign, both psychologically and physically, but that it cannot be expected to do the job alone. All consider it very important that strikes against the north be continued during any negotiation talks.

3. None of the participants foresees a dramatic improvement in the south in the immediate future. The strategy for achieving our objectives proposed by Ambassador Taylor, General Wheeler, Admiral Sharp, and General Westmoreland is to break the will of the North Vietnamese by denying them victory. Ambassador Taylor puts it in terms of a demonstration of Communist impotence, which will lead eventually to a political solution. The conferees see slow improvement in the south, but all emphasize the critical importance of holding on and avoiding, for psychological and morale reasons, a spectacular defeat of South Vietnamese or U. S. forces. All

suspect that the recent Viet Cong lull is but the quiet before the storm.

The foregoing is, in fact, a distortion of the view I took at that conference. However, as with most conferences that Secretary McNamara attended, the published results somehow tended to reflect his own views, not necessarily a consensus.

These early months of 1965 were, in retrospect, crucial ones. Our Rolling Thunder bombing program against North Vietnam got off to a painfully slow start and inched along with the most gradual increase in intensity. At the same time we decided to employ additional ground forces in South Vietnam and to use them in active combat operations against the enemy. Despite John McCone's perceptive warning vis-à-vis the implications of deploying those ground forces without making full use of our air power against the north, Secretary McNamara chose to do just exactly that; i.e., to downgrade the U. S. air effort in North Vietnam and to concentrate on air and ground action in the south. This fateful decision contributed to our ultimate loss of South Vietnam as much as any other single action we took during our involvement. And underlying it all was an almost frantic diplomatic activity directed at getting negotiations started. Hanoi would analyze such activity as an indication that we were lacking the will to fight. We were soon to give them yet another signal which would tend to confirm that analysis.

CHAPTER 7

A HALT TO BOMBING

THE PRESIDENT ADVISED Ambassador Taylor on 10 May 1965 that he had decided to call a brief halt to air attacks in the north, and instructed him to obtain Premier Phan Huy Quat's agreement to the plan. In follow-up, the Secretary of Defense, with the concurrence of the Secretary of State and the White House, sent a joint State/Defense message to Ambassador Taylor, CINCPAC, and COMUSMACV, as follows:

> In order to observe reaction of DRV rail and road transportation systems, bombing of targets within DRV will cease for several days, effective at 2400, 12 May, Saigon time. CINCPAC should issue the necessary instructions to U. S. forces and the Ambassador should seek to obtain compliance of the [South] Vietnamese Air Force.
>
> During the period in which bombing operations are suspended, photo and eyeball reconnaissance flights over the DRV, insofar as they can be carried out without flak suppression escorts and within currently approved rules relating to altitudes and latitudes, will be increased to the level required to permit a thorough study of lines of communication. The bombing sorties which would have been directed against the DRV during this period, to the extent practica-

ble, will be targeted against appropriate targets in South Vietnam. Rolling Thunder 15 has been approved. It is to be executed upon receipt of appropriate execution orders.[1]

The political purpose of the pause, which was to test Hanoi's reaction, was kept under very tight wraps and was not revealed to me at the time. However, a great effort was made to inform Hanoi of the fact of the pause and of its political intent. For one thing, Soviet Ambassador Anatoly F. Dobrynin was given an oral explanation by Secretary of State Dean Rusk, backed up by a written statement emphasizing that cessation of North Vietnam's attacks on South Vietnam was the key ingredient to a peaceful solution and we would be alert to any indication during the pause that such might be forthcoming. In addition, a similar statement was sent to U. S. Ambassador Foy D. Kohler in Moscow for delivery to the North Vietnamese ambassador there. This diplomatic maneuver was foiled at every turn, but there is no doubt that whether or not the written text of the U. S. State Department note was ever officially received by North Vietnam, the "message" it contained was well understood in Hanoi.

Once again, the response was predictable. Hanoi denounced the bombing halt as "a worn-out trick of deceit and threat," and the Soviet reaction was to call our approach to the North Vietnamese government "insulting." With the failure of yet another initiative toward negotiations, the President's next move was to order resumption of the bombing raids effective 18 May. Since the whole affair had been handled on a low-key basis, no public announcements were made of either the suspension or of the resumption (although several friendly governments were informed after the fact).

In line with the foregoing, I commented to the JCS on the subject of negotiations as it applied generally to the situation in Southeast Asia. I said our objective must be to maintain a position of strength to thwart Chinese Communist expansion since the cessation of fighting in South Vietnam alone would not solve all of our problems in Southeast Asia. I had three specific observations. First, the Communists might unilaterally suspend the insurgency without benefit of any negotiations, shift their attentions elsewhere, and wait for a suitable occasion to make a new effort in South Vietnam. Second, we had enough experience in negotiating with the Communists to know that military pressures must be sustained throughout the negotiating period. We should, therefore, be prepared to maintain air and naval action against North Vietnam during any negotiations with that country, despite expected pressures to suspend such operations in order to provide a propitious climate for settlement talks. And third, more effective control mechanisms than had been used in the past would be needed to ensure that North Vietnam fulfill any promises made incident to negotiations. (These observations—made in May of 1965—would in my opinion have been a good basis for the negotiations in which we eventually engaged for the purpose of winding up our action in South Vietnam. Unfortunately, such terms were not used.)

Toward the end of May, Walt Rostow, who was then a Counselor and Chairman of the Policy Planning Council in the State Department, authored a memorandum entitled "Victory and Defeat in Guerrilla Wars: The Case of South Vietnam." In this memorandum he maintained (against those voices insisting otherwise) that a clear-cut victory for the United States in Vietnam *was* a possibility and that it required mainly more pressure on the north and effective conduct of the battle in the south. He argued that in general guerrilla wars had historically been lost or won cleanly and that the same result was possible in this war.

Rostow set forth four routes by which a guerrilla victory could possibly be achieved in this case. The first would be going to all-out conventional war, as happened in China in 1947–49. Another would be the political collapse of the government of South Vietnam and takeover by the Communists. The third would be political collapse in the south and formation of a coalition government in which the Communists achieved control over the security machinery. And a fourth would be for the guerrillas to convert the bargaining pressure generated by their partial victory into political action to split the country as was done in Laos. Rostow went on to say that if we succeeded in blocking these four routes to victory, discouraged the Communist force in the south, and made continuance of the war sufficiently costly to North Vietnam by bombing, there was no reason why we could not win a clear victory in South Vietnam. Therefore, he argued that more, rather than less, pressure on the north while conducting the battle in the south was the way to make Viet Cong hopes for military and political progress wane.

In connection with this last point, Rostow had always supported a strong bombing program, especially one directed at elements of the North Vietnamese industrial system. He was convinced that Hanoi attached a high premium to the maintenance of its industrial establishment and that the optimum U. S. bombing objective should be not the destruction, but rather the paralysis, of North Vietnam's industrial and urban life.

Mid-1965 was marked by South Vietnamese Premier Quat's resignation on 12 June. On the twenty-fourth, Brig. Gen. Nguyen Cao Ky assumed power as Premier, and announced new measures to strengthen the South Vietnamese prosecution of the war. Gen. Nguyen Van Thieu was proclaimed Chief of State. The inauguration of this government marked the end of a long period of political turmoil, and the Thieu/Ky government remained in power until the general elections of 1967.

CHAPTER 8

THE CONCEPT OF THE CREEPING APPROACH

THROUGHOUT THE LATE spring and early summer of 1965 the Rolling Thunder bombing program was expanded, but with the rapidity of a tortoise. Even with this miniscule expansion, bombing was still restricted to the southern part of North Vietnam, south of twenty degrees latitude, where there were few *important* targets. The important targets, whose destruction would really have put significant pressure on North Vietnam, were located in the vital Hanoi/Haiphong area, *north* of twenty degrees latitude.

Armed reconnaissance sorties were increased to a maximum allowable rate of 40 per day, with no more than 200 per week being permitted. With Rolling Thunder 17, the weekly total was raised to 260, which was still well below existing capabilities and too small an effort to be effective. The authorization for armed reconnaissance was at least changed from stated routes to broadly defined geographical areas; all of these, however, were still south of twenty degrees latitude. At long last the people in the field were given just a little opportunity to use their initiative, but their freedom of action still was severely limited.

The kinds of armed reconnaissance targets that might be specified were also expanded somewhat during this period to include railroad rolling stock, trucks, ferries, lighters, barges, radar sites, secondary bridges, road repair equipment, North Vietnamese naval craft, bivouac and maintenance areas. (A plane on an armed reconnaissance mission flies over a certain route or into an assigned area searching for targets of opportunity to attack, but the kinds of targets are restrictively specified in the pilot's flight orders.) Emphasis was directed on armed reconnaisance routes emanating from Vinh in order to restrict traffic in and out of this communication hub.

At this point it is both pertinent and appropriate to describe the decision-making process for determining what targets in North Vietnam our pilots would be allowed to strike. After consultation with my subordinate commanders I would forward to the JCS a list of the targets in North Vietnam that I wanted to hit during the next Rolling Thunder period (which was usually still confined to a one- or two-week time frame), together with a discussion of the strategic reasons for hitting those particular targets. Although I was constrained by the current strategy of the bombing campaign and by the specific restrictions imposed by higher authority, I was, of course, free to request changes to those constraints and did so frequently. My proposals were considered by the JCS, some targets deleted and others added, and then the JCS recommendations were forwarded to the Secretary of Defense. Before reaching the Secretary, however, the JCS recommendations were reviewed by several layers of civilians from the Secretary's vast organizational staff and by various offices in the State Department. By the time the Secretary of Defense considered these JCS proposals, they were accompanied by many comments and suggestions for change.

The final decision on what targets were to be authorized, the number of sorties allowed, and in many instances even the tactics to be used by our pilots, was made at a Tuesday luncheon in the White House attended by the President, the Secretary of State, the Secretary of Defense, Presidential Assistant Walt Rostow, and the Presidential Press Secretary (first Bill Moyers, later George Christian). The significant point is that no professional military man, not even the Chairman of the JCS, was present at these luncheons until late in 1967. This omission, whether by the deliberate intent or with the indifferent acquiescence of Secretary McNamara, was in my view a grave and flagrant example of his persistent refusal to accept the civilian-military partnership in the conduct of our military operations.

Returning to the chronology of events, on 14 May 1965, General Westmoreland sent a message to me proposing the use of B-52 bombers in South Vietnam. His proposal, which had Ambassador Taylor's political blessing, was as follows:

(1) During recent months firm intelligence has been collected using all possible sources which confirms existence of various Viet Cong (V. C.) headquarters, complexes and troop concentrations in RVN. Each of these targets . . . is spread over a relatively large area and consists of groups of buildings or huts, foxholes, trenches, tunnels, etc., connected by trails. General topography is more suitable for area carpet than for pinpoint tactical fighter weapon delivery. In most areas two and three canopy jungle growth hides surface targets. Even if accurate coordinates [are] fixed on maps . . . or photos, solid jungle canopy provides few reasonable aiming points for delivery aircraft.

(2) Operation Black Virgin One on 15 April 1965 was an attack on the military component of the Central Office South Vietnam (COSVN), the main V. C. military headquarters. Four hundred and forty-three sorties were applied against an area of approximately 12 square kilometers, dropping approximately 900 tons of ordnance. As a result of this effort, the existence of a target complex was confirmed by the uncovering of over 100 buildings and the occurrence of several large secondary explosions. We have determined that the attack created a drastic effect within the V. C. military headquarters. Individual compounds were disrupted for several days and even though these components now appear to be functioning again, they have

not reassembled into an integrated headquarters complex as they were before the attack. . . .

(3) During the attack the target area was completely covered by smoke and resulting bomb pattern was spotty. Bomb damage assessment photography shows that the distribution of bombs throughout the target was poor. Some areas received a heavy concentration of bomb impacts while other parts of the target received no hits. If an attack could have been launched in which the bombs were evenly distributed, the results would have been far more effective. An attack compressed into a shorter period of time would also have been much more likely to kill V. C. before they could evacuate the area and would have allowed ground troops to enter the area the same day.

(4) It is essential that we keep these selected V. C. headquarters and units under attack. . . . We know from interrogation of V. C. captives and from agent reports that the V. C. fear our attacks. We also know that their plans can be upset by unexpected events. The best way for us to keep them off balance and prevent large-scale V. C. attacks is to keep them under constant pressure in their base areas.

(5) Continued use of tactical fighters for pattern bombing does not get the job done properly; it diverts them from other important work for which they are better suited. . . . We will, of course, continue to use tactical fighters [where they can be best used], but for attacks on V. C. base areas we must provide a capability which will permit us to deliver a well planned pattern of bombs over large areas and preferably within a short period of time.

(6) . . . I strongly recommend therefore that as a matter of urgency we be authorized to employ SAC B-52 aircraft against selected targets in RVN.[1]

I sent General Westmoreland's recommendations to the JCS with my own endorsement that it be approved. The JCS had considered using B-52s in South Vietnam a month or so earlier, but had concluded at the time that the big bombers should be reserved for use against important targets in North Vietnam. By now, however, Secretary McNamara had decreed that South Vietnam would have priority on air assets, and it was decided that the B-52s could be useful there, albeit not with the same shock effect they would have had if employed against North Vietnam.

On 18 June the first B-52 raid was authorized against a Viet Cong stronghold not far from Saigon, and the B-52 bombing program, which was designated "Arc Light," became a regular part of our operations in South Vietnam. At first the big bombers flew in from Guam, a distance of 2,200 miles. Later a fine base at Utapao in Thailand was completed and subsequently most B-52 raids came from there. The effectiveness of each B-52 bombing sortie was difficult to assess because of the lack of definitive intelligence, but there was no doubt that many of the B-52 raids did considerable damage to the enemy. Certainly, the threat of B-52 attacks did have a major influence on enemy movements, which was to our advantage.

In early June we had become very concerned that the Communists might be about ready to increase the intensity of the conflict. Evidence indicated that the North Vietnamese were now capable of mounting regimental-size operations in many locations throughout the country and battalion-size operations almost anyplace. Further, Viet Cong units were now equipped with a new family of weapons—received primarily from the Soviet Union, with lesser amounts from Communist China—which represented a great increase in their total firepower. Elements of one North Vietnamese regular-army regiment had shown up in the northern zone of the second corps area, and there were intelligence indications that perhaps two additional regiments were also in that area. It appeared that another North Vietnamese regiment was in southern Laos capable of moving into South Vietnam quite rapidly. The enemy had virtually isolated the Pleiku-Kontum area of the highlands, and a siege of Saigon was in progress and causing serious military and economic consequences. The South Vietnamese armed forces had been chewed up badly and were not in good position; we were worried about their ability to continue fighting.

Authorization had by now been given to go ahead with an increase of the South Vietnamese armed forces, but such action was deferred because the available men were needed to rebuild forces that had suffered heavy battle losses. Consequently, it was considered that a further increase in U. S. and allied forces in South Vietnam was required at the most rapid possible rate. We recommended then that the remaining ground forces of the Third Marine Amphibious Force be immediately deployed, along with U. S. army logistics units. It was also desirable that an air mobile division with all of its combat and logistics support forces arrive in South Vietnam as early as possible and, further, that four additional tactical fighter squadrons be brought in. I also requested that we intensify the air action against North Vietnam. In short, the idea was to save lives by bringing greater firepower to bear.

On 7 June, General Westmoreland sent me a message stating that the North Vietnamese summer offensive was underway to destroy South Vietnamese forces and to isolate and attack district and provincial towns. As he saw it, we had not yet felt the full force of the enemy, and he had serious reservations about the South Vietnamese capacity to handle the situation. Westmoreland considered our only course to be reinforcement by U. S. and third-country forces as rapidly as possible. He recommended that all forces then in the planning stages be approved for deployment. He also stated a requirement for additional troops consisting of nine maneuver battalions in a "division minus" (a division minus certain units) and one Marine expeditionary brigade, indicating that these might be needed later and that planning should begin now. In addition, he asked that the 173rd Airborne Brigade be held in South Vietnam until the air mobile division was operational.

I supported Westmoreland's request for more troops and reiterated the need for four additional tactical fighter squadrons, as well as for intensified air action against North Vietnam.

As a point of interest, General Westmoreland and I wound up in a rare disagreement at this juncture over the issue of how the air mobile division should be deployed in South Vietnam. His view was that the division should be quickly sent to the central highlands after having landed at Qui Nhon, anticipating it could be supplied once there by both the single ground-supply route (Route 19) and air operations. My view was that the division should be based in the Qui Nhon area until both this vital coastal area and Route 19 had been secured, primarily out of concern that the logistical backup problem of 600 to 800 tons resupply per day would severely overtax the existent limited airlift/airfield facilities in the area should the ground resupply route be closed off. Although criticized at the time as smacking of the "enclave strategy,"* my concerns were nothing more than those of prudence with respect to the logistical support situation involved, and consistency with regard to utilizing our forces to first secure our base areas. In any event, the JCS and Ambassador Taylor's views coincided with mine.[2] Ultimately, after further study of the issue, it was resolved that the CINCPAC/ MACV concepts were compatible in that deployment to the An Khe area (about thirty-five miles west of Qui Nhon) would provide a base that could be supplied by road and from which operations could be projected into the Pleiku highlands as well as into the surrounding countryside of Binh Dinh province.

The situation at the time typified our conduct of the war. North Vietnamese regular army units were engaged at numerous points in South Vietnam—aggression pure and simple. The South Vietnamese were in deep trouble; everyone realized they needed help. We were planning to bring in more American troops but this would take time—help was not going to arrive immediately—and, in the meantime, we had strong air forces on the spot ready to strike as soon as orders were received. The logical course would have been to unleash that air power against the homeland of the aggressor. In-

---

*The enclave strategy was seen as a way to get U. S. ground troops engaged at relatively low risk. The strategy proposed that U. S. troops occupy coastal enclaves, accept full responsibility for enclave security, and be prepared to go to the rescue of South Vietnamese forces within a fifty-mile radius.

stead we wasted our air strength on inconsequential targets while planning to commit still more of our men to the ground battle.

On 13 June, General Westmoreland sent another long message to me outlining his employment of the search-and-destroy strategy.* Although he has often been the center of controversy and criticism vis-à-vis this strategy, I considered it to be both well conceived and entirely appropriate to the ground-battle conditions under which he was compelled to fight. He got my full support in this matter, and search and destroy actually became the primary strategy during the remaining years of ground operations in South Vietnam.

In response to our force augmentation request, we were asked by the JCS to advise whether or not we considered that a forty-four battalion force deployment would enable us to achieve our objective of convincing the enemy that he could not win. In response, General Westmoreland expressed the view that whatever we did would probably have little persuasive impact on the enemy, at least in the next six months, but that the forty-four battalions should be enough to prevent a South Vietnamese collapse and establish a favorable balance of power by year's end.

In Washington, meanwhile, the seemingly endless policy discussions continued. On 1 July 1965, Undersecretary of State Ball sent a memo to the President describing the Vietnam War as one the United States could not win regardless of effort. Rather than pour our resources down the drain, he recommended that U. S. force levels be held at fifteen battalions and 72,000 men, the numbers that had been announced by the Secretary of Defense in June. Further, he considered that the combat role of U. S. forces should be restricted to base security and reserve in support of the South Vietnamese army. As rapidly as possible and in full realization of the diplomatic losses that might be incurred, the United States should exit from South Vietnam and thereby cut its losses. His recommendation was, of course, tantamount to defeat for the United States,

---

*The search-and-destroy strategy was essentially a traditional infantry attack mission: locate the enemy, try to bring him to battle, and either destroy him or force his surrender. Gen. W. C. Westmoreland, *A Soldier Reports* (New York: Doubleday & Co., Inc., 1976) p. 83.

defeat for the South Vietnamese, and a Communist takeover of South Vietnam.

The Undersecretary's point of view was not shared by his superior, Secretary of State Dean Rusk. In a memorandum written on the same day, Rusk stated: "The central objective of the United States in South Vietnam must be to ensure that North Vietnam not succeed in taking over or determining the future of South Vietnam by force. We must accomplish this objective without a general war, if possible." Rusk went on to explain why he felt that an absolute commitment was necessary:

> The integrity of the U. S. commitment is the principal pillar of peace throughout the world. If that commitment becomes unreliable, the Communist world would draw conclusions that would lead to our ruin and almost certainly to a catastrophic war. So long as the South Vietnamese are prepared to fight for themselves, we cannot abandon them without disaster to peace and to our interests throughout the world.[3]

In view of the increase in guerrilla activity in Thailand and Malaysia in the wake of the final tragedy enacted in South Vietnam, Secretary Rusk must, in my view, be credited with a clear grasp of the workings of world politics. His 1965 assessment of the situation is being borne out to this day.

Meanwhile, Secretary McNamara's staff was drafting a memorandum to the President concerning our Vietnam strategy. The original draft, also dated 1 July, recommended a total quarantine of the movement of war supplies into North Vietnam by sea, rail and road, to be accomplished through the mining of Haiphong and all other harbors, and the destruction of rail and road bridges leading from China to Hanoi. It also urged the destruction of airfields and surface-to-air missile sites as necessary.

Endorsing the views of this original draft version, the JCS once again recommended immediate implementation of an intensified bombing program against North Vietnam to support the additional deployments of troops that were under consideration (the total U. S. strength at completion of the deployments being recommended by the JCS was to have been 175,000). Furthermore, their program for destroying the war-making facilities of North Vietnam estimated that an increase from the current level of 2,000 attack sorties per month to about 5,000 would be required.

Secretary McNamara went to South Vietnam on 14 July and upon his return a week later came up with a revised version of the 1 July memorandum in which he backpedaled significantly from his earlier stand. Instead of the decisive proposal to mine North Vietnam's harbors as an offensive measure, the Secretary now recommended mining *only* as a possible "severe reprisal should the Viet Cong or North Vietnamese commit a particularly damaging or horrendous act, such as interdiction of the Saigon River." One is led to believe that his recent discussions in Saigon touched on fears that should the United States mine Haiphong, the Viet Cong might then mine the Saigon River. (Although I have no information to indicate who might have brought up this thought, the inference is certainly there.) In any event, his change of heart was most unfortunate since the offensive mining operation would have been the most useful action we could have taken at that time.

McNamara further noted in this revised memorandum to the President that his specific recommendations were concurred with by General Wheeler and Ambassador-designate Henry Cabot Lodge, who accompanied him on his trip to Vietnam, as well as by Ambassador Taylor, Ambassador Johnson, Admiral Sharp, and General Westmoreland. I must emphasize that although I did concur in the specific and precise recommendations the Secretary made concerning the increase of force levels, both regular and reserve, I most assuredly did not agree with all of his recommendations regarding strategy. Some of them were directly opposed to what I had gone on record as recommending—and continued to recommend.

In a follow-up memorandum sent to the President shortly thereafter, Secretary McNamara indicated that the present bombing program was on the way to accomplishing its purpose and should be continued. In summary, he indicated the future program should:

> (a) Emphasize the threat. It should be structured to capitalize on fear of future attacks. At any time pressure on North Vietnam depends not upon the current level of bombing, but rather upon the credible threat of future

destruction which could be avoided by agreeing to negotiate or agreeing to some settlement in negotiations.

(b) Minimize the loss of North Vietnamese face. The program should be designed to make it politically easy for North Vietnam to enter negotiations and to make concessions during the negotiations. It may be politically easier for North Vietnam to accept negotiations and/or to make concessions at a time when bombing of their territory is not currently taking place.

(c) Optimize interdiction versus political costs. Interdiction should be carried out so as to maximize effectiveness and to minimize the political repercussions from the methods used. Physically it makes no difference whether a rifle is interdicted on its way into North Vietnam, on its way out of North Vietnam, in Laos, or in South Vietnam. But different amounts of effort and different political prices may be paid, depending on how and where it is done. [Here he obviously was trying to justify pressing the bombing in the southern part of North Vietnam and Laos and South Vietnam rather than in the northeast sector of North Vietnam]. . . .

(d) Coordinate with other influences on North Vietnam. So long as full victory in the South appears likely, the effect of the bombing program in promoting negotiations or a settlement will probably be small. The bombing program should be designed for its influence on North Vietnam at that unknown time when North Vietnam becomes more optimistic about what they can achieve in a settlement acceptable to us, than about what they can achieve by continuation of the war.

(e) Avoid undue risks and costs. The program should avoid bombing which runs a high risk of escalation into war with the Soviets or China, and which is likely to appall allies and friends.[4]

It is obvious from the messages I had sent in before, and from ones I sent in later, that my disagreement with the generality of the dogma of Secretary of Defense McNamara was on the record.

Under that dogma, the bombing continued slowly to expand and intensify, but the objective of interdicting the flow of enemy troops and material into South Vietnam continued to influence target selection, and much caution was exercised with respect to sensitive targets, or at least what the Secretary *perceived* as sensitive. (His perception of target sensitivity is very much open to question in my mind.) The bottom line was simply that the Secretary refused to approve either the overall JCS concept for fighting the Vietnam war, which included effective Rolling Thunder strikes against key military and economic targets, and a blockade mining attack on North Vietnamese targets, or specific JCS proposals for attacks on major fuel depots, power plants, airfields, and other war-ending targets. His decisions, apparently, were made with the President's concurrence.

As I have indicated before, this was obviously a most critical decision point in the Vietnam War. We had decided to put major ground forces into South Vietnam and to use them in a broad range of offensive tasks, thus becoming committed to fighting on the ground in Asia; but, at the same time, we were not allowed to use our air and naval power to its maximum effectiveness in support of that ground effort. There is no question that the high-value targets, *which remained off limits*, were in the Hanoi/Haiphong area. In essence, all the traffic arteries came together in Hanoi, and the economy of North Vietnam was therefore dependent upon continued functioning of that city's industry, as well as its lines of control and communication. Accordingly, the North Vietnamese leadership was very vulnerable to a concentrated and sustained attack on this area. The U. S. forces, however, were not allowed to do more than peck at seemingly random individual targets in North Vietnam, and always under severe restrictions. We were denying ourselves the advantage of our immensely superior firepower and technology, fighting a war with one hand tied behind our backs. It was quite clear that with this policy we could expect a long, painful war with many more Americans being needlessly killed. What a difference had we been allowed to utilize fully our military-technological power!

Fighting in this strange no-win fashion created problems for our fighting men. One commander who clearly visualized the pitfalls and gave his men dramatic guidance was Cdr. James B. Stockdale, U. S. Navy, who was Commander of the Air Wing aboard the aircraft carrier USS *Oriskany*. Cdr. Stockdale had participated in the 1964 Gulf of Tonkin attacks and the subsequent air strikes against North Vietnam. In April 1965 he was returning to the Tonkin Gulf aboard *Oriskany*. The briefing he gave to his pilots at that time expressed a remarkably perceptive grasp of where the military man must stand vis-à-vis the political strategies to which he finds himself responding.

Having reviewed for you the terrain of Vietnam, the enemy's order of battle, the rules of engagement, and to some extent the modern history of the conflict and the evolution of America's strategy, I think I owe you in addition a straight from the shoulder discussion of pilots' mental attitudes and orientation in "limited war" circumstances. I saw the need for this last summer aboard *Ticonderoga* — after the start of the war had caught us by surprise and we had gone through those first, exciting days pretty much on adrenaline. In the lull that followed, as we prepared for a next round, I could sense that those fine young men who had measured up so well in the sudden reality of flak and burning targets wanted to talk and get their resources and value systems lined up for the long haul. Like most of you, they were well read, sensitive, sometimes skeptical — those educated in the American liberal tradition to think for themselves — those who are often our most productive citizens — and just as often, our best soldiers. They realized that bombing heavily defended targets is serious business and no game — that it is logically impossible, in the violence of a fight, to commit oneself, as an individual, only in some proportion of his total drive and combative instinct. It has to be all or nothing; dog eat dog over the target. I think they were asking themselves, as you might — Where do I as a person, a person of awareness, refinement and education, fit into this "limited war," "measured response" concept?

I want to level with you right now, so you can think it over here in mid-Pacific and not kid yourself into imagining "stark realizations" in the Gulf of Tonkin. Once you go "feet dry" over the beach, there can be nothing limited about your commitment. "Limited war" means to us that our target list has limits, our ordnance loadout has limits, our rules of engagement have limits, but that does *not* mean that there is anything "limited" about our personal obligations as fighting men to carry out assigned missions with all we've got. If you think it is possible for a man, in the heat of battle, to apply something less than total *personal* commitment—equated perhaps to your idea of the proportion of *national* potential being applied, you are wrong. It's contrary to human nature. So also is the idea I was alarmed to find suggested to me by a military friend in a letter recently: that the prisoner of war's Code of Conduct is some sort of a "total war" document. You can't go half way on that, either. The Code of Conduct was not written for "total wars" or "limited wars," it was written for all wars, and let it be understood that it applies with full force to this Air Wing—in *this* war.

What I am saying is that national commitment and personal commitment are two different things. All is not relative. You classical scholars know that even the celebrated "free thinker" Socrates was devoted to ridiculing the sophist idea that one can avoid black and white choices in arriving at personal commitments; one sooner or later comes to a fork in the road. As Harvard's philosophy great, Alfred North Whitehead, said: "I can't bring half an umbrella to work when the weatherman predicts a 50% chance of rain." We are all at the fork in the road this week. Think it over. If you find yourself rationalizing about moving your bomb release altitude up a thousand feet from where your strike leader briefs it, or adding a few hundred pounds fuel to your over target bingo because "the Navy needs you for greater things," or you must save the airplane for some "great war" of the future, you're in the wrong outfit. You owe it to yourself to have a talk with your skipper or me. It's better for both you and your shipmates that you face up to your fork in the road here at 140° east rather than later, 2000 miles west of here, on the line.

Let us all face our prospects squarely. We've got to be prepared to obey the rules and contribute without reservation. If political or religious conviction helps you do this, so much the better, but you're still going to be expected to press on with or without these comforting thoughts, simply because this uniform commits us to a military ethic— the ethic of personal pride and excellence that alone has supported some of the greatest fighting men in history. Don't require Hollywood answers to What are we fighting for? We're here to fight because it's in the interest of the United States that we do so. This may not be the most dramatic way to explain it, but it has the advantage of being absolutely correct.

Would that the audience listening to this insightful hard-hitting bit of philosophy could have included politico-strategic decision makers at every level!

Rolling Thunder expanded during the remainder of 1965 on a bit-by-piece basis. For example, we graduated to receiving target approval from Washington in two-week packages vice one-week packages. We were still not permitted the latitude in the field, however, of preparing extended air campaign plans. The intent was obviously to keep any increase in the intensity of the air war firmly in the hands of the political decision makers. In addition, the JCS list of major targets grew from 94 to 236 by the end of the year. This growth was caused by coordinated CINCPAC and JCS analysis of the various targets in North Vietnam, which added to the list progressively. Nevertheless, the targets authorized for attack continued to be selected in Washington by the Secretary of Defense and the White House. Few of these were ever high-value targets in that critical northeast quadrant, north of twenty degrees latitude, which contained the Hanoi/Haiphong military complexes and major port facilities, as well as the lines of communication to China. Further-

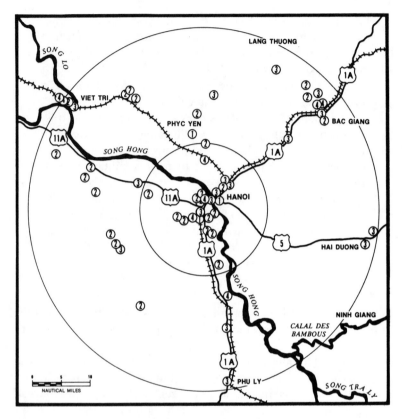

HANOI — PROHIBITED AND RESTRICTED AREAS. The concentration of important targets within the ten-mile Prohibited Area and the thirty-mile Restricted Area around Hanoi is dramatically illustrated on this chart. Note how all roads and railroads converge in the center of Hanoi and a heavily used waterway flows through the city. Highway number 5 between Hanoi and Haiphong is paralleled by a railroad that is not shown on this chart. The numbers indicate classifications of targets as follows: (1) airfields; (2) military installations including army barracks, military headquarters, supply depots, ammunition depots, and radio transmitters; (3) transportation targets — bridges, railroad yards, and locks; (4) industrial targets such as chemical plants, thermal power plants and transformer yards.

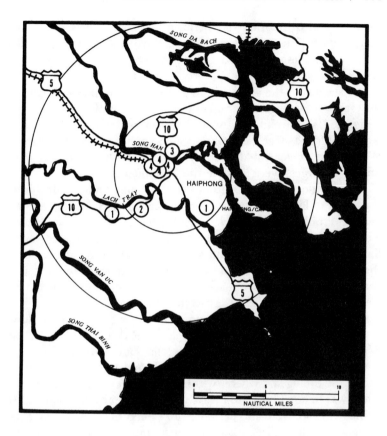

HAIPHONG — PROHIBITED AND RESTRICTED AREAS. The four-mile Prohibited Area and the ten-mile Restricted Area around Haiphong are shown on this chart. The numbers indicate target classifications similar to the Hanoi chart: (1) airfields; (2) military installations; (3) transportation; and (4) industrial.

more, virtual sanctuaries were permitted to exist in the areas around Hanoi and Haiphong, and in the areas thirty and twenty-five miles from the Chinese border in the northwest and in the northeast, respectively.

Specifically, the areas within a circle of ten-miles radius from the center of Hanoi and four miles from the center of Haiphong were designated as "Prohibited Areas." No target in these Prohibited Areas could be struck without specific approval from the JCS in Washington, which could seldom be obtained. Obviously, the most important targets were those in the Prohibited Areas.

In addition, the areas within a circle of thirty-miles radius from the center of Hanoi and ten miles of the center of Haiphong (excluding the Prohibited Areas) were designated as "Restricted Areas." The JCS, as directed by the Secretary of Defense, imposed severe limitations (which varied from week to week) on target attacks in these areas, and essentially no strikes were authorized without JCS permission. A large percentage of the remaining important targets were located within these Restricted Areas.

Such severe restrictions on air operations were lifted only slowly and never completely. For example, in Rolling Thunder 21 the Washington "controllers" raised the maximum armed reconnaissance sorties per week from 200 to 250, and they allowed me to decide the timing and where, within authorized areas, the weight of effort was to be. This was at least a crumb given to the commander in the field. We were also permitted to extend the armed reconnaissance area a short distance to the north, and we were given a little more latitude in restrike authority.

On 24 July 1965, we lost our first aircraft to a surface-to-air missile (SAM). As a result of this loss, a special strike against SAM sites was authorized, and, for the first time, we got authority to conduct low-altitude photography over the whole of North Vietnam to confirm or deny the existence of occupied SAM sites. Despite this new enemy threat, however, the sanctuary areas that I have previously defined were still off-limits, and Phuc Yen airfield near Hanoi was given a specific sanctuary ten miles in diameter. All these restrictions made it most difficult for our airmen to fly their assigned missions and made them more susceptible to enemy fire since they were, quite naturally, required to pay close attention to staying away from those areas. It soon became clear that the SAM sites were being moved around very frequently, but we were *forbidden* to hit them until we had analyzed photographs of suspected sites. By the time the photographs were analyzed, of course, the SAM sites had been moved elsewhere . . . and so the hunt was on again.

By degrees, but almost grudgingly, increases were made in the number of armed reconnaissance sorties and in the targets. One graphic example of a small concession to an otherwise incredibly restrictive operational climate is illustrated in a strike authorized in late September. We were allowed for the first time to hit two bridges northeast of Hanoi, but these targets had to be struck simultaneously and *only once*. And so, while this was the first time we had been authorized to attack lines of communication targets in the vital northeast quadrant, the immediate-case restrictions made it quite impossible to strike these targets effectively. At the same time, attacks on SAM sites within a thirty-nautical-mile radius of Hanoi were prohibited, thereby actually extending the already stringent ten-mile Prohibited Area restriction around that city. One had the feeling of being in Lewis Carroll's Wonderland—totally unrealistic.

In late October and early November, we were authorized for the first time to strike *one target* within the Restricted Area of Haiphong. And in late November the prohibition was removed against suppression strikes on SAM units inside the thirty-nautical-mile radius around Hanoi which had fired on U. S. aircraft. Even this was qualified since only *if* these sites were observed firing on a U. S. aircraft could the aircraft then return fire. Our pilots had just been given the right of self-defense!

On 26 November, I reiterated to the JCS my feeling that it was vital to destroy the source targets in the northeast part of North Vietnam, including those in the Hanoi/Haiphong area, and again recommended disruption of major port facilities and subsequent increased armed reconnaissance directed at the road, rail and coastal lines of communication from China and on the inland waterways. This was another of my many recommendations on stepping up the air war, which were usually turned down, but it was necessary to continue making them in order to get the restrictions lifted at least partially.

Earlier, in September, a JCS study group had assessed the Rolling Thunder achievements and revealed that despite the growing widespread damage to North Vietnam there was no indication of any willingness to negotiate or to terminate support to the Viet Cong in the south. In commenting on this study, I had emphasized that increased pressure was basic to the concept of Rolling Thunder, and that increasing pressure had *not* been maintained in either armed reconnaissance or fixed-target strikes. I pointed out that in fact the armed reconnaissance sorties had leveled off over the two previous months, partly because the authorized area contained fewer lucrative targets, and that strikes on fixed targets had actually been decreased. Thus we had in truth *lessened* pressure on North Vietnam, rather than increasing it. It was not surprising that the North Vietnamese were not evincing the slightest desire to negotiate under such conditions.

CHAPTER 9

BOMBING SUSPENDED, RETREAT FROM REALITY

I N THE FALL of 1965 there had been a great deal of debate on a new pause in the bombing. The debate started in July, became intense in November and December, and ultimately led to the pause commencing on Christmas Day. Secretary McNamara and his Assistant Secretary for Internal Security Affairs, John McNaughton, played leading roles in this discussion. At first Secretary McNamara had been thinking in terms of a six-to-eight week standdown, but by 30 November his position had changed somewhat. He summarized his views in a memorandum to the President:

> It is my belief that there should be a three or four week pause in the program of bombing the North before we either greatly increase our troop deployments to Vietnam or intensify our strikes against the North. The reasons for this belief are, first, we must lay a foundation in the minds of the American public and in world opinion for such an enlarged phase of the war, and second, we should give North Vietnam a face-saving chance to stop the aggression.[1]

Earlier that month a State Department memorandum had gone to the President with arguments for and against the pause. Briefly summarized, it set forth the following:

For the pause:

1. It would offer the North Vietnamese and the Viet Cong a chance to move toward a solution if they should be so inclined.
2. It would demonstrate to domestic and international critics that we had indeed tried for a peaceful settlement before proceeding to intensified actions.
3. It would probably tend to reduce the dangers of escalation after we resumed the bombing, at least insofar as the Soviets were concerned.
4. It would set the stage for another pause, perhaps in late 1966, which might produce a settlement.

Against the pause:

1. In the absence of any indication from Hanoi regarding reciprocal action, we could well find ourselves in the position of having played this very important card without receiving anything substantial in return.
2. A unilateral pause would offer an excellent opportunity for Hanoi to interpose obstacles to our resumption of bombing and to demoralize South Vietnam by dangling before us the prospect of negotiations with no intent of reaching an acceptable settlement.
3. Obtaining South Vietnamese acquiescence to a pause would be difficult since it could adversely affect the stability of the Saigon government.
4. Resuming a heavier Rolling Thunder series after a pause would make it seem more dramatic in character, both internationally and domestically, thereby perhaps heightening tension vis-à-vis the Soviets rather than lessening it.

After this exposition of pros and cons, the State Department memorandum went on to articulate Secretary Rusk's position:

On balance the arguments against the pause are convincing to the Secretary of State who recommends that it not be undertaken at the present time. The Secretary of State believes that a pause should be undertaken only when and if the chances were significantly greater than they now appear that Hanoi would respond by reciprocal actions, leading in the direction of a peaceful settlement. He further believes that from the standpoint of international and domestic opinion, a pause might become an overriding requirement only if we are about to reach the advance stages of an extrapolated Rolling Thunder program, involving extensive air operations in the Hanoi/Haiphong area. Since the Secretary of State believes that such advance stages are not in themselves desirable until the tide in the South is more favorable, he does not feel that, even accepting the point of view of the Secretary of Defense, there is now any international requirement to consider a "Pause."[2]

It is important to note that I was not aware of all the discussions in Washington about a bombing pause and had no knowledge of the foregoing ramifications until I reviewed the Pentagon Papers. I found it extremely interesting that the Secretary of Defense was the advocate of the pause, while the Secretary of State recommended against it. There was certainly a sufficiency of military reasons to mitigate against the pause, and one would normally expect to find the Secretary of Defense espousing the military line of reasoning, but McNamara's aversion to taking the offensive against North Vietnam was clearly *well* established by the end of 1965.

Furthermore, neither Ambassador Lodge (who by now had replaced General Taylor in Saigon) nor General Westmoreland nor myself had received advance indications that the suspension of air action over North Vietnam, which was actually initiated on 25 December, might continue for more than just a few days. We had no idea that Washington was considering a pause that would last several weeks; as a matter of fact, on 27 December General Westmoreland sent a message to the JCS and to me saying: "Although I am not aware of all the considerations leading to the continuation of the standdown of Rolling Thunder, I consider the immediate resumption is essential."

Ambassador Lodge submitted a recommendation similar to General Westmoreland's, and by then I had several times made my own case for resumption of the bombing. On 26 December I also commented on the difficulties faced by a commander in the field in the presence of an enemy when a cease-fire is extended on short notice. I emphasized that the advantages accrued to the enemy and suggested that any future cease-fire should therefore be planned in detail, well in advance. Further, I proposed that aerial observation of enemy installations in North Vietnam should most certainly continue during the present cease-fire.

Finally, in mid-January 1966, still attempting to get the air campaign against North Vietnam started again, I sent a long message to the JCS, which also spoke to our overall strategy in the war. Some of the points bear quoting:

> One of the key elements of the strategy in Vietnam has been the application of steadily increasing military pressure against North Vietnam to force cessation of support to the Viet Cong and to bring North Vietnam to the negotiating table. Surely, a negotiated solution to the problem of peace and security for South Vietnam is infinitely preferable to a long, bitter and costly war. We recognize that the effectiveness of military pressures depends partly on a significant combination of moves toward negotiation which clearly indicates to the DRV our continued readiness to negotiate. Based on reactions so far, Hanoi has shown no inclination to negotiate and may continue to spurn all of our efforts unless they are forced to take some other course. We should plan now to resume effective operations against North Vietnam, that is the way to get negotiations started.

> When we resume operations against North Vietnam, the air campaign should be conducted in the most effective manner to accomplish the denial of effective direction and assistance from North Vietnam. This will require operations quite different from those of 1965. The vital external

assistance to North Vietnam required to sustain effective internal military operations and external aggression must be denied. All known military materiel and facilities should be destroyed. Military activities and movements should be continuously harassed and disrupted. It appears that the very foundation of the enemy's morale and resultant tenacity stands squarely on the belief that our patience will run out before his.

The [Communists] know that we would choose to exploit full use of air power as a technological alternative to human loss. To prevent this they have staged a remarkable worldwide political and propaganda campaign. They anticipate that the Viet Cong, fully supported by North Vietnam, can inflict sufficient casualties to generate internal U. S. pressures to end the war far short of the objectives we seek. They have correctly determined that a crucial battle of the war is the political battle. They are now fighting to attain a permanent standdown. We must not permit them to win it.

In consonance with the overall concept, military operations against North Vietnam should: first, deny to North Vietnam assistance from external sources; second, destroy in depth those resources already in North Vietnam that contribute most to the support of aggression, destroy or deny use of all known permanent military facilities, and harass and disrupt dispersed military operations; and third, harass, disrupt and impede movement of men and materials through southern DRV into Laos and South Vietnam.

Denial of external assistance requires interdiction of land lines of communication from China and closing of the ports. Occasional attacks against bridges on the lines of communication in the northeast quadrant has had only limited success in disrupting the flow. This area must be opened up for armed reconnaissance with authority to attack transportation targets as necessary. Destruction of resources within North Vietnam should begin with POL [petroleum-oil-lubricants]. Every known POL facility and distribution activity should be destroyed and harassed until the war is concluded. Denial of electric power facilities should begin at an early date and continue until all plants are out of action. Complete destruction is not required. All large military facilities should be destroyed in northern North Vietnam as they have been in the southern area.

In summary, we strongly believe that air operations against North Vietnam should be resumed as one of the three main elements of our strategy in Vietnam. We should use all available force, with due regard to the President's intention at this time not to destroy the North Vietnamese people and nation, to eliminate Hanoi's capability to support the V. C. Success in all three elements of the strategy promises the most rapid progress toward achieving our objectives. Viewing this prospect from both sides, and in consideration of factors discussed, these three tasks well done will bring the enemy to the conference table or cause the insurgency to wither from lack of support. The alternative appears to be a long and costly counterinsurgency . . . costly in U. S. and South Vietnamese lives and material resources.[3]

This message outlined a course of action that in my judgment would have ended the war possibly by the end of 1966, and surely by the end of 1967.

By 24 January, the standdown was still in effect. After receiving another message from General Westmoreland recommending again that it be lifted, I sent a message to the JCS expressing my continued concurrence with his comments. I further advised that our reconnaissance had revealed clear evidence of unrestricted movement along all lines of communication in North Vietnam, resulting in many new and lucrative targets that could, however, disperse at any time. I recommended that these targets be struck with no warning when Rolling Thunder resumed, which, I added, should be immediately and on the scale previously suggested.

It was not until the last day of January that air strike operations against North Vietnam were in fact begun again. At that time Rolling Thunder 48 was executed, consisting only of armed reconnaissance strikes south of twenty-one degrees north and, as usual, prohibiting air operations in the vital Hanoi/Haiphong area and the northeast sector. Further, SAM suppression operations were now to be restricted to this armed reconnaissance area. We were starting 1966 with heavier restrictions than we had had in late 1965! The vacillating nature of the air campaign could not help but be readily apparent to the enemy and must have convinced him that his propaganda was having the desired effect.

In early February, I recommended to the JCS that we restore the earlier flexibility we had had in air operations as soon as possible. In mid-month I sent another message to the Chairman asking for no restrictions on sorties, and requesting approximately 10,000 to 11,000 sorties against Laos and North Vietnam combined, to be implemented according to the dictates of the weather.

I should comment that in our effort to get a better bombing campaign in North Vietnam, we in the field always had complete cooperation and assistance from the Joint Chiefs themselves and from the Joint Staff. In particular, Vice Adm. Lloyd Mustin, U.S. Navy, the Assistant Chief of Staff for Operations on the Joint Staff, and Maj. Gen. John McPherson, U.S. Air Force, his deputy, were extremely helpful in trying to push our projects through the decision-making structure and in suggesting ways we could possibly influence the Washington apparatus.

In March, with Rolling Thunder 49, the armed reconnaissance area was extended to include coastal armed reconnaissance to the limits in effect prior to the standdown. So we finally got back to where we had been in late 1965—and two relatively fruitless months of 1966 had gone by.

CHAPTER 10

OFF AGAIN, ON AGAIN
PRESSURES: AMERICAN
CASUALTIES MOUNT

THROUGHOUT THE NEXT few months of early 1966, we tried unremittingly to get authority to strike the North Vietnamese POL (petroleum-oil-lubricants) system and to close their ports. The JCS aggressively supported my stand on these two matters, recommending to the Secretary of Defense that the total POL system be struck and major ports be mined.

When Rolling Thunder 50 was executed on 1 April, we were allowed to strike four bridges, and armed reconnaissance along major lines of communication (LOCs) in the northeast quadrant was also permitted for the first time. The level of attack sorties was increased from 8,000 to 10,000 per month. So the strong efforts of CINCPAC and the JCS had, by then, resulted in at least some increased level of activity; the Hanoi/Haiphong heartland, however, was still off-limits.

During this time frame I became involved in one of the numerous efforts, which were made throughout the war, to change the manner of conducting the air campaign as far as the field commanders were concerned. At the beginning of 1966, General Westmoreland, COMUSMACV, expressed his desire to take cognizance of the lower part of North Vietnam and conduct the air campaign in that area as an extension of his battlefield responsibilites. This plan had some validity because the presence of enemy troops and supplies in the area, as well as their movement toward South Vietnam, was of vital concern to our ground-force commander. There was, however, some doubt in my mind that COMUSMACV could actually conduct this campaign with the same efficiency as my Component Commanders (CINCPACFLT and CINCPACAF), who had been giving targets in that area close attention and had plenty of air power available for this task. Therefore, I held off giving him authority along this line for a considerable period of time. Finally, on 1 April, I did change the basic operation order for Rolling Thunder and assigned COMUSMACV the primary responsibility for armed reconnaissance and intelligence analysis in the southernmost portion of North Vietnam, the area designated as Route Package 1.

My change to the Rolling Thunder operation order in due course came to the attention of the Secretary of Defense, and he promptly got into the act. He sent a message to me to the effect that—so there would be no doubt about where the emphasis might lie—operations north of Route Package 1 would be conducted *only* when they did not cause a reduction in required operations in the COMUSMACV extended-battlefield area. This was another example of the complete lack of appreciation by the Secretary of Defense for what the air campaign against North Vietnam could accomplish, and of his preoccupation with the ground campaign in South Vietnam. We were continually justifying and rejustifying the air campaign against the north, being very careful never to let the Secretary think that there was any restriction on the amount of air support being supplied to South Vietnam.

The subtleties of this situation were further compounded by the fact that COMUSMACV and his staff always had a certain amount of desire for more of the strike effort to be exerted in South Vietnam (although by mid-1966 sufficient air power was available in South Vietnam to take care of any contingency). A ground commander quite understandably would like to get the maximum amount of force applied to his objectives. In this case, however, considerable evidence existed that some of the sorties were dropping bombs on targets that could just barely be justified. While I had no objection to Westmoreland's using his in-country air power where he thought best, I did object to his indicating that he had additional requirements when it was apparent that adequate air strength was available. Any request by Westmoreland for more air power always got a sympathetic hearing from the Secretary of Defense, who was determined that all in-country requirements would be satisfied, no matter how inflated they were, before we used any effort against North Vietnam. His priorities for air strikes were (1) South Vietnam, (2) Laos, and (3) North Vietnam—and North Vietnam was a very poor third.

Trying to get the restrictions on the Rolling Thunder operations removed and the level of effort increased was a continuing, exasperating struggle, with Secretary McNamara never convinced that the air attacks against North Vietnam were doing any significant good. Furthermore, he expressed his views on this issue to everybody in Washington with whom he came in contact, so a general feeling grew among a great many civilians that the air campaign actually was not having much effect. In point of fact, it was not having as much effect as it could have had, because we were operating under severe restrictions seldom before applied in warfare. On the other hand, intelligence reports did reveal, as the war progressed, that the air war against North Vietnam was creating many problems for the enemy.

In April of 1966, the JCS forwarded a study to the Secretary of Defense in response to his request for an optimum air interdiction program against North Vietnam. The study recommended the same kind of strong campaign we had been trying to get all along and pointed out that, due to self-imposed restraints, the targets most critical to North Vietnam's support of the insurgency, as well as to its military capabilities and industrial output, had not been hit. It further observed that these restraints had permitted the enemy to receive war-supporting material from external sources through routes immune from attack and to then disperse and store this material in politically assured sanctuaries from which it could easily be infiltrated into South Vietnam and Laos. The JCS study went on to say that by the use of "off-limits" villages and towns, the Hanoi/Haiphong sanctuaries and the Chinese Communist border buffer areas, North Vietnam was protecting its forces and material from attack, and massing its air defense weapons in safety. The study concluded that the heavily restricted air campaign had undoubtedly contributed to Hanoi's belief in ultimate victory, and that it was therefore essential to initiate an intensified air campaign against specific target systems critical to North Vietnam's capability for continued aggression and support of insurgency.

One of the great debates in the first half of 1966 was whether or not to strike POL storage facilities in North Vietnam. A strike against these facilities had been recommended by CINCPAC and the JCS numerous times, and the idea had been studied by almost every agency in Washington. In the meantime, however, there had been enough publicity in the press about hitting the POL facilities that the Communists were sparing no effort to disperse their fuel supplies. The Hanoi and Haiphong POL storage complexes were still lucrative targets, but by now the North Vietnamese were storing fuel in barrels in caves and along the streets of villages in order to make such supplies immune from air attack (they knew we would not strike a populated area).

Rather surprisingly, Secretary McNamara's memorandum to the President on bombing operations for April found him in the JCS corner with a forceful recommendation to authorize attacks on seven of the nine POL storage facilities in the Hanoi/Haiphong area. Further, his recommendations included attacks on the Haiphong cement plant, and on roads, bridges and railroads connecting Hanoi with Haiphong and leading from the two cities to the Chinese border. One wonders what caused the Secretary of Defense to take such a strong stand at this point. It would appear he was now in sympathy with the marked escalation that CINCPAC and the JCS had been urging. The question remains in my mind, however: Did McNamara really want President Johnson to approve these recommendations? What he told the President in private may have been quite different from the message in his memorandum. Then again, there may well have been overriding reasons for this seeming about-face which are not discernible to me. In any event, the President did not approve all the recommendations. He restricted CINCPAC to a total of 900 sorties in the all-important northeast quadrant during April, and gave permission to strike roads, railroads, and bridges provided they were *outside* of the Prohibited Areas around Hanoi and Haiphong; but he did not approve attacks on the POL facilities or the cement plant.

Before the POL question was eventually settled, it had assumed the proportions of a major strategic issue. The political risks and military dangers had been brought up and carefully appraised. The hesitant decision makers had great difficulty coming to grips with this problem, which became the source of a significant policy dispute within the administration. Some saw it in the context of the overall bombing program as seriously risking war with China or the U. S. S. R., and some were more concerned over the risk of incurring severe domestic political repercussions. Some envisioned the POL targets as the first in a series of high-value targets that North Vietnam would consider crucial, and they worried that if these were hit, North Vietnam might call on its allies to intervene, or perhaps even strike the Saigon POL storage in reprisal. Official intelligence estimates were available, which said that, on balance, Chinese or Soviet intervention in the war was unlikely; but, of course, no one could say that such intervention was positively out of the question. In general, all of the well-worn reasons for inaction were repeatedly emphasized by the mid-level civilian hierarchy in the Defense and State Departments.

On 23 June, however, we finally got permission to strike the POL targets, and with it many exhortations to be careful. Because of the intense interest of both the President and the Secretary of Defense, and the great apprehension over what might happen, we were also directed to give Washington rapid and complete information, minute by minute, on how the strikes were going. The following day, moreover, we got word that news of the strike had been leaked to the press somehow, so the North Vietnamese—indeed, the world—were informed of our plans before we could even start. This was a flagrant example of another of the difficulties we had during the war: while we were being directed to take the utmost care to keep enemy civilian casualties to a minimum, someone in Washington would leak our plans to the press, thereby making the accomplishment of the mission many, many times more hazardous for our *own* pilots. To add to our frustration in this particular instance, authorization to strike the POL targets was canceled on 25 June with no explanation. Presumably the reason was the less-than-perfect weather that was forecast, since I was told new authority to strike would be issued as soon as the weather improved and our forces were ready. On the other hand, the strike may have been canceled, rather than merely postponed, for security reasons in anticipation of another press leak.

On the twenty-eighth, we sent word that our forces were ready and the weather forecast favorable, and requested permission to initiate the strikes. We were authorized to go ahead, and the strikes were finally launched on the thirtieth. The Hanoi strike by the air force was very successful, with about ninety-five percent of the POL facility extensively damaged. The navy's first strike group into the Haiphong storage area was not large enough and a second strike had to be launched, after which the evidence indicated that Haiphong's POL was also about ninety-five percent damaged. Following the Hanoi and Haiphong strikes, Washington initiated a campaign to destroy all the other small storage areas in North Vietnam that were not in populated areas. Interestingly enough, Washington was now impatient to get on with knocking off these POL targets. We considered that interdicting the railroad, road and waterborne traffic (all of which were engaged in moving POL supplies) would make a greater contribution to the overall campaign, and we wanted to hit the small, widely dispersed POL targets only as strike forces were available. However, the pressure was on to get every POL target right away—no doubt as the result of official Washington's delight over the success of the major POL strikes and the relatively mild reaction from the international community.

It became clear as the summer wore on that, although we had destroyed a goodly portion of the North Vietnamese major fuel-storage capacity, they could still meet requirements through their residual dispersed capacity, supplemented by continued imports that we were not permitted to stop. The fact that they could disperse POL stores in drums in populated areas was a great advantage to the enemy. We actually had photos of urban streets lined with oil drums, but were not allowed to hit them. Furthermore, the Secretary of Defense was disappointed that the POL campaign had not had a more dramatic effect on enemy operations. McNamara once more became disenchanted with the bombing program as a whole. In the meantime, we had not struck any important targets other than POL. Against mounting opposition, both CINCPAC and the JCS continued to press for permission to proceed with such a campaign. Rolling Thunder 51, which started on 9 July 1966, expanded the armed reconnaissance area to include all of North Vietnam *except* for a thirty-mile zone along the Chinese border and the Restricted Areas around Hanoi and Haiphong. The important armed reconnaissance targets, however, still remained within these sanctuaries. The number of sorties authorized per month was raised to 10,000. So we had a significant force available, but the vital targets were still "off limits." By September we had been given enough freedom so that armed reconnaissance was fairly successful in knocking off trucks and rail units outside the Restricted Areas, and by 25 September the interdiction effort had closed the northwest rail line. It stayed closed throughout the following month.

In early October, Secretary McNamara made a brief visit to South Vietnam and returned more convinced than ever that our present military policies and actions were essentially unproductive. His report to the President reflected his general pessimism and recommended that we level off the U. S. effort and seek a solution through diplomatic channels. His conclusion regarding the air war was that since the bombing had to date neither significantly reduced infiltration nor diminished Hanoi's will to continue the fight (in this he noted the concurrence of the intelligence community), we should avoid any further escalation in this program. As an alternative McNamara recommended construction of a physical anti-infiltration barrier just south of the Demilitarized Zone and in Laos. Noting that his views would not be easily accepted in some circles, he commented:

> Any limitation on the bombing of Vietnam would cause serious psychological problems among the men who are risking their lives to help achieve our political objectives;

among their commanders, up to and including the JCS; and among those of our people who cannot understand why we should withhold punishment from the enemy.[1]

The JCS, as could be expected, did not accept these views—easily or otherwise—and responded promptly on 14 October in a memorandum to the Secretary, which the Chiefs expressly requested be passed on to the President. Strongly worded, it said, in part:

> The Joint Chiefs of Staff do not concur in your recommendation that there should be no increase in the level of bombing effort and no modification in areas and targets subject to air attack. They believe our air campaign against North Vietnam to be an integral and indispensable part of our overall war effort. To be effective, the air campaign should be conducted with only those minimum constraints necessary to avoid indiscriminate killing of population. The Joint Chiefs of Staff do not concur with your proposal that as a carrot to induce negotiations, we should suspend or reduce our bombing campaign against North Vietnam. . . . Additionally, the Joint Chiefs of Staff believe that the likelihood of the war being settled by negotiation is small, and that, far from inducing negotiations, another bombing pause will be regarded by North Vietnamese leaders, and our allies, as renewed evidence of lack of U. S. determination to press the war to a successful conclusion.[2]

The Chiefs went on to state that they wished to provide the Secretary of Defense and the President with their unequivocal views on two salient aspects of the war situation: the search for peace and military pressures on North Vietnam. To begin with, it was their belief that further peace offers would be not only nonproductive, but would in fact be counterproductive. They suggested instead that the President make a statement of his unswerving determination to carry on the war until North Vietnam's aggression against South Vietnam ceased. They reiterated their recommendation for heavy strikes on North Vietnam's military assets and war-supporting facilities, rather than the campaign of slowly increasing pressure which had been adopted, pointing out that we had deprived ourselves of the military effects of an early weight of effort and shock, thereby giving the enemy time to adjust to increasing pressure. And finally, leaving no doubt as to intent, the JCS closed the memorandum with this explicit statement: "The Joint Chiefs of Staff request that their views as set forth above be provided to the President."[3]

There is no indication in the Pentagon Papers whether or not the JCS memorandum actually went to the President, but it is unlikely that the Secretary of Defense would have withheld it. It is evident, however, that the President did not accept the advice contained therein, for the strategy of gradualism continued.

In late October, having received indications that Washington was thinking about another standdown in the air campaign, I responded with a message to the JCS, which once more outlined my comprehensive philosophy on this subject. Quoted in full in Appendix B, some key points follow:

> Our air campaign in the North is a major military activity wherein we have the initiative and control over the intensity of combat. In South Vietnam the enemy can engage or disengage on the ground almost at will; thus, in a sense, pacing the ground war to his advantage. Such is not the case in the air over his homeland where he must make a concession if he is to gain any relief from the pressures being applied against him. It must be quite apparent to him that decisions which can increase his losses at home will not be of his own making. We cannot afford to relinquish these initiatives except under conditions clearly indicative of success in our overall objectives.
>
> There are very serious military risks attached to any form of a partial standdown, either in terms of reducing the targeting base or in restricting air operations to small geographical areas. As soon as such reductions became apparent in the past the enemy has reacted quickly by readjusting his air defenses and our attrition has increased proportionately. It is essential that we avoid any voluntary simplification or reduction of his air defense problems.

Rolling Thunder 52, authorized 12 November, increased the number of monthly attack sorties to 13,200 and authorized strikes against a bridge, a railroad classification yard and various other military targets, including a vehicle depot, a cement plant, two power plants, and elements of the Thai Nguyen steel plant. Some of these facilities, in fact, were *inside* the Hanoi Prohibited Area and thus required specific approval from Washington. However, authority to strike the steel plant, the cement plant, and the power plants was abruptly withdrawn before we were able to hit them. Then, on 15 December, we were prohibited from making restrikes on the railroad classification yards and the vehicle depot.

Such restraints on restrikes were particularly frustrating. Frequently we would make one or two strikes on a critical target, and then after it was hit (whether damaged or not) strike authorization would be retracted and permission to go back to that target would not be forthcoming for months—or maybe forever. It is important to realize that to keep a target out of action, you must go back frequently and hit it again; otherwise it will be repaired. The North Vietnamese were adept at quickly repairing or bypassing transportation facilities, but they were forced to use a tremendous amount of manpower to do so, thus reducing their ability to do other things. Regrettably we could not force them into this position with enough consistency to be damaging.

Later, on 23 December, as part of my continuing campaign to get more targets authorized and at least some of the restrictions removed, I requested authority to strike three ship-repair yards and the naval base at Haiphong. Just before Christmas, however, we got word from the JCS that we were not to conduct air operations involving *any* targets within the Hanoi Prohibited Area and that we were to avoid even the transit of this area by strike aircraft if possible.

In comment on the foregoing, I sent a message to General Wheeler, Chairman of the JCS, in which I said:

> We are just starting to put some real pressure on Hanoi. Our air strikes on the rail yard and the vehicle depot were hitting the enemy where it was beginning to hurt. Then,

Hanoi complains that we have killed a few civilians, hoping that they would get a favorable reaction. And they did, more than they could have hoped for. Not only do we say we regretted that any civilians were killed, but we also stop our pilots from striking within 10 miles of Hanoi. Hanoi has been successful once again in getting the pressure removed. They will be encouraged to continue their aggression, hoping to outlast us.

With nearly 400,000 U. S. fighting men in South Vietnam, it must be apparent to Hanoi that they can't take over the country by force. But they can fight a protracted guerrilla war, terrorize the countryside, make revolutionary development very difficult, and kill a lot of people, including Americans. This kind of war can go on for a long time if we let them get away with it. My limited sounding of public opinion, including the thoughts of quite a few members of Congress, leads me to believe that we had better do what we can to bring this war to a successful conclusion as rapidly as possible. The American people can become aroused either for or against this war. At the moment, with no end in sight, they are more apt to become aroused against it. It's up to us to convince our people and Hanoi that there is an end in sight and that it is clearly defeat for Hanoi. However, our action these last few days can only encourage the enemy to continue.

When Hanoi complains about civilians being killed, is it not possible to say, "Perhaps some were killed, we tried to avoid that, but this is a war and some civilians are bound to get killed. Hanoi can prevent it by calling off the aggression in South Vietnam."

If the enemy avoids major engagements in South Vietnam and gets back to Phase II of their plan, the guerrilla phase, then it becomes urgently important to step up the pressure in the North by hitting targets that hurt them. And if some civilians get killed in the course of these stepped-up air attacks, we should recognize it as a part of the increased pressure. This war is a dirty business, like all wars. We need to get hardheaded about it. That is the only kind of action that these tough Communists will respect. That is the way to get this war over soonest. Let's roll up our sleeves and get on with the war. We have the power, I would like to have authority to use it. We should be authorized to hit all Rolling Thunder 52 targets.

The restrictions should be removed. And then when Hanoi screams in anguish we should hit them again. I realize that there are other considerations which are important in Washington. It is my duty, however, to report to you my strong belief that we need to change some aspects of our current posture as the enemy must view it. This I have done.[4]

Thus 1966 came to a frustrating conclusion, capped off by forty-eight-hour standdowns observed on both Christmas and New Year's. CINCPAC and the JCS had made many attempts throughout the year to initiate a hard-hitting air campaign, but restrictions continued to dominate the Rolling Thunder program. I have no doubt in my mind that Secretary McNamara *understood* the military recommendations, but he was determined, in accordance with his own political view of the situation, to hold the air war against North Vietnam to what was in essence an ineffectual level. In this regard, although the foregoing message was officially addressed to the Chairman of the JCS, I knew, of course, that it would be read by McNamara. I did not expect a reply . . . nor did I receive one.

CHAPTER 11

VIGOROUS ACTION: WHY NOT?

I T WAS MY custom to start the new year by sending the JCS a message that reviewed recent progress in the war and then looked ahead to recommend what should be done in the coming year. My comments to the JCS in mid-January of 1967 are quoted in Appendix C. In essence, I summarized and reiterated my concerns regarding the restrictive nature of the 1966 Rolling Thunder campaign (pointing out, for example, that of the 104 lucrative targets in the northeast sector of North Vietnam, only twenty had been hit). I outlined emphatically what I considered must be our future concentration relative to the enemy's known strengths, and ended by saying that, in my opinion, the most important requirement for success was a demonstrated determination to stick to our guns.

This message was followed by a detailed proposed target package designed to systematically flatten North Vietnam's military and industrial base. My proposal emphasized attacks against target systems, as opposed to individual strikes against only a small part of any given capability, and asked for increased pressure through the steady application of air power against key target systems. It called for destruction of seven power plants and ten war-supporting indus-

125

tries, with the Thai Nguyen iron-and-steel plant at the head of the list. Also included were twenty transportation support facilities, forty-four military complexes, twenty-six POL targets, and twenty-eight targets such as docks and shipyards in Haiphong and other ports.

At this time, my arguments for a heavier bombing campaign were supported by a January 1967 CIA analysis, which concluded that "in the long term the uncertainties and difficulties resulting from the cumulative effect of [a hard-hitting] air campaign would probably cause Hanoi to undertake a basic reassessment of the probable course of the war and the extent of the regime's commitment to it." On the other hand, the CIA analysis postulated that restricting the bombing to the southern panhandle of North Vietnam and to Laos "would tend to strengthen Hanoi's will." North Vietnam would regard such a restricted bombing pattern as "a clear victory—evidence that international and domestic pressures on the U. S. were having an effect." Their leaders would be encouraged to believe that the U. S. was tiring of the war and was being forced to retreat.[1] This analysis was, of course, directly in line with what I had said in many previous dispatches to the JCS.

So we began 1967 on a bold, positive note at least insofar as our attitude and recommendations in the field were concerned—perhaps even a hopeful one in view of the objective reinforcement of our position, which the foregoing CIA study had provided. In retrospect, however, I had to conclude that 1966 had been a most trying year with respect to both the management of the air war and my relationships with official Washington in the process.

Insofar as my Component Commanders and COMUSMACV were concerned, we experienced no problems vis-à-vis either management or command relationships. I issued frequent directives on the air war and included them as information addressees on most messages I sent to the JCS. In this context, I should make it clear that, although I did not attempt to review in detail General Westmoreland's conduct of the ground war in South Vietnam, I did review very closely and instruct him in some detail as to the air war in Laos and North Vietnam. I considered this an essential part of my coordinating responsibility. After we gave COMUSMACV the authority to conduct air operations in Route Package 1, for example, we provided him with detailed instructions to ensure that his reporting and general operating procedures were in line with those we were using, since these procedures had proven most effective over a considerable period.

By contrast, the problems in dealing with Washington were myriad. One of the most aggravating was the frequently inordinate delay we experienced in receiving a reply from the JCS to proposals that required their approval. The reason was regrettably simple: the Chiefs could not get a decision from McNamara. On one occasion we wanted to strike a section of road in the Cam Pha-Hon Gai area. We had seen worthwhile targets on this line and wanted to hit them. So instead of asking for permission to attack, we sent a message to the JCS saying that unless they indicated otherwise within twenty-four hours we would go ahead and strike. This put the ball in Washington's court; they had to speak up promptly or be foreclosed by our action. (As I recall, in this particular case we did not hear from Washington and therefore proceeded as planned.) In any event, we began using this procedure occasionally, and I am convinced it met with JCS approval because it forced the Secretary of Defense to make a *timely* decision if he wished to disapprove our plans.

Another frustrating situation, which always accompanied our requests for authority to hit targets in the Hanoi/Haiphong area, involved the tricky business of trying to estimate the number of civilian casualties that might occur. I would be asked, for example, to advise Washington on just what steps we would take to keep casualties to a minimum, and then to predict the number of casualties I thought would result if we took these steps. The JCS had studied this problem in some detail and were predicting detailed figures—one civilian for this target, four for that one, and so forth. The CIA also apparently had a formula for estimating civilian casualties. There was even some thought given at one point to warning the civilian population ahead of time so that the casualties would be lower. (Needless to say, when you warn the civilian population you also warn the military that an attack is going to take place, so your own military forces are exposed to significantly higher risks.) In typical Communist fashion, however, Hanoi was continually protesting about our air attacks, the casualties they were causing, how we were hitting civilian targets, and so forth. Unfortunately, Washington continued to pay entirely too much attention to this propaganda.

We informed the Secretary of Defense that we would take the following steps to keep down casualties: We would conduct a strike only under favorable weather conditions, with good visibility unhampered by cloud cover, so that all targets could be readily identified; we would select the best access route for attack so that normal weapon dispersion would avoid populated areas to the maximum feasible extent; we would use weapons with optimum ballistic characteristics to provide the best assurance of precision; we would employ tactics to hamper the air-to-air missiles and anti-aircraft fire so that our pilots would be distracted as little as possible; and, finally, we would use the most experienced pilots available, ensuring that they were thoroughly briefed before the mission. (At that time, we did not have the so-called "smart bombs," the laser-guided and television-guided bombs and missiles that make it possible to conduct very precise strikes with fewer weapons.) Such precautionary measures would, undoubtedly, help to minimize the problem, but in my view it was an unrealistic and unproductive exercise to try to assess accurately the numbers of casualties that might result from their collective application in our air operations.

As a personal aside, let me say emphatically that it is tragic to have civilian casualties in any war. Washington decision-making circles did not appear to recognize, or at least to acknowledge publicly, however, that in the war in South Vietnam the North Vietnamese and Viet Cong were murdering civilians wantonly and purposely. The situation was a graphic indication of the effect propaganda can have on an administration that is hypersensitive to reactions of other nations and the media. The solution to this civilian-casualty obsession was, in my view, quite simple. Once the decision is made to use military power to settle a political issue, that power should be used to its full effectiveness to get the war over with as quickly as possible. All other considerations should be secondary. *That* is the way to reduce *civilian and military* casualties.

The Pentagon Papers contain a summary of the air campaign of 1966 which graphically underscores this frustrating, ever-widening gap between the points of view of the military and the civilian policymakers in Washington. It is important to note here who was writing the Pentagon Papers. The so-called Office of the Secretary of Defense (OSD) Vietnam Task Force was led by its Chairman, Leslie H. Gelb, and consisted primarily of civilians from the Office of the Secretary of Defense. I think it is well established by now that most of this group believed we should have cleared out of South Vietnam early in the game and left the South Vietnamese to struggle by themselves. It is also apparent that these members of the task force did not believe in the air war against North Vietnam. In the letter that forwarded the report to the Secretary of Defense, Mr. Gelb states, "Of course, we all had our prejudices and axes to grind and these shine through clearly at times. But we tried, we think, to suppress or compensate for them."

Mr. Gelb wrote the summary and analysis sections, in which he attempted to capture in narrative form the main themes and facts of the monographs and to make some judgments and speculations that may or may not have appeared in the chronological text itself. His summary of the air war in 1966 reads, in part, as follows:

> The military view of why Rolling Thunder had failed in its objectives in 1966 was most forcefully given by Admiral Sharp, U. S. CINCPAC, in a briefing for General Wheeler at Honolulu on January 12, 1967. Admiral Sharp described three tasks of the air campaign in achieving its objective of inducing Hanoi to "cease supporting, controlling and directing" the insurgency in the South: "(1) reduce or deny external assistance, (2) increase pressures by destroying in depth those resources that contributed most to support the aggression, and (3) harass, disrupt and impede movement of men and materials to South Vietnam." CINCPAC had developed and presented to the Secretary

of Defense an integrated plan to perform these tasks, but much of it had never been approved. Therein lay the cause of whatever failure could be attributed to the bombing, in Admiral Sharp's view.

The rest of the briefing was a long complaint about the lack of authorization to attack the Haiphong harbor in order to deny external assistance and the insignificant number of total sorties devoted to JCS numbered targets (one percent of some 81,000 sorties). Nevertheless, CINCPAC was convinced the concept of operations he had proposed could bring the DRV to give up the war if "self-generated U. S. constraints" were lifted in 1967.

Thus, as 1966 drew to a close, the lines were drawn for a long 15-month internal administration struggle over whether to stop the bombing and start negotiations. McNamara and his civilian advisers had been disillusioned in 1966 with the results of the bombing and held no sanguine hopes for the ability of air power massively applied to produce anything but the same inconclusive results at far higher levels of overall hostility with the significant risk of Chinese and/or Soviet intervention. The military, particularly CINCPAC, were ever more adamant that only civilian imposed restraints on targets had prevented the bombing from bringing the DRV to its knees and its senses about its aggression in the South. The principle remains sound, they argued; a removal of limitations would produce dramatic results. And so 1967 would be the year in which many of the previous restrictions were progressively lifted and the vaunting boosters of air power would be once again proven wrong. It would be the year in which we learned the negative lessons of previous wars on the ineffectiveness of strategic bombing.[2]

This quote from the Pentagon Papers not only indicates how many OSD civilians felt about the air war in general, but also reveals the predisposed set of mind concerning the air war in 1967. As I begin my analysis of that year, let me again quote from the Pentagon Papers:

During the first seven months of 1967 a running battle was fought within the Johnson Administration between the advocates of a greatly expanded air campaign against North Vietnam, one that might genuinely be called strategic, and the disillusioned doves who urged relaxation, if not complete suspension, of the bombing in the interest of greater effectiveness and the possibilities for peace. The hawks, of course, were primarily the military, but in wartime their power and influence with an incumbent administration is disproportionate. McNamara, supported quantitatively by John McNaughton in ISA (International Security Affairs, Defense Department), led the attempt to de-escalate the bombing. Treading the uncertain middle ground at different times in the debate were William Bundy at State, Air Force Secretary Harold Brown, and most importantly, the President himself. Buffeted from right and left, he determinedly tried to pursue the temperate course, escalating gradually in the late spring but leveling off again in the summer. To do so was far from easy because such a course really pleased no one (and it should be added, did not offer much prospect of a breakthrough one way or the other). It was an unhappy, contentious time in which the decibel level of the debate went up markedly but the difficult decision was not taken—it was avoided.[3]

In any kind of endeavor, avoiding the difficult decision, treading the mushy ground of the middle road, is guaranteed to produce something less than notable success. In war it is guaranteed to produce a true strategy for defeat.

CHAPTER 12

STUDIES, NOT ACTION

IN MID-JANUARY OF 1967 we received word that a group comprised of State, Defense, and CIA personnel had been formed in Washington to study alternatives to the current and projected strategies for prosecuting the war in Vietnam. The group was dominated by civilians, and although Brig. Gen. Theodore H. Andrews, U. S. Army, from the JCS Joint Staff, was involved, he apparently had little influence on the discussions. Considerations included construction of the previously mentioned barrier in Laos and South Vietnam to prevent infiltration, redirection of air and naval action against military targets in North Vietnam, and unilateral de-escalation measures highlighted by suspension of the bombing either in all of North Vietnam or north of a stated line.

We, who would have to implement whatever new strategies might be forthcoming, viewed this study with great apprehension. One thing in particular that heightened our feelings of apprehension was that some of the participants were avowed anti-war advocates. Notable in my memory was Richard Steadman, who worked in International Security Affairs in the Office of the Secretary of Defense. A lawyer by training, he was a bright young man with absolutely no military experience, who nevertheless seemed to believe that he was better at strategic planning than the military. Let me emphatically clarify that because I or any other military professional view the anti-war advocate with suspicion, it does *not* follow that we are pro-war militarists in our thinking. It only means we consider that the anti-war advocate must wage his philosophical battle by seeking to influence the political decision-making arena, not by seeking to weaken or distort the capability of the military to implement political decisions once made.

On 25 January I sent a message to General Wheeler in reply to a JCS request for comments and recommendations on how we might improve the anti-infiltration aspect of our overall strategy. Once again Washington—that is, of course, Secretary McNamara—was on the tack that the object of the air war was to stop infiltration, and since it had not done so we needed to look at more productive alternatives. I had made the point many times that air attacks on lines of communication have never been able to stop infiltration, only hinder it. The primary objective of using air power should not be to try to stop infiltration, but rather to destroy the sources of the material being infiltrated. That is the way to use air power properly, and it has been so used in other wars, very effectively. But you are doing the job in a most difficult manner if you allow the enemy to import material into his country and do not attack it at that point, and then you let him stockpile it in a central location in a base area, such as Hanoi or Haiphong, and still do not strike at it until it is dispersed into small segments and moved along roads, trails and waterways.

I reiterated this basic premise in my comments to General Wheeler. I then went on to say that what was at issue was a balanced program of military operations in Southeast Asia, which included the objective of countering infiltration without undue reliance on *any one* specific measure such as, for example, the proposed ground-barrier system. For one thing, a barrier system is a defensive measure, and although it could most certainly slow down North Vietnamese infiltration into the south by making their lines of communication longer, it could not stop the flow altogether. There were too many other lines of communication available, including the sea routes into South Vietnam and Cambodia, the river systems of Laos and Cambodia, and the air routes into Cambodia. Another important concern was that our strategy for Vietnam needed to stress the offense, and any such defensively oriented anti-infiltration system would have to be one that could be emplaced, manned, operated, and defended without degradation of our offensive operations. (The last part is most important—*if* it could be manned and operated without degradation of our offensive operations.)

My comments to General Wheeler concluded as follows:

> The enemy's capability to supply his forces in South Vietnam has been degraded by our air interdiction campaign in South Vietnam, Laos, and North Vietnam, and by our offensive ground operations in South Vietnam. The condition of his supply situation may account in part for his attempts to avoid significant contact with our forces. The enemy is dependent upon external sources for most of his weapons, ammunition, medical supplies, and assorted technical equipment. The closing of Haiphong would disrupt the enemy's logistical capability to supply these items to South Vietnam. Therefore, I recommend closing the port of Haiphong and other minor ports in North Vietnam. This would be the single most effective and economical method of drastically reducing the enemy's capability to carry on the war in South Vietnam. The military advantages of this action would be manifold. It would still be necessary, however, to recognize the significance of infiltration through Cambodia. The more successful our operations in North Vietnam and Laos become, the more Communist pressure will be brought to bear on Cambodia to increase use of her ports and LOC's for infiltration of supplies into South Vietnam.
>
> The measures to improve the counter-infiltration aspects of our current program are aimed at striking at the enemy's vulnerabilities and countering his strikes, and we were doing this by destroying his military logistics bases, by interdicting his LOC's, by forcing the enemy to sustain combat operations, by providing security for the South Vietnamese population to prevent impressment into the

V. C., by assisting economic and political development, and by inhibiting the enemy's effective use of Laos and Cambodia sanctuaries.

During this same time period, toward the end of January, General Westmoreland issued command guidance to his subordinate commanders on the conduct of the war in 1967. His text pointed out that during 1966 the buildup and successes of U. S./Free World forces had created a new climate in South Vietnam. Having spent much of 1966 engaged in a holding action characterized by border surveillance to detect and prevent infiltration, by reconnaissance to locate threatening enemy forces, and by spoiling attacks to disrupt enemy plans before they could be executed, he indicated that we were now entering a new phase in the conflict. Strategies had to be reexamined to ensure that they were taking full advantage of the existing strategic opportunities.

Since the Viet Cong and North Vietnamese forces no longer appeared capable of achieving a military victory, Westmoreland emphasized that 1967 must be the year to make it evident to the enemy and the world that we could and would achieve our military objectives. Recognizing that military success alone would not achieve Free World objectives in South Vietnam, and that a political, economic, and psychological victory must be considered equally important, he outlined his intention to mount a general offensive designed to (1) maintain the momentum of the offensive on a seven-day-a-week, around-the-clock basis, (2) decimate enemy forces, destroy his base areas, and disrupt the Viet Cong infrastructures, (3) interdict enemy land and water lines of communication, denying him the opportunity to resupply and reinforce his units and bases in South Vietnam, (4) open, secure, and use land and water lines of communication, (5) convince the enemy through the vigor of our offensive and accompanying psychological operations that he faces defeat, and (6) support political and economic progress in South Vietnam.

In early February 1967 four of the principals of the State/Defense/CIA study group came through Honolulu on their way to South Vietnam and stopped for a conference with me. They were Joseph A. Yager from the State Department, Richard C. Steadman from the Defense Department, George A. Carver, Jr., from CIA, and Brigadier General Andrews, U. S. Army, from the Joint Staff. At the outset, Yager requested that the discussions be limited to alternatives concerning South Vietnam, presumably to avoid getting into a discussion of the bombing program in the north. As might be expected, I was adamant that the war could not be discussed without viewing the situation as a whole. We had only a limited initiative in South Vietnam because of the enemy's sanctuaries in Laos, Cambodia, and the Demilitarized Zone. Our strategy therefore necessarily was, and had to remain, a three-pronged one, including maintenance and intensification of our pressure on the source of the aggression in North Vietnam. Yager went on to describe the background mission of the group, indicating that it had high-level support and stressing that its purpose was not to assess the manner in which the war was being conducted, but to analyze alternative approaches. The alternatives, he said, could be complementary to existing programs.

The first alternative that the group desired to discuss was the defensive anti-infiltration barrier concept. I reiterated my position regarding the unrealistic nature of most such concepts, adding that given the current "state of the art" for laying the barrier from the air, I was quite concerned about the probable losses if we tried to sow sensors and ordnance from slow, low-flying aircraft. We then talked about the feasibility of obtaining additional foreign troops, and also about unilateral de-escalation measures. With respect to the latter, I indicated that I was generally opposed to all such measures since they would demonstrate a weakness on our part, which could only serve to encourage Communist belief that U. S. resolve was not strong. I especially emphasized the long-range cost of suspending bombing in North Vietnam: considering the ultimate result in extending the duration of the war, the cost in dollars alone would be astronomical and the cost in lives would be unforgivably multiplied.

The study group also presented alternatives vis-à-vis reciprocal de-escalation measures, none of which I considered realistic. For example, since North Vietnam had never even admitted having forces in South Vietnam, any reciprocal de-escalation would have to come from the Viet Cong—this was completely infeasible in my opinion. The subject of improvements in the army of South Vietnam was discussed. I indicated that further improvement was indeed desirable and we were doing our best along this line, but that further progress would take time. There needed to be more training, more schools, and much new equipment, including the M-16 rifle.

Overall, the study group's visit intensified our apprehension about its efforts. The alternatives these men had in mind could do little but encourage the enemy and reduce our chances of concluding the war satisfactorily.

CHAPTER 13

NAVAL OPERATIONS

A BRIEF OVERVIEW of naval operations during this general time frame is pertinent to a thorough appreciation of the military situation as a whole. Naval interdiction operations in North Vietnamese waters were first authorized in October 1966 and were limited at that time to a belt of water twelve miles wide off the coast, from the DMZ to latitude seventeen degrees thirty minutes north, an area of thirty miles. These operations, called "Sea Dragon," exacted a considerable toll on North Vietnamese coastal shipping, which quickly decreased in that zone to almost nothing. From the first day operations started, the ships encountered shore battery fire and were authorized to fire back in self-defense.

Although our ships were fired at on almost every mission, no casualties occurred until 23 December 1966 when the destroyer *O'Brien* was hit, with two men killed and three wounded. The area of operations had been extended by then to eighteen degress north latitude, and we were trying both to get the area extended farther northward and to be given permission to bombard whenever we desired. Regrettably, this authority was not forthcoming immediately—another case in point of how reluctant Washington was to authorize any offensive operations against North Vietnam. Although ships were used almost from the start of the Vietnam War for shore bombardment into South Vietnam, and we were permitted by this time to use counter-battery fire north of the DMZ, no bombardment directly into the DMZ was allowed. So this became a sanctuary for the enemy, and he was using it. Only when we finally convinced authorities in Washington that the North Vietnamese were in fact using the DMZ as a sanctuary were we authorized to use shore bombardment to counter the threat of North Vietnamese infiltration through that area. We could take such action, however, only against that portion south of the demarcation line that runs through the middle of the DMZ—a restriction that defies reason! The enemy could thus establish fortifications north of the demarcation line with impunity, and that is exactly what he did.

Another naval operation, called "Game Warden," was designed to patrol the rivers in South Vietnam. Designated Task Force 116, it was under General Westmoreland's operational control. The first boats came to South Vietnam in April 1966—two river patrol-boat sections, ten boats to a section. One section was deployed to Nha Be on the Mekong and the other to the river patrol-boat support ship at Dong Tau for patrols in the Saigon River. By mid-September of that year, ninety-five boats were operating on the major rivers of the Mekong Delta in coordination with six armed helicopters. In addition, there were twelve minesweeping boats working on the river approaches to Saigon, as well as a Seal (Sea Air Land) Team Detachment (commonly known as frog men) conducting surveillance and raiding operations in the area. The force built up quite rapidly until by the end of 1966 there were in operation some 120 river patrol boats, three air-cushion vehicles, eleven minesweeping boats (one had been destroyed by a Viet Cong mine), eight helicopters, and numerous support craft.

"Market Time" was the title for a naval operation that had the mission of interdicting the waterborne infiltration of men and especially material from North Vietnam into the coastal areas of South Vietnam. This operation was conducted under COMUSMACV by his Naval Component Commander, and by the end of 1966 there were 220 combined U. S. and South Vietnamese navy ships on patrol. Overall, the effort was quite successful in keeping the enemy from using the coastal waters to infiltrate to the south, which he had been doing extensively prior to the establishment of "Market Time."

In my mind, however, the most significant naval operation we could have mounted was the closing of North Vietnamese ports. So, in February 1967, having previously made several fruitless recommendations to mine Haiphong, I nonetheless considered it worth bringing to the attention of Washington again. I sent a message to the JCS outlining once more the advantages that would accrue. The message sank as usual into the Washington quagmire, but I quote it here since it gives a compilation of alternative methods of port closure.

A drastic reduction of external support to the enemy would be a major influence in achieving our objectives in North Vietnam. Despite fewer ship arrivals in 1966 compared to recent years, the tonnage of imports increased in 1966. This increase demonstrated the rising need for external support in North Vietnam. So while the nature of the cargoes discharged cannot be stated with precision, there is little doubt that a major portion contained war-supporting material. Additionally, the ability of North Vietnam to export products to other nations through its seaports, contributes significantly to its capability to support hostilities in South Vietnam. The closure of selected North Vietnamese ports would result in a severely strained economy and reduce Hanoi's capability to support military actions in South Vietnam.

The closing of the port of Haiphong to ocean-going ships is of paramount importance and would be effective in compounding North Vietnamese logistic problems for these reasons: First, 85 percent of the imports come through Haiphong and there is no satisfactory alternate port; second, Soviet cargo presently entering North Vietnam through Haiphong would have to be rerouted through Communist China or offloaded in time-consuming barge operations. Thus far the Chicoms have not permitted the Soviets unlimited use of their rail systems. And third, the ability of the Chicom-North Vietnamese rail systems to function as a substitute means to provide logistic support is marginal. A demand for increased rolling stock as well as new port facilities would be generated. For another thing, the closure of North Vietnamese ports would be a sign of U. S. determination to prosecute the war successfully, thus bringing increased pressure on Hanoi to terminate the hostilities.

Three courses of action are available to close the ports. First, blockade; an effective naval blockade will require the commitment of substantial forces to a comparatively static operation over a long period of time. These forces would have to be withdrawn from other high priority operations such as Rolling Thunder, Sea Dragon and naval gunfire support. Due to the geography of the northern portion of the Gulf of Tonkin, the attendant risk of Chicom intervention must be considered. Direct confrontation between U. S. Naval ships and Soviet or other third nation ships would have certain international political ramifications.

The second method would be using air strikes against port facilities. I have already proposed attacking 25 selected lucrative targets in the Haiphong port area as a target package. These attacks would probably be successful in forcing most shipping out of the area; however, they would not achieve this result as rapidly as would mining of key areas. A primary advantage of air attacks in the area, in addition to seriously disrupting the port, would be the destruction of concentrated quantities of critical materials that are already ashore. Accordingly, it is considered that mining of Haiphong and air attacks against the Haiphong package complement each other and should be undertaken.

The third method is aerial mining. Mining can effectively close North Vietnamese ports without requiring direct involvement with third countries. Offensive mining imposes a heavy burden upon the enemy with little expenditure on our part. Only a few aircraft are required for the initial plant and even fewer are required for reseeding the mine field. Assets required to conduct an effective mining campaign against shallow and medium draft shipping are available in the Western Pacific. Accurate planting could be accomplished by A-6 aircraft during darkness and under cover of diversionary air strikes. Diversionary strikes would be designed to assure minimal exposure to AA fire by the mine-planting aircraft. Mining is also attractive because it presents the least threat to civilians. In order to achieve the maximum economic impact, the ports of Haiphong, Cam Pha, Port Wallut, Hon Gai, Phuc Loi, Quang Khe and Ben Tuy would be included in overall mining effort. However, the mining of Haiphong alone would curtail North Vietnam's imports to a degree that would severely impair the war-making capacity of North Vietnam, since about 95 percent of all North Vietnamese shipping is handled at this single port. Should the North Vietnamese resort to barge offloading operations seaward of the mine field, this traffic would be subject to interdiction by air strikes and additional mining.

I recommend authorization to conduct offensive mining against North Vietnam ports with initial efforts at Haiphong. This action would provide an effective means of depriving the enemy of imports required to continue the war. If it is used in conjunction with Rolling Thunder air strikes against the port system, Haiphong can be virtually sealed as a source of war supplies.[1]

Although I had made this same recommendation many times before, it was still my professional duty to continue putting before my superiors those proposals which in my experienced judgment would best serve our strategic goals. Viewed in retrospect, however, I must admit that I find it not at all surprising and certainly ruefully amusing to see that the description of the foregoing message contained in the Pentagon Papers chronology begins: "Keeping up his barrage of cables, Sharp urges . . . "!

CHAPTER 14

THE TET PAUSE AND THE
GUAM CONFERENCE

PERIODICALLY DURING THE war we had standdowns of all action against North Vietnam, and the enemy had learned to take maximum advantage of them. In particular, during the recent 1966 Christmas and New Year's truces there were not only significant resupply gains made by the enemy, but our forces had sustained some losses as well. I had earlier recorded my opposition to any truce or military standdown for this reason; the JCS had done so to the Secretary of Defense in late November 1966; and on 2 January 1967, General Westmoreland specifically recommended against the proposed standdown for the upcoming Vietnamese religious holidays (called Tet), which would fall on 8–12 February. I endorsed Westmoreland's message, concurring with his views, and the JCS agreed, pointing out that our experience with such holiday suspensions of operations was that the Viet Cong and North Vietnamese had increasingly exploited them to resupply, prepare for attacks, redeploy forces and commit violations. It seemed pointless to allow the enemy the luxury of such respites, which, in the end, would only translate to higher casualties on our side.

In this case, although I did not know it at the time, the President and his advisers had already committed the U. S. to a four-day truce. On 14 January, Ambassador Lodge had been instructed to obtain South Vietnamese government agreement to the ninety-six hour standdown, and had forewarned them that we might extend the period if promising negotiating contacts developed.

Political considerations notwithstanding, the JCS advised the Secretary of Defense on 18 January that they desired a set of conditions to be attached to the standdown, namely: that Sea Dragon counter-sea infiltration operations be continued up to nineteen degrees latitude, that CINCPAC be authorized to resume air attacks if major land-resupply efforts south of nineteen degrees were observed, that operations be resumed in the Demilitarized Zone to counter any major resupply or infiltration, and that warnings be given to the enemy that violations of the standdown or other North Vietnamese efforts to gain tactical advantage in South Vietnam during the period would prompt direct military counteractions. This recommendation went unheeded, however. The order for suspension of hostilities authorized CINCPAC to execute strikes *only* in the case of an immediate and direct threat to U. S. forces, and directed simply that major military resupply activity in North Vietnam south of nineteen degrees latitude be reported immediately to the JCS, indicating that decisions on how to respond to such activity would be made in Washington.

In conjunction with the standdown, the President wrote to the North Vietnamese leader, Ho Chi Minh, advising that he was prepared to order a cessation of bombing and to stop further augmentation of U. S. forces in South Vietnam if he could be assured that infiltration into South Vietnam by land and sea had stopped. The hope was, of course, that an answer would be forthcoming during the time of Tet so that peace talks might begin in the atmosphere of truce.

There were vigorous efforts within civilian circles in Washington to prolong the standdown even before it began. One Defense Department memorandum on the subject offered a recommended course of action: at the end of four days we should extend the standdown to seven and at the end of seven . . . just keep pausing!

The international community spoke out as well, and even the Pope expressed his hope that the suspension of hostilities could be extended to open the way to peace. Soviet Premier Kosygin, who was visiting in London at the time, joined with Prime Minister Wilson in a rare indulgence of mutual cooperation to seek some means of bringing the two sides together.

Two days into the standdown, on 10 February, the Defense Intelligence Agency sent Secretary McNamara a summary of the North Vietnamese resupply situation during the opening forty-eight hours of the truce, indicating that if the present pattern continued the enemy would move some 34,000 tons of material southward over the course of the truce, the equivalent of 340 division days of supply. This information brought considerable pressure to bear on President Johnson to resume the bombing, but when the truce ended on 12 February, the pause continued. Moreover, no announcement of the continued bombing standdown was made. Finally, the whole abortive peace-seeking endeavor was brought to a close on 15 February when Ho Chi Minh sent President Johnson a reply in which he unequivocally rejected the notion that the U. S. should expect any reciprocity from North Vietnam and made it clear that we must unconditionally halt the bombing before any other issues could be considered.

Not only had our attempt to get to the negotiating table failed dismally, but the North Vietnamese had also taken full advantage of the Tet truce with unprecedented resupply activity, as the military had consistently predicted would happen during any such standdown. The daily sightings of watercraft and trucks between seventeen and eighteen degrees north latitude were the highest ever seen, and truck traffic moving south from the Mugia Pass area during Tet was the highest ever observed in a four-day period. Resupply operations of such volume, which were in marked contrast to the normal logistic flow, were obviously the result of extensive planning and coordination. Movements of supplies southward were well under way by the early morning of 8 February, attesting to the advanced state of readiness that had been reached in the staging areas by the pre-positioning of watercraft, trucks, pontoon bridges, and equipment to repair roads and highway bridges. The use of both truck and watercraft to ship and transship supplies farther southward showed the flexibility of the North Vietnamese in utilizing all means of transportation within the limited time allowed. In all, during the 1967 Tet, between 22,300 and 25,100 tons of supplies were moved from the north into the area below nineteen degrees.

In Washington the focus returned once again to a consideration of possible escalatory actions that would bring pressure to bear on the North Vietnamese. On 21 February, apparently in response to the President's request, Cyrus Vance, Deputy Secretary of Defense, forwarded a package of proposed options to Undersecretary Nicholas D. Katzenbach at the State Department for comment. The package, most probably put together by John McNaughton, set forth eight specific recommendations for air, ground and naval actions against targets in North Vietnam and in Laos. Although in each case the supporting discussions indicated the designated targets could in fact be either heavily damaged or destroyed, the conclusion was that even the cumulative effect would have little impact on the reduction of the war-supporting flow of men and material into the south. The "inescapable" fact that apparently forced this conclusion was that North Vietnam's import potential far exceeded its requirements and could sustain considerable contraction without impairing the war effort. (This was a familiar line of reasoning from Secretary McNamara and John McNaughton, but I maintain the argument was faulty because it did not ever take into account the damaging effect we could have imposed on North Vietnam's *overall economy*.)

As usual, the likely Soviet reaction to our actions was evaluated, and in the case of the proposed mining of major ports was adjudged as follows:

> To the U. S. S. R. the mining of the ports would be particularly challenging. Last year they moved some 530,000 tons of goods to North Vietnam by sea. If the ports remained closed almost all of their deliveries— military and civilian—would be at the sufferance of Pei-ping, with whom they are having increasing difficulties. They would be severely embarrassed by their inability to prevent or counter the U. S. move. It is an open question

whether they would be willing to take the risks involved in committing their own ships and aircraft to an effort to reopen the ports.

In these circumstances the Soviets would at least send a token number of "volunteers" to North Vietnam if Hanoi asked for them and would provide Hanoi with new forms of military assistance—e.g., floating mines and probably cruise missiles (land-based or on komar boats), which could appear as a direct response to the U. S. mining and which would endanger our ships in the area.

The Soviets would be likely to strike back at the U. S. in their bilateral relations, severely reducing what remains of normal contacts on other issues. They would focus their propaganda and diplomatic campaign to get U. S. allies in Europe to repudiate the U. S. action. They would prob-ably also make other tension promoting gestures such as pressure on Berlin. The situation could, of course, become explosive if the mining operations resulted in serious dam-age to a Soviet ship.[1]

At the State Department, Assistant Secretary William Bundy drafted comments on the Vance proposals, which were generally supportive. He noted that the State Department would be inclined to separate the mining of ports used by Soviet shipping from the mining of coastal or internal waterways used mostly by the North Vietnamese. While it was admitted that mining of the coastal/ internal waterways would have a more limited effect on Hanoi's will and capacity, this action would also clearly be much less disturbing to the Soviets and less likely to either throw Hanoi into the arms of China or induce the Soviets into fuller cooperation with the Chinese. (This distinction apparently was important to the President because he did eventually approve limited mining of internal waterways but deferred any decision on mining the ports.)

At this point we were at a very important phase in determining the course of our strategy for the Vietnam War. As the senior mili-tary commander in the field, I had made strong proposals for effec-tive action with the forces we had available. The JCS, in turn, had made similar recommendations to the Secretary of Defense. The U. S. government had tried a standdown as an inducement to the North Vietnamese to start negotiations, only to be turned down contemptuously. But the memorandum answering the President's request for alternatives was really nothing more than a half-heartedly presented list of things that might possibly be done; it avoided a viable, forceful presentation of *positive* options. Certainly Secretary McNamara's policies and influence were strongly felt and were reflected in the varying degrees of negativism that accompanied discussion of the bombing and mining actions. Worries about possible Soviet and Chinese reactions were expounded upon in great detail.

In the end, as would be expected, the President approved only a few of the actions outlined, obviously choosing the ones that offered the least risk of counter-escalation. Naval gunfire up to the twentieth parallel was authorized against targets ashore and afloat, as was artillery fire across the DMZ. There was a slight expansion of operations in Laos, and the mining of rivers and estuaries south of twenty degrees was permitted. And, finally, new bombing targets for Rolling Thunder 54 were authorized, to include the remaining power plants (except those in the center of Hanoi and in Haiphong), the Thai Nguyen steel plant and the Haiphong cement plant.

Implementation of these measures was begun immediately in the field, but since this was still a period of bad weather and we had very few all-weather bombers, it took a long time to get things moving. Overall, although the inclement weather over North Vietnam somewhat hampered our air operations, twelve of the sixteen most recently authorized targets were struck during the month of March. As an aside, it is worthwhile noting that because the mining operation was authorized only for inland waterways, only shallow-water mines could be used. These mines were converted 500-pound bombs, and while they harassed the North Vietnamese, they were not a big factor in the long run because of their small explosive content, and because they could easily be swept (exploded harmlessly).

In mid-March, the President convened a high-level conference on Guam. His purpose was to bring together the members of his

South Vietnam "team," new and old, to discuss the problems at hand. Among the principals were Ambassador Ellsworth Bunker, who was to succeed Ambassador Lodge, and Gen. Creighton W. Abrams, U. S. Army, who was to be deputy to General Westmoreland, as well as South Vietnamese Generals Thieu and Ky. The latter presented to the conferees the draft constitution that the South Vietnamese constituent assembly had just completed, and there was considerable discussion of its various provisions. Of the military issues, General Westmoreland's recent request for additional forces was given some attention, and the bombing program was touched upon, although the principals were not particularly interested in the latter at the time.

The Guam conference was highlighted by Hanoi's unexpected action of publicly publishing the exchange of letters between President Johnson and Ho Chi Minh, which had taken place during the Tet truce. Presumably intended to embarrass the President, the contrast in attitudes—the President's solicitous, positive style and Ho Chi Minh's blunt negativism—actually turned the whole episode into a plus for the United States. It indicated conspicuously that the United States did intend to do anything in its power to gain peace, while North Vietnam was not in the slightest interested.

Inspection tour of South Vietnam. *Left to right:* Admiral Sharp; Maj. Gen. Lewis W. Walt, Commanding General Third Marine Amphibious Force; and General Westmoreland. *U. S. Marine Corps.*

Honolulu Conference, 20 April 1965, at CINCPAC Headquarters. *Left to right*:
General Earl G. Wheeler, U. S. Army (Chairman, Joint Chiefs of Staff),
Ambassador Maxwell D. Taylor, Secretary of Defense Robert S. McNamara,
Assistant Secretary of State William Bundy, Admiral Sharp, and Assistant Secretary
of Defense John McNaughton.

Strategic Air Command B-52 releasing its large load of bombs on enemy targets in
South Vietnam. *U. S. Air Force.*

Pilots of an attack squadron being briefed in their ready room aboard an aircraft carrier in the Tonkin Gulf prior to an air strike on North Vietnam. *U. S. Navy.*

Secretary of Defense Robert S. McNamara and Gen. Earl G. Wheeler, Chairman Joint Chiefs of Staff, listen to a debriefing of strike pilots aboard the attack carrier U.S.S. *Oriskany* in the Tonkin Gulf. *U. S. Navy.*

Maj. Gen. William B. Rosson, U. S. Army, briefing Admiral Sharp en route from Tan Son Nhut Airport to Cam Ranh Bay. At extreme left is Capt. Rembrandt C. Robinson, U. S. Navy, Admiral Sharp's Executive Assistant.

Admiral Sharp, General Wheeler and General Westmoreland conferring at CINCPAC Headquarters in Honolulu.

Repeated bombings destroyed two bridges and cratered roads on this important supply route in North Vietnam, forcing the enemy to build bypass fords. *U. S. Air Force.*

The Haiphong docks, with ships unloading and large amounts of supplies stored in the area. *U. S. Air Force.*

The Guam Conference on Vietnam, 20 March 1967.

Flight deck crewmen ready an A-6A Intruder attack aircraft of Attack Squadron 165 for launching from the flight deck of the aircraft carrier U. S. S. *Constellation*. *U. S. Navy.*

Ordnancemen strain to hoist a bomb to the rack of an Intruder attack aircraft. *U. S. Navy.*

Air force tactical fighters dropped six of eleven spans of the Lang Giai bridge, using 2,000-pound guided bombs ("smart" bombs) that permit an almost surgical approach to precision bombing. *U. S. Air Force.*

Kinh No railroad yard after B-52 "Linebacker II" strikes, December 1972. This yard is located seven miles north of Hanoi. *U. S. Air Force.*

Bomb damage to Hanoi Storage Area Bac Mai during "Linebacker II" operations. *Department of Defense.*

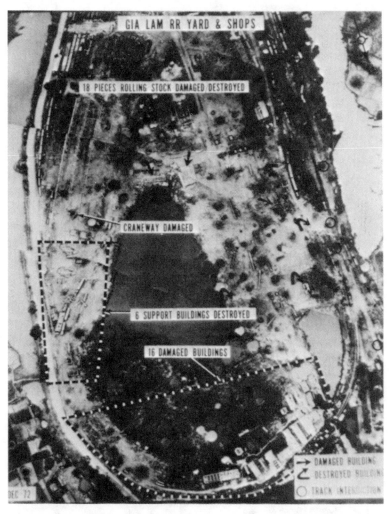

GIA LAM RR YARD & SHOPS

18 PIECES ROLLING STOCK DAMAGED DESTROYED

CRANEWAY DAMAGED

6 SUPPORT BUILDINGS DESTROYED

16 DAMAGED BUILDINGS

→ DAMAGED BUILDING
⤳ DESTROYED BUILDING
○ TRACK INTERSECTION

DEC 72

Bomb damage to Gia Lam railroad yard and shops during "Linebacker II" operations. *Department of Defense.*

The Hanoi thermal power plant, a very important target, before and after "Linebacker II" operations. *Department of Defense.*

HANOI THERMAL POWER PLANT

AFTER

22 DEC 7.

CHAPTER 15

WHEN WE NEGOTIATE:
KEEP THE PRESSURE ON

AT THIS POINT in the narrative, I want to interrupt briefly the chronology of events to examine the case for negotiation. In February 1967, Gen. Maxwell Taylor, who was then serving as Special Military Advisor to the President, undertook to provide such an examination in a memorandum which considered some of the difficulties of negotiations. One of his key points was "that it was in the U. S. interest to adopt a 'fight and talk' strategy in which the political issues were settled first and the cease-fire arranged afterward, hopefully conducting the actual negotiations in secret while we continued to vigorously press the Viet Cong and the North Vietnamese in combat."[1]

General Taylor's memorandum was circulated to the Secretaries of State and Defense and the Chairman of the JCS for their comments, and I was subsequently requested to give my views and recommendations. My answer to this particular memorandum was prophetic:

> In general, any settlement of the conflict in Vietnam must be viewed in the context of our future posture

throughout Southeast Asia and the Western Pacific. We must continue to maintain a position of strength to deter Chicom aggression and defeat it if it should occur. Cessation of fighting in South Vietnam will not in itself solve our problems in Southeast Asia. There are two general comments in this regard.

First, we have had enough experience in negotiations with the Communists to know that pressures must be maintained during negotiations. We should, therefore, continue air and naval action against North Vietnam during any negotiations despite pressure to suspend such operations in order to provide an ostensibly more favorable climate for negotiations.

Second, our military operations against the aggressors in Vietnam should be pursued to the point where they will be prepared to make major concessions in exchange for relief from the pressures being applied against them. Cessations of these pressures without exacting major concessions would provide the enemy with the incentive to sustain and increase his support of the aggression in South Vietnam.

Within the framework of these general observations, I would then make specific comments.

There have been discussions in the past in terms of what are the maximum and minimum conditions which might apply to a cessation of the bombing. In my view we have reached a point where further consideration of a wide range of alternative conditions is no longer necessary. The air campaign in North Vietnam has resulted in significant disruption and destruction of enemy material and continuing operations are intensifying effects which could soon become unacceptable to him. To ensure that the war concludes on acceptable terms, bombing attacks in North Vietnam should continue and be intensified until South Vietnam is free from aggression. This objective can be achieved if North Vietnam strictly observes the 1954 Accords with respect to South Vietnam and the 1962 Agreement with respect to Laos; that is, if North Vietnam stops infiltration and brings about a cessation of armed insurgency in both countries. The bombing in North Vietnam should not be stopped until Hanoi has, first, stopped infiltrating personnel and material into South Vietnam and Laos; and, second, demonstrated conclusively that all North Vietnamese Army units are being withdrawn from South Vietnam and Laos; and, third, stopped its support and direction of the V. C. and the Pathet Lao insurgencies.

The air campaign in the North is a major military activity where more than any other place we have the initiative and can control the intensity of combat. This is not the time for relaxation of pressure. The air campaign disrupts daily life in North Vietnam and causes multiple and ever-increasing management and logistics problems. The United States has the power to force Hanoi to cease support of the insurgencies in Laos and South Vietnam. We should use that power. Any relaxation of pressure would encourage the Communists to increase their aggressive efforts throughout Southeast Asia. Moreover, our allies would consider the U. S. irresolute in its determination to force Hanoi to stop supporting the insurgency.

I have previously proposed a targeting concept which should be approved and the measures for conducting the air campaign that I had previously proposed should be implemented, and that's the soundest approach toward early achievement of an end to the conflict in South Vietnam and Laos on terms favorable to the United States, to the Republic of Vietnam and to our allies. Premature cessation of bombing would forfeit major strategic and tactical advantanges to the enemy. To ensure that Hanoi complies fully with all the conditions indicated above, there must be a system of positive and continuing verification. In dealing with the Communists, control commissions and similar bodies cannot be relied on to exact compliance with the terms of an agreement. There is no substitute for clear and present force with the determination to use it. Experience with the International Control Commission (the ICC) in Laos and Vietnam supports this judgment. An international inspection force must police the roads, trails and combat areas in Laos and South Vietnam to ensure that infiltration has in fact ceased and withdrawals taken place. Probably the best procedure for initial negotiations would be to have the governments of South Vietnam and North Vietnam meet at the military level with the U. S. in the role of observer to reach an agreement on the mechanics of carrying out the talks. Such exploratory talks could be held in the DMZ. The future of Laos is a vital issue to be resolved if long-term peace and stability are to be achieved in Vietnam. The provisions for safeguarding the sovereignty of Laos must be considered in any negotiations. In establishing the ground rules for the negotiations, we should insist that concurrent discussions be held between Laos and North Vietnam. The site for negotiations should be outside the area of conflict in a neutral country. In Korea the initial choice of Kaesong was in Communist-controlled territory and invited and encouraged enemy arrogance.

Admiral Charles Turner Joy in his book, *How Communists Negotiate*, stated: "Never weaken your pressure when the enemy sues for armistice, increase it." The relaxation of pressure in Korea permitted a buildup of artillery and construction of defenses in depth which resulted in two more years of war. To avoid a stalemate in negotiations we should maintain pressure on North Vietnam and if an acceptable agreement is not reached by a set, early deadline, discussions should be terminated and attacks against North Vietnam intensified until the enemy again indicates the desire for an armistice.

Allied mistakes in the negotiations in Korea should be given wide publicity to prepare U. S. and international public opinion for the position which should be taken by the United States during negotiations. In 1951 just prior to the initiation of the Korean armistice talks, the U. S. mounted a major offensive which, by June 13, had penetrated deep into the iron triangle of North Korea and resulted in the capture of Chorwon and Kumhwha. To this point in the war 12,000 U. S. personnel had been killed. As soon as negotiations began the momentum of this offensive was unilaterally curtailed by the United States. And, subsequently, the Communists were able to prolong the negotiations for two years and the number of United States forces killed was 21,000 during that two-year period, which far exceeded the casualties we would have sustained had we maintained the momentum of our successful offensive and forced the Communists to conclude the negotiations in a reasonable time.

In the present instance, the Communists' immediate aim will be to cause the United States to cease its air and naval attacks against North Vietnam. The only way to prevent long and fruitless negotiations will be to continue these attacks against North Vietnam until the conditions outlined above have been fulfilled by Hanoi; that is, withdraw from South Vietnam and cease supporting the insurgency. A program should be initiated now to educate the U. S. public and the world on the Communist use of negotiations as a tool to gain their objectives and the necessity to maintain our military pressures on North Vietnam until it ceases its support and direction of the insurgencies in South Vietnam and Laos. However, termination of Hanoi's aggression under effective verification will result in withdrawal of free world forces from South Vietnam in accordance with the terms of the Manila Communique.[2]

If the United States had followed the recommendations in this message, the Vietnam affair could have ended quite differently. Perhaps political considerations would have prevented our doing so, but I believe we should have approached negotiations with a much tougher stance than we did. In concert with my beliefs, I quote from Alexander Solzhenitsyn, who says on this point: "The Communist leaders respect only firmness and have contempt and laugh at persons who continually retreat. You are told . . . that power without any attempt at conciliation will lead to a world conflict. But I would say that power with continual compliance, continual retreat, is no power at all."

CHAPTER 16

INCREASED BOMBING PRESSURE: THEN MORE RESTRICTIONS

I N THE WAKE of the mild escalation of the air effort against North Vietnam which the President had authorized in February, we entered the second quarter of 1967 with an improvement in weather conditions and an increase in attack sorties, but with a markedly higher level of North Vietnamese defense efforts against our strikes.

Over 30,000 attack sorties were flown during this quarter as compared to about 20,000 during the previous quarter. Although late March through early April generally marks the end of the northeastern monsoonal weather in North Vietnam, this year the monsoon persisted in the northern areas until 18 April, when favorable weather finally began and steadily improved throughout the quarter. As the weather improved, the air activity accelerated, and by the end of April a total of almost 9,000 attack sorties had been flown. May and June approached the record highs flown in August and September of 1966, with sorties averaging more than 11,000 each month. However, the number of strike aircraft in the general

Hanoi/Haiphong area during the latter part of April and all of May resulted in an intense defensive reaction by the enemy. During April there were fifty engagements, which resulted in nine MiGs being shot down and the loss of seven U. S. aircraft, the highest U. S. loss for any single month of the war to date. At the same time, a new high of 246 SAM firings were reported, resulting in five U. S. losses. In May there were seventy-two MiG engagements, with twenty-two MiGs shot down and two U. S. aircraft lost.

Concurrently, two new Rolling Thunder operations began— Rolling Thunder 55 on 24 April and Rolling Thunder 56 on 2 May—which authorized strikes against seventeen JCS-approved targets in the northeast quadrant of North Vietnam. Since these JCS-designated targets represented significant war-supporting activities, each new authorization helped to keep on the pressure.

After the record level of MiG and SAM activity during the first weeks of May, defense reactions noticeably decreased later that month. SAM firings were down, with only two U. S. aircraft lost. During the period of 2–10 June, there was a brief flare-up of twenty-five engagements, with five MiGs shot down and no U. S. losses, but after 10 June, although our pilots reported sighting MiG aircraft, no attempts were made to engage U. S. aircraft. This hesitancy to attack probably reflected a lack of confidence and also quite possibly a reduced inventory following the heavy losses experienced during May and early June.

Destruction of important thermal power plants in the Hanoi/ Haiphong industrial complex caused a drastic curtailment of electrical power in this area in the second quarter of 1967. As of mid-June, it was estimated that approximately eighty-five percent of the total electrical power capacity of the country was inoperative. Since the major portion of this power shortage was incurred in the industrial complex, some industrial processes had to be fragmented to permit the use of diesel generators, and some production processes ceased completely. Further, there were indications that the large chemical plants at Viet Tri and Vac Giang were inoperative. The shutdown of such plants would affect the production of munitions as well as fertilizers, and the indirect effects would include, ultimately, shortages of food and the necessity to increase imports of munitions and fertilizers. Overall, the damage inflicted on the North Vietnamese targets by the Rolling Thunder operations continued to be cumulative in nature, and there were strong indications of increasing hardships on the population in the form of the aforementioned food shortages, in addition to travel restrictions and the lack of electrical power. Most importantly, continued presence over the area was wearing down the enemy.

Meanwhile, the evacuation of Haiphong continued during this quarter, with the population down from 400,000 to about 250,000, so that most of the people in Haiphong were now able-bodied workers. The city's population was exposed to numerous air-raid alerts which caused interruptions in work schedules and backlogs of cargo in the port. In an attempt to avoid detection and destruction during daylight hours, the North Vietnamese resorted to nighttime movement along their lines of communication, and several witnesses reported being impressed by the heavy columns of truck traffic abroad during these hours. Reports of decreased industrial production indicated that as much as fifty percent of the planned output had not taken place. This decrease was attributed primarily to the electrical power shortage and, to some degree, to the diversion of labor for repair of disrupted lines of communication. In addition, the most recent campaign against the northern railroad system had produced excellent results, particularly in the entrapment of rolling stock and its subsequent destruction. Although the flow of supplies and personnel into South Vietnam still continued in sufficient quantity to sustain the insurgency, North Vietnam was now at least unable to mount a major offensive and had to rely primarily upon increased guerrilla activity and small-scale actions.

In the second week of April 1967, I had told the JCS that we needed an improved all-weather bombing capability. The majority of our fighter-bomber aircraft being used against North Vietnam at this time were designed to attack targets that the pilot could see—he had to acquire the target visually to get it in his bombing sights. On the other hand, an all-weather bomber has a radar system that allows the pilot to attack a target using his radar alone, whether or not he picks it up visually. The Grumman A-6 aircraft, which we had in limited number aboard our carriers, was our only all-weather attack aircraft, but strikes by these planes in bad weather and at night had already confirmed that, given more of them, we could conduct around-the-clock harassment and disruption strikes in North Vietnam. During Rolling Thunder 54, A-6s had conducted radar-system air strikes against seven of thirteen authorized JCS targets, with five of the seven being rendered inoperative or heavily damaged. I therefore recommended increasing as soon as possible the number of A-6s assigned to the attack aircraft carrier (CVA) squadrons deployed to Southeast Asia, indicating that we should have fifteen per CVA, with a minimum total of thirty aboard those CVAs operating in the Gulf of Tonkin off the coast of North Vietnam.

Despite the fact that we did get more lucrative targets in the northern part of North Vietnam during this period, we still had many restrictions, and I was in constant dialogue with the JCS to have them removed. In mid-April I tried again to get increased strike flexibility, pointing out that as the weather improved we should have maximum freedom of action to assure increasing pressure on the vital northeastern sector. There were twenty-four especially important targets within the Hanoi Prohibited Area, which we were not yet permitted to hit but which were still considered essential for attainment of our objectives against selected target systems. Again I recommended that the Prohibited Areas be eliminated and that the Hanoi and Haiphong Restricted Areas be reduced from thirty to ten and from ten to four nautical miles respectively.

It was always necessary virtually to beg target authorization out of Washington bit by piece, and we had to be extremely careful not to set off a new negative reaction. For example, I received word from the JCS in late April that they were worried that our air attacks on Hoa Lac and Kep airfields were heavier than needed just to harass and attrite aircraft. They indicated that overly strong action on these fields might jeopardize our chances to get authorization to attack other airfields. In reply, I told the Chairman I had already advised my Component Commanders to be careful not to overdo these harassing attacks for the very reason he had cited, and they had agreed.

At about this same time, I informed the JCS that the number of enemy fighter aircraft that had engaged our pilots during recent strikes against important targets in the northeast area indicated an increasing MiG threat. As a counter step I wanted permission to hit the rest of the airfields (Kien An, Cat Bi and Phuc Yen). Phuc Yen was the most important—and most heavily defended—airfield in North Vietnam because most of the MiGs were based there. Normally the first step a commander would take would be to knock out the principal airfields, but we had not been permitted to do so. Furthermore, most installations do not stay disabled after one strike. For example, the North Vietnamese, using hoards of laborers, would rapidly repair important railroad yards that we had disrupted. To keep the yard out of commission we needed to strike it again once it was repaired and in use.

I also advised the Chairman, General Wheeler, of my concern about a recent message from the Secretary of State, which contained remarks he intended to use in a briefing. It included a statement that there were not many targets in North Vietnam that had not been hit. I pointed out that in our recent briefing at the Guam conference we had clearly identified 274 significant targets within the Hanoi/ Haiphong Restricted Areas. Moreover, by reducing these Restricted Areas to ten and four nautical miles, as I had just requested, we would open up some 184 targets currently denied to armed reconnaissance. I was emphatic in noting there was no shortage of targets in North Vietnam.

In early May, I sent further word to General Wheeler that we had noticed some interesting things on aerial photographs of certain North Vietnamese target areas. For example, a photograph of a village near one of the airfields indicated that it was being extensively, indeed almost exclusively, used by military elements. Heavy vehicular track activity, numerous trenches, foxholes, vehicle revetments, and defensive positions had been identified, to include a probable communications site on the edge of the village. It was quite obvious that the enemy had taken full advantage of our reluctance to attack pseudo-civilian areas, even those completely taken over by the military, and had thereby acquired a large number of sanctuaries where his support of aggression was immune to attack. Recognizing the many political problems associated with any modification of the current restrictions on civilian areas, I nonetheless inquired as to whether this would be a propitious time to seek such modification. I received an early reply saying that we needed to document the situation carefully and then let it go up the line to see if we could get the rules of engagement changed. We followed that suggestion but, as I recall, were not successful.

On 23 May, we received word from the JCS that no further targets would be authorized within the Hanoi Prohibited Area. When I promptly fired back "why?", I was advised by General Wheeler that it was indirectly related to the present strategy of cutting back our air campaign north of twenty degrees latitude, although there were other factors involved. These included the feeling in high circles that our recent strikes in the Hanoi area had raised the temperature of the war to a degree that might elicit additional Soviet assistance to the North Vietnamese, as well as a perception that the losses sustained by our forces were not commensurate with the results obtained. Also, there was that old recurrent desire to let the dust settle while we watched for Soviet and Chinese Communist reaction. The Chairman indicated, however, that he agreed our strikes were hurting the North Vietnamese and that this view was shared by foreign observers in Hanoi who were reporting such to their European headquarters. He added that the JCS had made a strong recommendation on the continuing need to obstruct and reduce the flow of war-supporting material into South Vietnam through various actions against the ports, the airfields and the rail lines.

And so once more the political decision makers evidenced the same stultifying combination of attitudes—a complete lack of understanding of the results of the air campaign, and a tendency to be more influenced by possible Soviet reaction than by what we could do to end the war. There evidently continued to be a myopic hope at some levels in Washington that the Soviets might do something to resolve this conflict. I believe history will document clearly that the Soviets did nothing to end the war and did everything possible to aid the North Vietnamese.

CHAPTER 17

STRATEGY DEBATE IN WASHINGTON

I N MID-MAY 1967 we had at long last been authorized to strike the Hanoi power plant, and the results had been immensely productive both in the amount of damage inflicted and the vehement North Vietnamese propaganda induced. The latter combined with the growing dissidence at home to bring on another series of high-level deliberations in Washington on the future course of U. S. strategy in the war.

As usual, the deliberations continued to be generally hampered by the basic lack of understanding of the bombing program in the Office of the Secretary of Defense. The majority of the civilian staff seemed to have a blind adherence to Secretary McNamara's directive that the primary purpose of the bombing was to stop infiltration into South Vietnam. Whether out of ignorance of the most elementary principles of military warfare or out of obsessive political fears (i.e., a super-sensitivity to the reactions of anti-war dissidents, and Soviet as well as world public opinion), they simply could not or would not recognize the utility of the effective strategic attacks on military-industrial targets in the heartland of the enemy. While these people were not necessarily decision makers, they had much influence since most recommendations from the military were staffed (processed) through them.

The strategy deliberations at this time were further aggravated by a request for more troops, which had been transmitted to the Secretary of Defense by the JCS on 20 April. General Westmoreland had asked for 100,000 troops immediately, and a total of 200,000 over the long term. So the nagging question of whether to escalate or level off was once again up front. The JCS had proposed mobilization of the reserves; major new troop commitments in the south; extension of the ground war into the North Vietnamese sanctuaries of Laos, Cambodia and possibly North Vietnam as well; mining of the North Vietnamese ports; and a solid deployment of manpower and resources to achieve military victory. Their hard-hitting recommendations provided the impetus for another look at our options.

To start the policy debate, Undersecretary of State Katzenbach forwarded a memorandum to John McNaughton at the Defense Department on 24 May in which he outlined the problem and assigned responsibility for the preparation of various policy papers to Defense, CIA and the White House staff. He asked the Department of Defense to consider two alternative courses of action: Course A, the kind of escalation proposed by the JCS; and Course B, the leveling off of U. S. troop commitment with no more than an additional 10,000 men authorized. He further requested the preparation of bombing strategies in the north appropriate to each course, suggesting, however, that for Course B the bombing be limited to areas south of twenty degrees latitude.

Vis-à-vis the continuing harangue over the pros and cons of the bombing program, General Westmoreland had said in a conversation with the President during the latter part of April, "I am frankly dismayed at even the thought of stopping the bombing program." General Wheeler, who was present at the discussion, took advantage of the opening to press for closing the ports as the next logical step. He also mentioned extending the war into the Laotian and Cambodian sanctuaries and the possible invasion of North Vietnam. I should note here that while we had studied the possibility of invading North Vietnam, I had never recommended it. In my view it was not necessary, since with proper use of air power we could bring the North Vietnamese to heel.

My first-hand knowledge of this major strategy review was minimal at the time, since relatively little information filtered through to Honolulu, but the Pentagon Papers make it clear that attention centered on cutting back the bombing program, an outgrowth of the prevalent negative assessment of its effectiveness.

Of the various memoranda circulating in Washington during this period, one written by Assistant Secretary of State William Bundy was especially pertinent. Although he was generally reluctant to give positive support to significantly increased bombing in the north or to mining the ports, he presented an interesting perspective with respect to the negotiations issue. In a summary paragraph titled "A Steady Firm Course" he stated:

> Since roughly the 1st of December, I think we have given a very jerky and impatient impression to Hanoi. This is related more to the timing and suddenness of our bombing and negotiating actions than to the substance of what we have done. I think Hanoi in any event believes that the 1968 elections could cause us to change our position or even lose heart completely. Our actions since early December may well have encouraged and greatly strengthened the belief that we wish to get the war over by 1968 at all costs. Our major thrust must be now to persuade him that we are prepared to stick it out if necessary. This means a steady and considered program of action for the next nine months.[1]

William Bundy's brother, McGeorge Bundy, who was president of the Ford Foundation, also got into the act. In a long letter to the President he analyzed the pros and cons of strategic bombing and generally advised against major escalation (specifically noting that he was opposed to closing the port of Haiphong). In his view, escalation would not bring a visible victory over Hanoi before our 1968 election:

> If we assume that the war will still be going on in November of '68 and that Hanoi will not give us the plea-

sure of consenting to negotiations sometime before then, what we must plan to offer as a defense of Administration policy is not victory over Hanoi, but growing success—and self-reliance—in the South. This we can do with luck. And on this side of the parallel the Vietnamese authorities should be prepared to help us out.

He went on to say:

If we can avoid escalation-that-does-not-seem-to-work, we can focus attention on the great and central achievement of these last two years: on the defeat we have prevented. The fact that South Vietnam has not been lost and is not going to be lost, is a fact of truly massive importance in the history of Asia, the Pacific and the U. S. . . . Under this Administration the United States has already saved the hope of freedom for hundreds of millions—in this sense, the largest part of the job is done. This critically important achievement is obscured by [our] seeming to act as if we have to do much more lest we fail.[2]

In effect, he was counseling that we concentrate on continuing to simply prevent defeat rather than taking decisive strategic action to achieve a clear and early military victory.

Predictably, the Joint Chiefs were in complete disagreement with the thrust of McGeorge Bundy's analysis and assertions. In providing the President with their views, the Chairman took particular issue with the recommendation against interdicting Haiphong harbor:

As a matter of cold fact, the Haiphong port is the single most vulnerable and important point in the lines of communication system of North Vietnam. During the first quarter of 1967 general cargo deliveries through Haiphong have set new records. In March 142,700 metric tons of cargo passed through the port. During the month of April there was a slight decline to 132,000 metric tons. Nevertheless, it is noteworthy that in April 31,900 metric tons of bulk foodstuffs passed through the port bringing the total of foodstuffs delivered in the first four months of 1967 to 100,680 metric tons as compared to 77,100 metric tons of food received during all of calendar 1966. These tonnages underscore the importance of the port of Haiphong to the war effort of North Vietnam and support my statement that Haiphong is the most important point in the entire North Vietnamese lines of communication system. Unless and until we find some means of obstructing and reducing the flow of war-supporting material through Haiphong, the North Vietnamese will continue to be able to support their war effort, both in North Vietnam and in South Vietnam.[3]

From another corner, Walt Rostow at the White House published his position in a paper entitled "U. S. Strategy in Vietnam." He began by stating that the United States was attempting to frustrate a Communist takeover by defeating their main force units in the south, attacking the guerrilla infrastructure, and concurrently building a sound South Vietnamese governmental and security framework. As he saw it, the purpose of the air war in the north was to hasten the North Vietnamese decision to abandon their aggression. We had never held that bombing the Hanoi/Haiphong area *alone* would lead them to abandon the effort in the south, or that it would *directly* stop or cut back infiltration. We had, he maintained, considered that the degree of military and civilian cost felt in the north and the diversion of resources to deal with our bombing could at least contribute marginally, and perhaps even significantly, to the timing of their decision to end the war. But it was no substitute for making progress in the south.

Rostow went on to postulate three broad strategy options with respect to the air war. Under the first, Option A, we would mine the major harbors, perhaps bomb port facilities, and even consider blockade. In addition, we would systematically attack the rail lines between Hanoi and mainland China. In analyzing the various ramifications of such actions, he noted, "I myself do not believe that the Soviet Union would go to war with us over Vietnam unless we sought to occupy North Vietnam, and even then a military response from Moscow would not be certain." He concluded his presentation of this option by predicting that tension between the United States, the Soviet Union and Communist China would increase, but the outcome was *less* rather than *more* likely to be a general war.

In Option B, Rostow called for bombing in the Hanoi/Haiphong area as we had been doing, explicitly disagreeing with the notion that these attacks had no bearing on the war in the south. He held, instead, that they diverted massive amounts of resources, energies and attention to keeping the civil and military establishment going, that they imposed general economic, political and psychological difficulties on the North Vietnamese, and, further, that they did *not* harden the will of the enemy. In his judgment, our bombing of the north up to this point had been "a painful additional cost which they [the North Vietnamese] had thus far been willing to bear to pursue their efforts in the South."

Option C suggested concentrating the bombing effort in Route Packages 1 and 2—that is, in the lower half of North Vietnam, south of twenty degrees. This would have the advantages of cutting our loss rate of pilots and planes, improving somewhat our direct harassment of infiltration into South Vietnam, and diminishing (relative to Options A and B) the risk of counter-escalatory action by the Soviet Union and Communist China.

In general, Rostow's thesis was that we had to date achieved significant results in increasing the pressure on Hanoi and raising the cost to them of continuing aggression in the south. We should not therefore lightly abandon what had been accomplished.[4]

Meanwhile, at the Department of Defense, the weight of effort was now directed at the preparation of a Draft Presidential Memorandum (DPM) on the issue. (The "courses of action" exercise directed earlier by Katzenbach was apparently dropped in favor of the DPM.) In view of its ultimate impact, it is important to note that a DPM is more than a statement of the views of the signator (in this case the Secretary of Defense). Its intent is to put on record the pertinent views of all the cognizant officials, hopefully by consensus.

The first draft of this DPM was authored by John McNaughton. It opened with a statement that the question was whether to continue the bombing program in the Hanoi/Haiphong area or to concentrate all air attacks for an indefinite period on the lines of communication in the lower half of North Vietnam, south of twenty degrees. The postulate behind this question was that, supposedly, there were few important targets left in the north exclusive of the ports, and attacking the ports had been rejected as risking confrontation with the Soviet Union. In addition, the alternative of striking minor targets, in conjunction with continuing armed reconnaissance against the transportation system north of twenty degrees, was viewed as relatively costly, risky and unprofitable. Here again, the same incredibly skewed perception of what air strategy is all about, what its objectives are, and how it should be pursued, prevailed.

In any case, this first draft was eventually superseded by a second, which pulled together the thinking of top civilians in the Defense Department on the issues of both the bombing program and General Westmoreland's troop request. This DPM presented two broad alternative courses of action, as follows:

> Course A: Grant the request for increased numbers of troops, adding a minimum of 200,000 men and possibly more later to fulfill the JCS ultimate requirement for Vietnam. Along with these force increases, greatly intensify military actions, especially against the north.
>
> Course B: Limit force increases to no more than 30,000, avoid extending the ground conflict beyond the borders of South Vietnam, and concentrate the bombing on the infiltration routes south of twenty degrees. This would involve termination of bombing in the Hanoi/Haiphong area unless military developments necessitated it, and concentration of all sorties in North Vietnam on the infiltration routes in the neck of North Vietnam between seventeen degrees and twenty degrees latitude.

In developing the pros and cons of the respective courses of action, all of the usual defensive reasons for not extending the bombing, not mining the harbors, not intensifying air attacks, not contemplating ground actions in North Vietnam, etc., were marshalled. In the end, Course A was rejected.

Perhaps most importantly, the DPM boldly proceeded to reconsider and restate U. S. objectives in the Vietnam War, noting in part:

The time has come for us to eliminate the ambiguities from our minimum objectives—our commitments—in Vietnam. Specifically, two principles must be articulated and policies and actions brought into line with them. (1) Our commitment is only to see that the people of South Vietnam are permitted to determine their own future. (2) This commitment ceases if the country ceases to help itself.[5]

In elaboration, the point was made that we were committed to stopping or offsetting the effect of North Vietnam's application of force in the south because it denied the South Vietnamese the ability to determine their own future. The importance of nailing down and understanding the implications of these limited objectives could not, therefore, be over-emphasized, since this related intimately to our strategy against the north, to troop requirements and missions in the south, to our handling of the Saigon government, to settlement terms, and to U. S. domestic and international opinion regarding the justification and success of our efforts on behalf of South Vietnam. It was strongly recommended that the President officially accept and document the foregoing as U. S. policy.

Interestingly, the Pentagon Papers indicate that Secretary McNamara showed the draft of this DPM to the President on 19 May, but there is no record of the President's reaction. They further note that, coincidentally,

May 19 was the day the U. S. planes struck the Hanoi power plant just one mile north of the center of Hanoi. That the President did not promptly endorse the McNamara recommendations as he had on occasions in the past is not surprising. This time he was faced with a situation where the Joint Chiefs were in ardent opposition to anything other than a significant escalation of the war with a call-up of Reserves. This put them in direct opposition to Secretary McNamara and his civilian aides, and created a genuine policy dilemma for the President, who wanted to keep the military "on board" in any new direction of the U. S. effort in Southeast Asia.[6]

The JCS, of course, were not without voice throughout this critical debate. On 20 May, the Chiefs forwarded a memorandum to Secretary McNamara setting forth the case for expanded operations against North Vietnam, with the request that the document be sent to the President. (Here the Chiefs were exercising their legal right to advise the President on military affairs.) They argued that the twin objectives of causing North Vietnam to pay an increasing price for support of the war in the south and of interdicting such support had only been partially achieved, because the incremental and restrained application of air power had enabled North Vietnam to anticipate U. S. actions and accommodate to the slow increase in pressure. What was needed to change that picture was an immediate expansion of the bombing to include attacks on all airfields, all port complexes, all land and sea lines of communication in the Hanoi/ Haiphong area, as well as the mining of all coastal harbors and coastal waters. Such action should be initiated during the favorable May to September weather season before the onset of poor flying conditions over North Vietnam, and should seek destruction of those targets that would have the most far-reaching effect on North Vietnam's capability to fight—i.e., electric power plants, ports, airfields, barracks, supply depots, and transportation facilities. To facilitate these operations the thirty-mile Restricted Area around Hanoi and the ten-mile Haiphong Restricted Area should be reduced to ten and four miles, respectively, and armed reconnaissance should be authorized throughout North Vietnam and adjacent coastal waters, except in populated areas in the China buffer zone and in the reduced Hanoi/Haiphong circles.[7]

The Chairman of the JCS also went on record with his views and those of the Chiefs in response to a request from Deputy Secretary Vance for comments on the following specific strategy options: (1) Add 250,000 troops in South Vietnam and intensify the bombing against North Vietnam, or (2) limit the troop increase to 70,000 and hold the bombing below twenty degrees latitude unless required by military necessity, or, if essential to provide an opportunity for a negotiated settlement, stop the bombing altogether. In countering the latter, General Wheeler took the position, not surprisingly, that any degree of standdown of the bombing in the north would allow

North Vietnam to recoup its losses, expand its stockpiles, and continue to support the war from a sanctuary. This would not only be costly to our forces and prolong the war, but also could easily be interpreted as a North Vietnamese victory, an "aerial Dien Bien Phu." As an alternative, adoption of the JCS program for the conduct of the war was again recommended, including air strikes to reduce external aid to North Vietnam, to destroy its in-country resources, and to disrupt movement into the south. The strikes would be designed to isolate the Hanoi/Haiphong logistics base by interdicting the lines of communication and concurrently attacking the main reservoirs of war-supporting resources.[8]

Finally, at the end of May, the Chiefs aired their strongest concerns in a memorandum to the Secretary of Defense dealing with his recent DPM. To begin with, they noted that Course A and its supporting arguments were labeled as the views of the military, whereas, in fact, they were a distortion of those views, which had been accurately detailed in numerous JCS memoranda on this subject at various times in the past. Furthermore, the Chiefs took the gravest exception to the compromising of U. S. objectives as restated in the DPM, noting that such was consistent neither with NSAM #288 nor with the explicit public statements of U. S. policies and objectives. The language of the DPM would in effect limit U. S. objectives to merely guaranteeing the South Vietnamese the right to determine their own future, and offsetting the effect of North Vietnam's application of force in South Vietnam; and the United States would be committed to those objectives only so long as the South Vietnamese continued to help themselves. In the Chiefs' view, such a modification of previously defined objectives not only sidestepped the full implication for the Free World of a failure to achieve successful resolution to the conflict in Southeast Asia, but would also undermine the basic rationale for our presence in South Vietnam and much of our effort there over the past two years.

The JCS critique of the DPM went on to oppose the concept of confining air operations to that part of North Vietnam south of twenty degrees, emphasizing that the arguments in support thereof were misleading and incorrect since the Communists were supplying their forces in South Vietnam from all sides—through the DMZ, through Laos, from the coast, from Cambodia and from the rivers in the delta. The proposed concentration of air operations solely in the neck or panhandle of southern North Vietnam would essentially, therefore, grant the enemy immunity for all these other lines of communication and distribution systems. It would permit him rapid recovery from the damage sustained to date, would allow an increase in movement capability, would reduce his requirement for total supplies in the pipeline, would enable him to concentrate air defenses in the panhandle, and would allow him to release personnel and equipment for increased efforts in the infiltration of South Vietnam. It also would relieve the Hanoi leadership from continuing to experience first hand those very real pressures that our recent air operations had imposed and could, therefore, result only in strengthening the enemy's resolve to keep on with the war.

In conclusion, apparently unaware that the President had seen the DPM ten days before, the Chiefs recommended that it not be forwarded to the President and that U. S. national objectives as expressed in NSAM #288 be maintained.[9] (This was typical of the way Secretary McNamara operated: often taking a controversial issue directly to the President before obtaining comments from the JCS.)

So the debate, if little else, continued to escalate, with no decision yet forthcoming to change our strategy one way or the other.

CHAPTER 18

McNamara's Conference
in Saigon

IN MID-JUNE 1967, word came that the Secretary of Defense and numerous other officials from Washington were about to make a trip to the western Pacific, and would hold a conference in Saigon that could have considerable bearing on the future of Rolling Thunder. I promptly advised my Component Commanders (CINCPACFLT, Adm. Roy L. Johnson, U. S. Navy; CINCPACAF, Gen. John D. Ryan, U. S. Air Force); COMUS-MACV, General Westmoreland; Commander 7th Air Force, Lt. Gen. William W. Momyer, U. S. Air Force; and Commander 7th Fleet, Vice Adm. John J. Hyland, U. S. Navy, cautioning them that there were indications the Secretary of Defense was departing from Washington with a leaning toward more restrictive alternatives for the air war. I told them that at the Saigon conference I would give my views on the importance of our air campaign in North Vietnam, particularly in the northeast quadrant, and that the firsthand knowledge of commanders on the scene would be most helpful. The importance of our conviction that we needed to continue the air campaign in the northeast could not be overemphasized. Accordingly, I forwarded to each of them a brief summary of my presentation, which highlighted the changed situation in North Vietnam; i.e., the air defense situation had improved in our favor, we had received indications of delays in getting material through the enemy ports so that supplies were piling up there, we had made inroads into the enemy's rolling stock and truck inventories, and power shortages were progressively interfering with North Vietnamese industrial activity. I asked Admiral Hyland and General Momyer to be prepared to amplify my analysis, with Momyer, in particular, pointing out the success of our armed reconnaissance along the northeast rail lines since the first of May. Statistics, I stressed, would be essential.

On 28 June, I made a special trip to Saigon to hold a pre-conference planning session with General Westmoreland, General Momyer and Admiral Hyland. It was important that Westmoreland participate in all of our preliminary meetings so that he would be thoroughly knowledgeable about the briefings we planned to give. After returning to touch base in Honolulu, I flew back to Saigon on 5 July in time for the start of the conference. Those present were Secretary McNamara, Undersecretary of State Katzenbach, Ambassador Bunker, General Wheeler, General Westmoreland, General Momyer, Admiral Hyland, and quite a number of other officials from the State and Defense Departments, and the Joint Staff.

The substance of my briefing was crucial to the continuation of the Rolling Thunder campaign. In the interest of readability, I have summarized the key points in the paragraphs that follow; the verbatim text is quoted in Appendix D.

I began by reviewing the air campaign briefly, stressing that since January 1966 I had been recommending an air campaign centered around attacks on vital target systems in the north and marked by sufficient weight of effort to convince the enemy that his aggression was not worthwhile in view of the damage he was suffering. I reminded the conferees, for example, that we had been authorized to strike the North Vietnamese POL system in June of 1966, but the enemy had been publicly forewarned of our intent and had therefore been able to disperse his POL supplies widely enough that our strikes were not as effective as they could have been with the element of surprise in our favor. Then in February 1967 targets from several of the six basic systems (electricity, maritime ports, airfields, transportation, military complexes, and war-supporting industry), including some important power plant targets, had been approved for strikes. Bad weather, however, had reduced the potential impact. By April, the weather had improved and permission had been given to hit a few targets in all six systems. Nine of the ten newly authorized targets had been hit by 1 May, five of them more than once. Favorable weather had continued and ten additional targets had been authorized, so by mid-May the bombing program was putting greater pressure on the Hanoi government than ever before. In fact, on 19–20 May, we had struck the vitally important Hanoi thermal-power plant in the center of the city. However, the immediate outcry from the North Vietnamese government had been so effective in Washington that on 23 May we were again told not to operate within ten miles of Hanoi. Strikes against such significant targets had thus been interrupted and real pressure on the enemy had once more been removed. I concluded this portion of my remarks by emphasizing that the sector within ten miles of Hanoi was the enemy's most important base support area—vital from his point of view—and our continued failure to strike decisively in that area gave him a virtual sanctuary from which to operate.

I then went on to highlight what I considered to be some significant trends in the air war. Of real importance, I noted, was the fact that we were beginning to see marked changes in the resistance the enemy was offering. Thirty of his fighter aircraft had been destroyed in air combat over the last five weeks, and now his MiGs were not challenging our planes. Three of his airfields had been damaged to the point that operating capacity was limited. We had also seen a lessened effectiveness of the enemy's surface-to-air missiles. Some, for example, had obviously been launched without proper guidance control, and we had noted occasional random-scatter, or barrage-type, firings, seemingly in desperation. His antiaircraft artillery (AAA) fire was also less intense and less effective, and as a result our aircraft loss rate was down.

I also briefed the conferees on some new weapons that we now had in useful quantities, making our air attacks more efficient. Included in these weapons was a bomb containing a cluster of bomblets, which had proven most successful against gun implacements, and another bomb that homed on its target thus making it possible to conduct a small, precise raid to destroy a target with minimum collateral damage. In addition, more of our planes were now equipped with electronic countermeasures that helped our pilots evade the enemy's surface-to-air missiles. Thus, in my view, the trend of the air war in the north was changing in our favor, and our current presence in some degree of force in the general vicinity of Hanoi and Haiphong was obviously having a marked effect on the North Vietnamese. We, of course, wanted to maintain our momentum by continued presence in that northeast quadrant, but we felt hampered by the imposition of the Prohibited and Restricted Areas around those cities—strictures that were tightly controlled in Washington.

As a final point, I emphasized that the job yet to be done was significant. The majority of those targets that had not been struck were those that were not authorized—fifty-nine percent of the military-complex targets, for example, and nearly seventy percent of the transportation targets. I explained, moreover, that we believed diversified attacks against *all* the various target systems would have the greatest impact on the enemy. We should not concentrate our attacks solely on one system, such as transportation targets, despite their priority of importance, but rather should strike at as many elements as possible of all systems so as to avoid establishing patterns and to heighten the enemy's management problems. I reiterated that the best way to convince Ho Chi Minh to stop his aggression against the south was to impress upon him the consequences to North Vietnam if he did not desist; over and above any other valid reasons, I maintained this was the primary reason we should not divert even the modest effort now devoted to the northeast quadrant, in an attempt to further interdict the infiltration routes to and in the south.

General Momyer and Admiral Hyland took over the briefing platform next with summaries of the Rolling Thunder campaign from their point of view, which entirely supported the theme I was presenting.

I then continued with a concluding "salvo," which summarized the essential elements we were trying to impress upon the Secretary of Defense:

During these past 18 months we have flown about 38,000 attack sorties in the northern areas and about 185,000 in the south, including Laos. Large numbers of vehicles, rolling stock and watercraft have been destroyed or damaged in both areas. The extent of LOC [lines of communication] disruption is partially indicated by the number of bridges and ferries destroyed, although some of the trucks and rolling stock and watercraft have been replaced, and many bridges have been repaired. The 20,000 secondary explosions observed in Laos and the lower route packages indicate significant losses are encountered in moving his supplies through those areas. Operations in the northern areas are increasing the cost of aggression to both the North Vietnamese and the people who are supporting them. Eighty-six percent of their primary electric power capacity is destroyed. Thirty to fifty percent of their war-supporting industry has been disrupted. Forty percent of the major military installations in the north and all fixed installations in the south have been destroyed or disrupted. Eighty-one MiGs have been shot down or destroyed on the ground. Operations from three of his jet bases are no longer possible. Their POL stocks are widely dispersed and distribution has become a problem. While we have no way of measuring the amount of war material actually destroyed in the northeast sector, a reliable source in Hanoi estimates that thirty percent of the war material supplied is being destroyed en route to Hanoi by U. S. air strikes. The following is quoted from the same source: "The effectiveness of American air action and the seemingly infinite capacity of the Americans to escalate to the degree necessary to overcome any increased support rendered are the principal causes of the disillusionment among Soviet and Bloc officials in Hanoi and their conviction that the North Vietnamese cannot win. They also feel that the problem must be negotiated if the complete destruction of North Vietnam is to be avoided."

It is again emphasized that not until late April did Rolling Thunder begin to reach the level of intensity in the northeast quadrant considered necessary to do the job. However, since late May, maximum effectiveness is not being achieved because of restrictions and the lack of authority to hit the more vital targets. These restrictions come at a time when two factors are in our favor: first, the good weather months; and, second, the important and perhaps decisive changes in enemy capability to defend himself. A momentum has been established. This momentum will be lost if we do not lift restrictions and strike the more vital targets. To retrench even further and limit our attacks to the south of the 20th parallel will have adverse and, I believe, disastrous effects. War-supporting industry in the north would be brought back to maximum output. Morale of our own forces would decline while that of the enemy would be greatly enhanced. It would allow North Vietnam to operate out of a virtual sanctuary with complete freedom to move supplies to the south without damage. The losses of material they are experiencing en route to Hanoi would cease. Trucks, rolling stock, watercraft and POL would be conserved. Such limitations would also permit redistribution of a large portion of his AAA and SAM order of battle creating a defense environment similar to that in Route Package 6. Armed reconnaissance and interdiction operations under such conditions would be greatly hampered.

We are at an important point in this conflict and an incisive air campaign, including sustained attacks in the northeast quadrant against all the target systems would assure interrelated effects against the enemy's military, political, economic and psychological posture. There is ample evidence that the enemy is hurting. I consider it essential that we continue this effective, successful air campaign. The widest latitude in planning and execution during the remaining months of good weather is requested.

In closing, I would like to emphasize one point that General Westmoreland has already made. The importance of our air and sea campaign against North Vietnam must be assessed within the broader aspects of the overall war in

Southeast Asia. The United States and North Vietnam each are engaged strategically in both an offensive and a defensive campaign. On the ground in the south North Vietnam is engaged in a strategic offensive campaign. The combat area is limited basically to the political boundaries of South Vietnam and the enemy moves his forces at will in and out of combat across those borders. While we have blunted his initiative by tactical offensive operations, political restraints rule out any assumption of a strategic offensive on our part. We must await his moves at places and times of his own choosing.

The opposite holds for the air war in the north. Here *we* hold the initiative. We are conducting a strategic offensive forcing the enemy into a defensive posture. He is forced to react at places and times of *our* choosing. If we eliminate the only offensive element of our strategy, I do not see how we can expect to win. My recommendations are on these charts. You will recognize that they are essentially the same actions proposed by the Joint Chiefs of Staff.

The charts I showed them contained the following recommendations, as well as necessary changes and additions to the operating rules:

Recommendations:

1. Close the Haiphong harbor to deep-water shipping by bombing and/or mining.
2. Destroy the six basic target systems (electricity, maritime ports, airfields, transportation, military complexes, war-supporting industry).
3. Conduct integrated attacks against entire target base, including interdiction in North Vietnam and Laos.

Necessary Changes and Additions to Rolling Thunder Operating Rules:

1. Delete Hanoi ten-nautical-mile Prohibited Area.
2. Reduce Hanoi Restricted Area to ten nautical miles.

3. Reduce Haipong Restricted Area to four nautical miles.
4. Move the northern boundary of the special coastal armed-reconnaissance area to include Haiphong area.
5. Authorize armed reconnaissance throughout North Vietnam and coastal waters (except populated areas, buffer zone, restricted areas).
6. Mine inland waterways to Communist China buffer zone as MK-36 Destructors become available.
7. Extend Sea Dragon to Communist China buffer zone as forces become available.
8. Implement now to exploit good weather.

In a somewhat caustic personal aside, I should note that when all the briefings were finished, Secretary McNamara commented, "General Westmoreland, that was a fine presentation." The next day I remarked to General Wheeler that I was damned annoyed at McNamara for turning to Westy at the end of the presentation where I was the senior officer present, to say that he had made a fine presentation, without saying anything to me. Bus Wheeler replied, "The reason he didn't say anything to you was that he was furious at you because of your presentation." It had, of course, been contrary to the theme the Secretary wanted to take back to Washington. When McNamara went to a conference, he usually had already decided what he wanted to report—and so, when I gave him facts and positions in opposition to those he had predetermined, he was soundly displeased!

As a result of the solid front we upheld in Saigon, Rolling Thunder continued. Secretary McNamara had been quite prepared to cut off the air war in the north if anybody had agreed with him, but nobody did. Westmoreland, Momyer, Hyland, Wheeler and the JCS all agreed with the stand I took on the issue. In the face of united opposition, McNamara could not possibly go back and report a consensus to stop the air campaign.

Back in Washington, the Secretary received approval from the President to authorize the additional troop deployments that had been discussed in Saigon. Although it seems likely that he would also have discussed with the President the problem of the next phase of the air campaign, there is no record of his recommendation. In any event, a decision on this issue would unquestionably have been made at the White House, and subsequent events point to a presidential decision that opted for keeping the bombing program essentially as it was, continuing the piecemeal expansion of armed reconnaissance, striking some new targets in each Rolling Thunder series, but still refraining from closing the ports and consistently hitting sensitive targets such as the MiG airfields.

The next Rolling Thunder series, number 57, which was authorized on 20 July 1967, characterized the foregoing parameters. The sixteen targets designated (including one airfield, one rail yard, two bridges, and twelve barracks and supply areas) were all within the Hanoi and Haiphong Restricted Areas but still outside the crucial Prohibited Areas around the centers of Hanoi and Haiphong.

And so, once again, the increasingly divisive issue of the air war in the north had been brought to a boil only to be pushed onto the back burner and allowed to simmer, to no one's satisfaction. To make matters worse, this was the best part of the good-weather period in North Vietnam—the ideal time to take the strong action I had proposed. In what can only be called the continuing strategy of equivocation, we continued to throttle the tremendous capacity of our air power to bring the war to a successful, early conclusion.

CHAPTER 19

THE STENNIS HEARINGS

SOMETIME AFTER SECRETARY McNamara returned
from his July conference in Saigon, he was informed by Sen.
John C. Stennis that the Preparedness Subcommittee of the
Senate Armed Services Committee intended to conduct extensive
hearings in August into the conduct of the air war against North
Vietnam. Senator Stennis told the Secretary that he would be called
upon to testify, as would all the top military leaders involved in the
Rolling Thunder campaign, including CINCPAC. The subcommit-
tee consisted of Senators Stennis (Chairman), Stuart Symington,
Henry M. Jackson, Howard W. Cannon, Robert C. Byrd of West
Virginia, Margaret Chase Smith, Strom Thurmond and Jack Miller.
The authors of the Pentagon Papers say this about the sub-
committee:

> They were known for their hardline views and military
> sympathies. They were defenders of "air power" and had
> often aligned themselves with the "professional military
> experts" against what they considered "unskilled civilian
> amateurs." They viewed the restraints on bombing as irra-
> tional, the shackling of a major instrument which could
> help win victory. With Vietnam blown up into a major
> war, with more than half a million U. S. troops, a cost of

187

more than $2 billion a month, and with no clear end in sight, their patience with the restrained bombing program was beginning to wear thin. But more was involved than a disagreement over the conduct of the war. Some passionately held convictions had been belittled and some members of the Subcommittee were on the warpath.[1]

As for my participation, I prepared for my meeting with the Senate subcommittee by having my staff make up a situation report on the accomplishments of our Rolling Thunder campaign vis-à-vis fixed targets up to this point, using a cutoff date of 15 July 1967 for this information. The report indicated that the following percentages of the national capacity of North Vietnam had been at least temporarily destroyed: military barracks—26 percent; ammunition depots—76 percent; POL storage—87 percent; supply depots —18 percent; power plants—78 percent; maritime ports—12 percent; railroad yards—36 percent; railroad shops—22 percent; explosive plants—100 percent; iron and steel plants—100 percent; cement plant—90 percent; airfields—23 percent; naval bases—20 percent; communications installations—20 percent; and, of the bridges targeted—56 percent.

The report further pointed out that the sustained relatively high intensity of recent air strikes against military and economic targets had resulted in a major increase in the level of damage inflicted on North Vietnam. There was widespread disruption of economic activity. Over 500,000 people were engaged in repairing lines of communication. Some large-hatch cargo ships had taken nearly sixty days to turn around in Haiphong. Port congestion was evidenced by the vast quantities of goods stacked in temporary holding areas. Attacks against the rail lines were reported to have destroyed nearly thirty percent of the supplies in transit in the northern area. Through railroad traffic was continually disrupted, and formidable repair problems were obvious, as was a substantial increase in expenditure of labor and materials allotted to this task. There were ever-growing reports of food shortages, difficult working conditions, and transportion problems. Preliminary estimates of the harvest showed it to be mediocre to poor, so that relatively large imports of foodstuffs would continue to be required.

In addition, the report detailed the extensive North Vietnamese air-defense system at this time. The enemy had about 200 SAM sites, of which we estimated twenty-five were occupied at any one time. These missile sites were mainly concentrated in the Hanoi/Haiphong area, with two or three located in the vicinity of Vinh. (The North Vietnamese had tried to establish a site near the DMZ, but had been unsuccessful because of immediate detection and destruction by our air strikes.) There were also an estimated 7,000 enemy anti-aircraft artillery weapons in North Vietnam, of which forty percent were in the Hanoi/Haiphong and the Kep areas. We estimated a little over sixty MiG-15s and MiG-17s, and about fifteen to twenty MiG-21s in North Vietnam. Most of these aircraft were based in South China and flown in daily, since the North Vietnamese airfields at Kep and Hoa Lac had been struck. Heavy MIG losses had been incurred in May, and since then the enemy had seldom challenged our aircraft. We considered, however, that this standdown was probably only temporary, until new pilots had been trained. Further, the North Vietnamese had an extensive, widespread system of early warning, ground-control intercept and acquisition radars, all of which were integrated into the overall aircontrol system.

In combination with the background data provided by this staff report, it is pertinent to the context of my appearance before the congressional committee to also consider the restrictions under which we were operating in early August 1967.

First of all, no strikes were authorized in the Communist China buffer zone, a strip along the northern border of North Vietnam, which was thirty to thirty-five miles wide and extended from Laos to the Gulf of Tonkin. Our aircraft could penetrate this buffer zone in transit, but only to within twenty miles of the Chinese border, and any of our aircraft that had engaged the enemy outside the zone could pursue the attack into this zone only to within twelve miles of the Chinese border.

Furthermore, the limitations on target strikes in the Prohibited Areas and Restricted Areas around Hanoi and Haiphong were still in effect. At this point in time, photo reconnaissance within the Prohibited Areas was permitted. Strike aircraft could penetrate through these areas if necessary when making a strike *outside* the areas, but it was obviously the intent that this be avoided. Often we were directed to stay clear of these areas completely, under any circumstances.

Finally, there were specific categories of targets that could not be struck under any circumstances—dikes, dams, hydropower plants, fishing boats, sampans and houseboats, and, most importantly, populated areas. Overall, we had a general exhortation to use caution during all attacks to avoid striking any populated areas and to keep collateral damage to a minimum at all times, consistent with the desired objectives. (It had, of course, become painfully obvious that the North Vietnamese readily understood all these restrictions and had therefore not only placed all of their POL and most of their SAM-support facilities in populated areas, but were also generally very careful to stay close to Hanoi and Haiphong with *any* valuable cargo.)

That was the situation with respect to the air war when the Stennis hearings began on 9 August. The Chairman, Senator Stennis, opened the first session with an important statement that I quote in full:

> Today we open our hearing on the conduct and effectiveness of the air war against North Vietnam with Adm. Ulysses S. G. Sharp, Commander in Chief of U. S. forces in the Pacific, as our principal witness. He is accompanied by Gen. John Ryan, Commander in Chief of the Pacific Air Force, and Adm. Roy Johnson, Commander in Chief of the Pacific Fleet.*
>
> This is an extremely important hearing. It could have a direct effect on the war in Southeast Asia. Although it is directed specifically toward the air war against North Vietnam, it will necessarily involve the overall policy and philosophy governing and controlling the conduct of the entire war.

---

*Also with me was my Executive Assistant, Capt. Rembrandt C. Robinson, U. S. Navy, an outstanding officer who was my principal staff man on all my trips.

Admiral Sharp is the chief operational commander of our forces in the Pacific. He has overall responsibility for the air war and controls and directs the Navy, Air Force, and Marine Corps aviation forces which carry out the operational missions against North Vietnam. Because of this and from the wealth of his military experience and professional expertise, he can give us firsthand authoritative information and advice on the very difficult problems and important questions involved in our inquiry.

We are going to inquire into all of the important aspects of the air war, including the processes for the selection and approval of targets, the effectiveness of the air campaign, the lucrative targets which have not yet been struck, the probable consequences of either increasing or decreasing the bombing, and particularly the impact on our fighting men in South Vietnam, and all related matters.

We plan to call on many qualified persons and sources for the information and counsel which we need. Our future witnesses will include Secretary of Defense Robert S. McNamara; Gen. Earle G. Wheeler, Chairman of the Joint Chiefs of Staff; Gen. Harold K. Johnson, Chief of Staff, U. S. Army; Adm. T. H. Moorer, Chief of Naval Operations; Gen. John P. McConnell, Chief of Staff, U.S. Air Force; and Gen. Wallace M. Greene, Commandant, U. S. Marine Corps. This is by no means intended as a complete witness list.

My own personal opinion, which I have expressed many times in the past is that it would be a tragic and perhaps fatal mistake for us to suspend or restrict the bombing. I am gratified by the step-up in the air operations which has occurred since this hearing was announced. It has brought increased pressure on the enemy. I hope this pressure will be further increased and expanded and that it will hasten the end of this unhappy war.

By slowing, reducing, and restricting the flow of supplies to the south the bombing of North Vietnam has saved the lives of many brave Americans. We know from the bitter experience of previous suspensions of the bombing during truce periods that such lulls are used by the enemy to build up forces and supplies that are used to kill and wound many valiant Americans.

In my opinion this is no time to reduce or diminish the pressure or to throw away any military advantage.

The effectiveness or impact of the bombing cannot be measured alone by the number of missions flown or the number of bombs dropped. The real question is whether we are doing what we can and should do in the opinion of our military experts to hit the enemy when and where and in a manner that will end the war soonest and thus save American lives.

Admiral, we have a number of reports about what our allies are doing, and what they are going to do. We are not expecting you to pass on that, but CBS news from Saigon yesterday morning and again last night said they weren't going to do anything more. Those things disturb me and they disturb the American people.

I made a short statement, members of the subcommittee, this morning on television because I have learned that if someone doesn't speak for the subcommittee, when it is sitting, they will put on somebody they can find out there in the hall and let them speak for the subcommittee, even though they are not members. Therefore, I made a few remarks for the subcommittee.

I said I thought the question was growing in Congress as to whether it is wise to send more men if we are going to just leave them at the mercy of the guerrilla war without trying to cut off the enemy's supplies more effectively. I think that is something that will come within the field of this inquiry.[2]

I then gave the committee a long opening statement, describing the current situation pretty much as stated earlier in this chapter, and forecasting our plans. I stressed that we wanted to press on into the Hanoi and Haiphong Prohibited and Restricted Areas to destroy the high-value military targets, concentrating on transportation systems but including rail rolling stock, vehicle repair facilities, military supply depots, and war-supporting industries. At Haiphong we wanted to destroy port facilities, warehouses, rail yards, and, in principle, isolate Haiphong from the remainder of North Vietnam to the maximum possible extent. We also hoped to increase pressure on both the northeast and northwest rail lines, including targets in the buffer zone. In the south, we would, of course, want to continue to seek out and destroy men and material infiltrating into South Vietnam.

Having outlined our overall strategy for the conduct of the war in Southeast Asia, I summarized our accomplishments to date in the air campaign, concluding with the point that during the last three months—under an expanded target list but with no significant departure from the broad restraints to which we had long been held—we had begun to hurt the enemy in his home territory. He was suffering painful military, economic and psychological strains, and now was the time to increase our pressure. The best way to persuade the ruling element in North Vietnam to stop the aggression was to make the consequences of not stopping readily and ever more painfully apparent.

The hearing was very interesting, and the senators were a most sympathetic audience. All subcommittee members attended most of the sessions, while other senators came in and out. Since these were closed hearings, all questions were answered as asked, whether or not classified information was involved. Furthermore, all testimony was given under oath.

To return for a moment to the comment made by Senator Stennis in his opening statement, concerning "the step-up in the air operations which has occurred since this hearing was announced," the following excerpt from the Pentagon Papers best explains his reference. I am delighted to note that the opinion of the historian in this particular instance is in complete agreement with my own thoughts.

In July the President had decided against both an escalatory and a de-escalatory option in favor of continuing the prevailing level and intensity of bombing. However, the prospect of having his bombing policies submitted to the harsh scrutiny of the Stennis Committee, taking tes-

timony from such unhappy military men as Admiral
Sharp, must have forced a recalculation on the President.
It is surely no coincidence that on August 9, the very day
the Stennis hearings opened, an addendum to Rolling
Thunder 57 was issued authorizing an additional 16 fixed
targets and an expansion of armed reconnaissance. Significantly, 6 of the targets were within the sacred 10-mile
Hanoi inner circle. They included the thermal power
plant, 3 rail yards, and 2 bridges. Nine targets were located
on the northeast rail line in the China buffer zone, the
closest one 8 miles from the border, and consisted of 4
bridges and 5 rail yards or sidings. The 10th was a naval
base also within the China buffer zone. Armed reconnaissance was authorized along 8 road, rail and waterway segments between the 10-mile and 4-mile circle around Haiphong, and the attacks were permitted against railroad rolling stock within the China buffer zone up to within 8 miles
of the border. The power of Congress was not to be denied. Where the military alone had tried unsuccessfully for
so long to erode the Hanoi/Haiphong sanctuaries, the
pressure implicit in the impending hearings where military
men would be asked to speak their minds to a friendly
audience was enough to succeed, at least for the moment. [3]

It was indeed no mere coincidence of timing that we had that
very morning finally received permission to strike various targets I
had been asking to hit for months. It was obvious to me that the
Secretary of Defense had hoped to spike my guns by granting these
new targets right before I was to testify. That hope proved futile,
however, since it came out almost with the first question that we had
just received not only the authority to strike certain lucrative targets
heretofore denied us, but also to restrike some targets that had been
removed from the authorized list. The significance of this turn of
events was not lost on the senators, and they made quite a point of it.
    After the first morning session, I had a private meeting with
Senators Stennis, Symington, Jackson and Margaret Chase Smith,
during which I gave them more detailed information about the

targets we had been authorized to hit that morning. We also had a general discussion on the conduct of the war, which was both enlightening and, I think, helpful to the senators. In fact, it was my general perception throughout my testimony before the committee that the members enthusiastically accepted my philosophy for the conduct of the air war. Certainly, they were most gracious in their comments.

Secretary McNamara's position as the final witness on 25 August was an unenviable one since he found himself lined up in opposition to the military witnesses who had preceded him, as well as to a significant number of subcommittee members. He took issue with the military view of the air war, and defended the bombing campaign to date as being carefully tailored to our limited purposes in Southeast Asia, aimed at selected targets of strictly military significance, which were primarily the routes of infiltration. In McNamara's conception of the objectives of the bombing program, the primary goal was to reduce the flow and/or increase the cost of continued infiltration of men and supplies from North Vietnam to South Vietnam. As a corollary, he included a secondary goal, which was to raise the morale of the South Vietnamese people, who, at the time the bombing had started, were under severe military pressure. And, as a final goal, he hoped to make clear to the North Vietnamese leadership that so long as they continued their aggression against the south they would have to pay a price in the north. The bombing of North Vietnam, he emphasized, had always been considered a supplement to, not a substitute for, an effective counterinsurgency land and air campaign in South Vietnam.

It was McNamara's opinion that in this light the bombing campaign had been successful. He further defended the targeting decisions that had been made in carrying out the program, insisting that the target selection had not inhibited the use of air power against targets of military significance.

The Secretary also held that the critics of such a limited bombing campaign were in fact looking towards objectives that were unrealizable. He perceived these critics as believing that our air power could win the war in the south either by breaking the will of North Vietnam or by cutting off the source of the war-supporting supplies needed in the south; their approach would use the air attack against the north not as a supplement to, but as a substitute for, the ground war, which needed to be forcefully waged in the south. McNamara then went on to say that, in his estimation, the air war would be unable either to break the will of the north or to stop the flow of supplies to the south.[4]

Overall, the Secretary spent the day on the witness stand engaged in an articulate, insistent, but in the end unsuccessful defense of his views. At times, his answers to some of the more pointed questions were, to say the least, evasive. For example, he was asked: "General Wheeler testified that in his opinion the proposal to limit the air campign in the south to 20 degrees north latitude is dead. Do you concur, sir?" Secretary McNamara replied: "I don't know that it was ever a proposal. I did ask that these three alternatives be studied, and I will continue to ask that we consider alternatives to the present program." It has, of course, been brought out in great detail in earlier parts of this narrative that the concept of limiting the bombing to south of twenty degrees north was indeed a proposal and had been considered in great depth in many offices of the Departments of Defense and State.

The subcommittee issued its report on 31 August, castigating the administration's conduct of the bombing campaign, deferring to the authority of the professional military judgments it had heard, accepting virtually all the military criticisms of the program, and advocating a switch-over to an escalating pressure concept.

Excerpts from the report are particularly revealing. At one point, Secretary McNamara had emphasized the inability of the bombing program to accomplish much more than it already had, given the nature of U. S. objectives as he viewed them. The subcommittee disagreed:

> That the air campaign has not achieved its objectives to a greater extent cannot be attributed to inability or impotence of air power. It attests, rather, to the fragmentation of our air might by overly restrictive controls, limitations, and a doctrine of "gradualism" placed on our aviation forces which prevented them from waging the air cam-

paign in the manner and according to the timetable which was best calculated to achieve maximum results.[5]

At another juncture, McNamara had discounted the value of closing Haiphong, though all the military witnesses had said it could and should be done since it would contribute significantly to an early conclusion of the war in the south. In this, and in other areas of discussion, the subcommittee considered that the military view was sounder and should prevail. In fact, the subcommittee's report was emphatic on this point:

> In our hearings we found a sharp difference of opinion between the civilian authority and the top level military witnesses, who appeared before the subcommittee, over how and when our air power should be employed against North Vietnam. In that difference we believe we also found the roots of the persistent deterioration of public confidence in our air power because the plain facts, as they unfolded in the testimony, demonstrated clearly that civilian authority consistently overruled the unanimous recommendations of the military commander and the Joint Chiefs of Staff for a systematic, timely, and hard-hitting integrated air campaign against the vital North Vietnam targets. Instead, for policy reasons, we have employed military aviation in a carefully controlled, restricted and graduated build-up of bombing pressure which discounted the professional judgment of our best military experts and substituted civilian judgment in the details of target selection and the timing of strikes. We shackled the true potential of air power and permitted the build-up of what has become the world's most formidable anti-aircraft defenses.
>
> It is not our intention to point a finger or to second guess those who determined this policy, but the cold fact is that this policy has not done the job and it has been contrary to the best military judgment. What is needed now is a hard decision to do whatever is necessary, take the risks that have to be taken, and apply the force that is required to see the job through.

As between these diametrically opposed views (of the SECDEF and the military experts) and in view of the unsatisfactory progress of the war, logic and prudence requires that the decision be with the unanimous weight of professional military judgment.

It is high time, we believe, to allow the military voice to be heard in connection with the tactical details of military operations.[6]

As a final note, the Pentagon Papers include this additional comment on the aftermath of the hearings:

The Stennis report also raised a furor by exposing the policy rift within the Administration. In an attempt to dampen its effects, the President called an unscheduled news conference on September 1 to deny differences among his advisors and to generally overrule his Secretary of Defense on the bombing. More stinging for McNamara, however, than this oral repudiation must have been the subsequent escalatory decisions against his advice. On September 10, for instance, North Vietnam's third port at Cam Pha, a target he had specifically counseled against in his testimony, was struck for the first time. McNamara's year-end resignation seems in retrospect the only logical course for someone who found himself so far out of line with the direction of Administration policy.[7]

These seeming rebuffs by the President did not deter Secretary McNamara in his determination to counter aggressively any proposals for a stronger bombing program so long as he remained in office. He was apparently determined to resist accepting JCS military advice at his level and to use every possible influence in urging that it not be accepted by the President.

CHAPTER 20

ANOTHER ATTEMPT TO NEGOTIATE . . . RESTRICTIONS ANEW

IN THE AFTERMATH of the Stennis hearings, the President was being pushed hard to escalate the air war in the north. Then, with an almost uncanny sense of timing, there suddenly came an opportunity for contact with the government of North Vietnam on terms for peace. In mid-August 1967, a channel to the North Vietnamese opened up in Paris, and the United States eagerly picked up the opportunity to test Hanoi. In line with this possible opportunity for negotiations, a cessation of attacks in the Hanoi Prohibited Area was ordered for a ten-day period to begin on 24 August. Apparently no reply was received from Hanoi by 1 September, so the cessation was extended for seventy-two hours, and then belatedly on 7 September it was officially extended again. The cessation order, incidentally, was sent out to the military command with no explanation of its purpose, since every effort was being made to maintain the secrecy of the contacts in Paris.

Later that month, on the twenty-ninth, the President delivered a speech in San Antonio, Texas, in which he dramatically appealed to the North Vietnamese leaders to begin peace talks. In essence, he was repeating publicly the language of the negotiations proposal that had been transmitted in August. After the speech, although it must be assumed that the Paris contacts remained viable, no official response was apparently received. On 3 October, however, the so-called San Antonio formula was rejected in scathing terms in the North Vietnamese party newspaper, *Nham Dan*.

In the meantime, since I had not been aware of the attempts to contact Hanoi, I of course had complained about this new limitation on the bombing program and sought, in many messages to the JCS, to have the cessation lifted.

Also during this time frame, but unrelated to the "peace feeler" issue, the JCS had requested that I provide my views and recommendations as to an optimum air campaign against North Vietnam for a twelve-month period, to begin in November of 1967. I had come up with a well-conceived, thoroughly staffed concept for an extended air campaign several times before, but this was another opportunity to get our thoughts into the JCS and on up to the Secretary of Defense. My response reconfirmed and restated our basic objectives of denying external assistance to North Vietnam through closure of the ports and destroying its war-making resources through essentially unrestricted, offensive-oriented target allocation. Detailed elements of this response are included in Appendix E. Incidentally, this exercise precipitated an interesting exchange with respect to the mission statement that would be used in the preparation of our air-campaign plans.

The exchange began when I advised General Wheeler that we understood the mission statement, as prepared by the Joint Staff, would be in accordance with Secretary McNamara's statement before the Preparedness Subcommittee at the Stennis hearings. I indicated that in my view McNamara's statement of the objectives for a bombing campaign was weak and imprecise, since it did not allude in any way to the most vitally important aspect, i.e., the denial of external assistance to North Vietnam with the specific objective of choking the entire economy. I stressed that we needed to emphasize that the denial of external assistance was *not* designed just to stop the importation of military supplies to be infiltrated into South Vietnam. By far the more important effect to be achieved was the widespread disruption and deterioration of North Vietnamese economy, coupled with creation of severe internal control-and-management problems. Such pressures and their effects would be cumulative and, if applied over an extended period of time, would be much more decisive in breaking Hanoi's determination to continue aggression in the south, than would a mere reduction of flow of arms into South Vietnam. My main point was that if we could rephrase the mission statement to bring out the foregoing objective, we might gain some ground in overcoming the frustrating misconception that the greatest contribution to be gained from the air campaign was to inflict much greater attrition and restriction on infiltration.

General Wheeler replied that, in essence, I was correct in my understanding of the source of the mission statement, but that any attempt to change it would inevitably produce a loud explosion in the administration. The JCS would immediately be cast in the role of irresponsible militarists attempting to expand the war. In his opinion, furthermore, a change in the language of the mission statement was really unimportant since it is what we do, not what we say, that impacts on the enemy. Wheeler pointed out that one of the tasks of our forces, using the mission statement as planned, would be to isolate Hanoi and Haiphong from each other and from the rest of Vietnam, which was what the increased level of air effort against an expanded target base had been designed to accomplish. While he agreed that mining or otherwise crippling the ports was militarily cheaper, more direct, and more effective, he advised me that the JCS believed this more direct approach was not politically in the cards.

Returning to the matter of the latest bombing cessation, I requested authority on 20 September to strike the Phuc Yen airfield, and the next day I made an urgent request to lift the ban on striking in the Hanoi area, which had been in effect now since 24 August. Gen. Harold Johnson, Army Chief of Staff, who was acting Chairman of the JCS in General Wheeler's absence (General Wheeler had had a moderate heart attack), affirmatively endorsed my request. Secretary McNamara's reply, written in his own hand, said merely, "The Hanoi restriction remains in effect, so this strike has not been approved." On 26 September, approval was given to hit Phuc

Yen, but before a strike could be launched the authorization was rescinded.

During October, the JCS, under General Johnson's interim leadership, continued to press for lifting the Hanoi restrictions and for permission to attack Phuc Yen. On the seventh, I used the forum of my monthly summary of the Rolling Thunder program to reiterate the cumulative detrimental effects of maintaining the Hanoi restriction. The following day I fired off yet another message to the JCS specifically requesting strikes against Phuc Yen:

> The morale of our air crews understandably rose when briefed to strike Phuc Yen airfield and its MiGs, a target which has continually jeopardized their well-being. The unexplained revocation of that authority coupled with the increasing numbers and aggressiveness of MiG-21 attacks, cannot help but impact adversely on air crew morale. Air crews flying combat missions through the intense North Vietnamese defenses, air-to-air and ground-to-air, have demonstrated repeatedly their courage and determination to press home their attack against vital targets. Every effort should be made to reduce the hazard to them, particularly from a threat in which the enemy is afforded a sanctuary so that he can attack at times of his own choosing.[1]

As it became undeniably evident that the hoped-for peace talks were not in the offing, the President approved six new targets in early October, including five in or near Haiphong. Then on 24 October, the strike on Phuc Yen was finally approved, along with a restrike on the Hanoi power transformer and a temporary lifting of Hanoi restrictions. The following day the MiGs at Phuc Yen were attacked for the first time, and Hanoi was at long last struck again after an extended period of grace.

Earlier in the month, the JCS had forwarded for transmittal to the President the requested plan for a twelve-month air campaign against North Vietnam. The President had asked what could be done to put more pressure on Hanoi, and the Chiefs had responded in their usual decisive, forthright manner. They first outlined their understanding of the objectives of the war, the constraints within which the political leadership wished it to be fought, and the self-imposed operational restrictions that they saw as hindering achievement of the objectives. They then proposed a recommended list of ten measures calculated to convince the enemy we meant business. This was one of the final expositions of the military argument for a strategy that could lead us to a clear victory over North Vietnam before U. S. de-escalation action began in March of 1968. It was an excellent articulation of the JCS point of view, with which I, of course, wholeheartedly concurred.

The ten actions recommended by the JCS were:

1. remove restrictions on the air campaign against all militarily significant targets in North Vietnam.
2. mine North Vietnamese deep-water ports.
3. mine inland waterways and estuaries in North Vietnam north of twenty degrees north.
4. extend naval surface operations.
5. use U. S. surface-to-air missiles from ships against combat aircraft.
6. increase air interdiction in Laos and along North Vietnamese borders.
7. eliminate operational restrictions on B-52s with regard to Laos.
8. expand operations in Laos.
9. expand operations in Cambodia.
10. expand covert programs in North Vietnam.[2]

Days after this joint memorandum from the JCS went forward, General Wheeler, who had by then returned to his duties as Chairman, sent forward his own proposal for expansion of the air war. Among his more significant recommendations was the reduction of the Hanoi and Haiphong Prohibited Areas to three and one and one-half miles respectively, thereby opening up an additional fifteen vital targets that could be struck on the authority of the field commander. However, on the basis of a recommendation from the Assistant Secretary of Defense for International Security Affairs (ISA), Paul Warnke, who was and still is a noted dove, this recommendation was rejected.[3]

In late November, the JCS sent Secretary McNamara another memorandum describing their plans for the conduct of all aspects of the war over the next four months. The Chiefs proposed the addition of twenty-four new targets to the authorized target list, and again requested authorization to mine the harbors of Haiphong, Hon Gai, and Cam Pha and removal of the general restrictions associated with attacks in the Hanoi and Haiphong areas. The twenty-four-target proposal was considered at the Tuesday lunch of 5 December, but no action was taken until the sixteenth when McNamara and Rusk did reach agreement to approve ten of the twenty-four, including seven within the ten-mile Hanoi radius and two within the four-mile Haiphong radius.

The President had taken some guarded steps toward military expansion of the air war in the fall of 1967, undoubtedly as a result of the Stennis hearings and in spite of Secretary McNamara's strong position against any such action. In the military view, however, we were not moving far enough fast enough, and we continued to press our position upon the decision makers, albeit with an increasing sense of futility.

CHAPTER 21

Pressure to De-escalate

LTHOUGH PRESIDENT JOHNSON'S San Antonio speech had obviously failed in its primary purpose in that no peace talks were forthcoming, it had certainly succeeded in heightening the tenor of the public debate over the war. Moreover, the slight escalation of the air war had not really satisfied the hawks, but it had most assuredly agitated the doves. On 12 October, thirty dovish congressmen had sent a message to the President urging him to stop the bombing and start negotiations, and on the twenty-first, leaders of the "new left" had assembled some 50,000 anti-war protesters in the capital and staged a massive march on the Pentagon.

In November, sensing that the increasing public clamor to do something different in the war—namely, stop the bombing—gave every indication of being persuasive, I had commented to the JCS on the effects of a cessation in the bombing of North Vietnam at that time. Although my concerns were not new, they needed to be reiterated for continued emphasis. I reminded the Chiefs that cessation would lead to the military, economic and psychological recovery of the enemy and would be a resounding political victory for North Vietnam, and I outlined the gains in those areas that we would be handing Hanoi. My conclusion was that we should not throw away one of our best means for shortening the war. The complete text of this important message is included as Appendix F.

By early winter of 1967–68 several new studies of the bombing program had been completed by both government and contract researchers. All of these had some bearing on the deliberations of February and March 1968, when the next major policy reassessment took place. The first study was done by the Joint Staff and the Office of International Security Affairs (ISA) in the Defense Department, and was entitled "Sea Cabin," a rather contrived acronym for "Study of the Political, Military Implications in Southeast Asia of the Cessation of Aerial Bombardment and the Initiation of Negotiations." It specifically addressed the question of what could be expected from a cessation of bombing and the beginning of negotiations.

Despite the fact that the general attitude in ISA was anti-war, and especially anti-bombing, the study was relatively objective. It listed the implications of cessation in terms of advantages to North Vietnam and risks to the United States, and the assessment was quite similar to the one I had given the JCS in November. In its summary of findings and conclusions, the "Sea Cabin" report had this comment on the bombing:

> It is clear that the air and naval campaigns against North Vietnam are making it difficult and costly for the DRV to continue effective support of the V. C. Our operations have inflicted heavy damage on equipment and facilities, inhibited resupply, compounded distribution problems, and limited the DRV's capability to undertake sustained large-scale military operations in South Vietnam. The economic situation in North Vietnam is becoming increasingly difficult for the enemy. However, as the result of extensive diversion of manpower and receipt of large-scale military and economic assistance from Communist countries, the DRV has retained the capability to support military operations in South Vietnam at current levels. A cessation of the bombing program would make it possible for the DRV to regenerate its military and economic posture and substantially increase the flow of personnel and supplies from North Vietnam to South Vietnam.[1]

In this same time frame, a Washington-based research group, the Institute for Defense Analyses, reassembled many of the people who had participated in a similar study in 1966 to once again consider whether the bombing program was viable in comparison to other military programs that might be more productive. This group was almost one hundred percent against the bombing, and the assessment indicated the members' personal viewpoints. The "Jason" study, as it was called, put forth a decidedly negative conclusion about the results of Rolling Thunder.

Briefly, this study indicated that U. S. bombing of North Vietnam had had no measurable effect on Hanoi's ability to mount and support military operations in South Vietnam, nor had it discernibly weakened the determination of the North Vietnamese leaders to continue to direct and support the insurgency in the south. The study maintained that the bombing had inflicted heavy costs not so much to North Vietnam's military capability or its infiltration system as to the economy as a whole. Measurable physical damage now appeared to exceed $370 million, and the regime had diverted 300,000 to 600,000 people from agricultural and other tasks to counter and cope with the effects of the bombing. In the final analysis, the study group concluded that it was unable to devise a bombing campaign in the north that would actually reduce the flow of infiltrating personnel into South Vietnam.

The "Jason" study was forwarded to Secretary McNamara on 3 January 1968, with a notation from Assistant Secretary Warnke that, together with the "Sea Cabin" study, it supported the proposition that a bombing pause, even for a significant period of time, would not add appreciably to the strength of our adversary.[2] I do not, and did not then, agree with that conclusion, but it was to be expected from Warnke, who was emphatically against offensive actions against North Vietnam.

In early January a study of the economic effects of the bombing of North Vietnam was completed by the Systems Analysis Division of the Office of the Secretary of Defense. This report was also decidedly negative about the productiveness of the air war, even to the point of suggesting that it might be counterproductive in pure economic terms. So, the forces were being marshalled to pressure the administration into stopping the bombing, and regrettably, the "Sea Cabin" study was grouped with the adverse studies despite its rational and persuasive outline of the dangers of a cessation in the bombing program.

That winter, during what had now become the routine standdowns for the Christmas and New Year periods, we made what had also now become the expected report to the JCS of the North Vietnamese maximum utilization of these "holidays" to move critical supplies southward. Further, in my annual 1967 overall progress report to the JCS (quoted in part in Appendix G) we included pertinent intelligence supporting the statement that "recent large deployments from North Vietnam indicate that the enemy may be seeking a spectacular win in South Vietnam in the near future." Information relative to high rates of artillery, rocket and mortar infiltration was included. Further, on 23 January 1968, General Westmoreland and I conferred in Da Nang about the growing seriousness of the situation around Khe Sanh. There were indications of an impending major attack in that vicinity, and we discussed what should be done in that event. The enemy buildup was obvious—and we were aware of it.

CHAPTER 22

MORE PEACE FEELERS

NEGOTIATIONS, NOT MILITARY operations, continued to hold the spotlight as we crossed from 1967 into 1968. On 29 December, North Vietnamese Foreign Minister Nguyen Duy Trinh made a public statement as follows: "After the United States has ended the bombing and all other acts of war, North Vietnam will hold talks with the United States on questions concerned." The change from his previous statements was that he had said North Vietnam "will" rather than "could" hold talks. Undoubtedly some response was sent to Hanoi, and although I have seen no record of it, the fact that on 3 January we received orders prohibiting bombing within five nautical miles of both Hanoi and Haiphong appears to confirm that such was the case. In any event, the President did go on public record in his annual State of the Union Address as calling for serious negotiations, stressing that the North Vietnamese must not take advantage of our restraint as they had done in the past. His appeal received a contemptous response on 21 January when *Nham Dan*, the official North Vietnamese newspaper, once again condemned his earlier offer (the so-called San Antonio formula) as a trick of the U. S. President, who was attempting to impose very insulting conditions on Hanoi, alleging that the United States had no right to ask for reciprocity before a cessation of the bombing since it was the aggressor.

Later that month during his confirmation hearings before the Senate, the new Secretary of Defense (designate), Clark McAdams Clifford, made a crucial statement in regard to the use of a bombing halt to induce negotiations. In response to questioning he said, "I would express the fervent hope that we could stop the bombing if we had some kind of reciprocal word from North Vietnam that they wanted to sit down and, in good faith, negotiate . . . the deepest desire that I have is to bring hostilities in Vietnam to a conclusion under those circumstances that permit us to have a dignified and honorable result that in turn will obtain for the South Vietnamese that goal which we have made such sacrifices to attain."

Senator Thurmond then asked, "When you spoke of negotiating, in which case you would be willing to have a cessation of bombing, I presume you would contemplate that they would stop their military activities, too, in return for a cessation of the bombing?"

Mr. Clifford replied, "No, that is not what I said. I do not expect them to stop their military activities. I would expect to follow the language of the President when he said that if they would agree to start negotiations promptly, and not take advantage of the pause in the bombing."

Senator Thurmond: "What do you mean by taking advantage if they continue their military activities?"

Mr. Clifford: "Their military activity will continue in South Vietnam, I assume, until there is a cease-fire agreed upon. I assume that they will continue to transport the normal amount of goods, munitions and men to South Vietnam. I assume that we will continue to maintain our forces and support our forces during that period. So what I am suggesting, in the language of the President, is that he would insist that they not take advantage of the suspension of the bombing."[1]

Several days later, this testimony was confirmed by the State Department as the position of the U. S. government. It was undeniably a weakening of our stance vis-à-vis negotiating preconditions and, in my opinion, entirely unacceptable.

Aware of what was in the offing and what was at stake, I fired off another message to the JCS with my views on the subject, briefly as follows:

If we stopped bombing North Vietnam simply because the Communists had said they would then enter into talks, we would have tossed away our most effective means of applying necessary pressure on the enemy. Although it is agreed that in such a situation we should maintain our momentum in South Vietnam, we would be doing so with our right hand tied behind our back; that is, engaging in a land war on a land mass of Asia without fully utilizing our air and naval offensive power. Such a defensive strategy would be disastrous for the achievement of our objectives in Southeast Asia.

I recognize that there are tremendous pressures being exerted by some who would jump at any opportunity to end the war, regardless of the long-term impact. To them I would say that negotiations are not an end in themselves, but rather a means to an end. Before entering any negotiations, the U. S. and our allies should agree upon and publicize the conditions with which the North Vietnamese and the V. C. must comply before our military pressures upon North Vietnam will be stopped. These military pressures should be maintained at a high pitch until the Communists meet our conditions in exchange for relief from these pressures. In summary, I can perceive no advantage, and on the contrary, the greatest disadvantage from a cessation of our bombing of North Vietnam. Time is on our side; we can win the war if we continue our present strategy. Negotiations will only serve our interests when they are undertaken because North Vietnam has determined that the war effort is no longer supportable and agrees to conditions jointly established by the U. S. Government and the Government of South Vietnam. The conditions upon which we should insist prior to any lessening of pressure are that Hanoi must stop infiltrating personnel and material to South Vietnam and Laos, and demonstrate conclusively that all North Vietnamese units have ceased their aggression and are being withdrawn from South Vietnam, Laos and the DMZ, and, further, they should stop the support and direction of the V. C. and the Pathet Lao insurgencies.

Unfortunately, this practical formula for negotiating the war to a *successful* conclusion required more political backbone than the administration was apparently willing or able to muster. The President, in his San Antonio speech, had "conceded" that we were ready to talk peace any time, any place, any where, and our new official negotiating position had "conceded" that we would cease our bombing but in reciprocity expected no cessation of enemy military activity. The Communists had simply to wait for more concessions, and it appeared at this rate that time was going to be on their side, not ours. We were soon to learn that they would not stand idly by while they waited.

CHAPTER 23

THE TET OFFENSIVE
ERODES U.S. PEACE
EFFORTS

O
N 29 JANUARY 1968, U. S., South Vietnamese and allied forces began a thirty-six-hour cease-fire for the Tet
religious holidays, with many South Vietnamese troops
going on leave. However, significant enemy activity in the northern
provinces, including thrusts at Da Nang, Nha Trang and Hue,
forced cancellation of the cease-fire in short order. Then, two days
later, capitalizing on the element of surprise, Viet Cong and North
Vietnamese forces attacked nearly every important city, provincial
capital, and military installation in South Vietnam. The suddenness
of the enemy's attacks was so effective that in Saigon enemy forces
actually entered the grounds of both the American embassy and the
palace temporarily, and many sections of the city were subjected to
severe Viet Cong harassment. United States and South Vietnamese
forces, however, regained control quite rapidly. In Hue, a part of
the city including the Citadel, seat of the ancient capital of Vietnam,
was captured. Overall, the enemy action was characterized by heavy
rocket and mortar attacks that inflicted considerable damage.

This was a major offensive, well planned and executed, with a highly effective logistics organization that had been prepared in obviously successful secrecy. Its objective was to destroy both the administrative structure and the political base of the South Vietnamese government to the point where it could not function, even with U. S. assistance. The Communists expected their attacks to initiate a general uprising against the Thieu government and to cause large defections from the South Vietnamese army, after which they hoped to take over large areas of South Vietnam. In this they were thwarted, however. No popular uprising in support of the Communists materialized and, indeed, the South Vietnamese people demonstrated that they were unwilling to cooperate at all. The constitutional government continued to function both in Saigon and in the provinces, manifesting a continuity of leadership and control, which indicated that the past two years of political evolution in South Vietnam had produced a government capable of meeting the emergency. Furthermore, the South Vietnamese, with a few exceptions, fought very well. There were no defections of military units to the enemy, as Hanoi had expected. The integrity of the armed forces was preserved and the chain of command functioned.

In the main, we were able in fairly short order to counter the attacks on Saigon, Da Nang and elsewhere and to cause the enemy heavy casualties. Only in Hue did the Communist forces succeed in holding on for nearly a month, during which time they slaughtered more than 3,000 innocent civilians. And so, despite the spectacular effect of this offensive, the enemy failed to achieve his objectives.

The heavy fighting that accompanied this offensive, moreover, saw large numbers of Viet Cong and North Vietnamese killed because, for the first time, they came out in the open enabling our forces to use their superior firepower with maximum effectiveness. It has been reported that from 29 January through 11 February the Communists lost 32,000 killed and 5,800 captured, close to half of the troops actively committed. American forces lost 1,001 killed, while South Vietnamese and allied losses were put at 2,082.[1]

The impact on South Vietnam was, of course, not negligible. All of the development programs in the countryside suffered, and while the government was forced to cope with the emergency, normal functions were neglected. The large number of refugees fleeing from the beleagured areas created a serious problem, and there was a pervasive feeling of insecurity and fear of further attacks. There was however, an overriding show of unity in the country, with key leaders and major anti-Communist elements responding in conspicuous support of the government. By the end of February the situation in South Vietnam was under control.

Not so in Washington, where the greatest effect of the Tet offensive was felt. Despite several messages from General Westmoreland warning that some sort of major enemy action was brewing, the administration went into a state of shock when the size and nature of the attack became apparent. Further, the people here at home were subjected to the rampant sensationalism of the media. The emotional coverage of this crisis paid little heed to balanced reporting, indeed, often paying even less attention to ensuring that the reporting was factual. The distorted picture that thus emerged was succinctly characterized by Gen. Maxwell Taylor in one of his recent books:

> In forming the popular concept of what had happened during the Tet offensive, TV was the dominant factor. The picture of a few flaming Saigon houses, presented by a gloomy-voiced telecaster as an instance of the destruction caused in the capital, created the inevitable impression that this was the way it was in all or most of Saigon. This human tendency to generalize from a single fact to a universal conclusion has always been a prime cause for the distorted views regarding Vietnam and certainly contributed to the pessimism in the United States after the Tet offensive in 1968.[2]

Most unfortunate of all, the administration seemed to be paying more attention to television and newspapers than to reports from the field, and so a traumatic aura of defeatism was generated at the seat of government.

From a military point of view, the most logical step to have taken after the Tet offensive began would have been a heavy air strike against the source of the aggression—the enemy's heartland, the Hanoi/Haiphong center of North Vietnamese power. The JCS therefore immediately renewed their earlier proposal to reduce the Prohibited Areas around Hanoi and Haiphong to three and one and one-half miles respectively, with field authority to make strikes as required. Once again, the proposal was turned down after another negative recommendation by Assistant Secretary Warnke of ISA. By now the civilian strategists in Washington were blindly entrenched against the full use of our air power even in retaliation. They compromised by authorizing some token strikes on targets in Haiphong, which were carried out on 10 February, the first such raids in over a month.

The Tet offensive did, however, heat up the controversy over a troop buildup in South Vietnam. General Wheeler visited General Westmoreland in Saigon in mid-February and returned to Washington with their jointly conceived plan to increase our forces by a substantial number. I was bypassed in this particular instance, most likely because of the perception of urgency generated by both the Tet offensive and the current enemy siege of Khe Sanh, but I was, as always, in favor of giving the field commander what he needed to do his job. In this case Westmoreland thought he needed an increase of about 25,000 troops at the present time, with an eventual overall increase of about 206,000 to handle expanded contingency plans. Westmoreland had estimated his optimum force requirements as any field commander would, i.e., the number of troops he could readily use, but in Washington that optimum force request was immediately translated into firm requirements. Everyone promptly went into a tailspin because to provide the number of troops indicated would mean mobilization, and mobilization at this point, with elections coming up later in the year and in a time of great domestic dissent, was unthinkable to the politicians.

In response to a myriad of questions from the JCS, General Westmoreland submitted a message delineating very precisely how his various proposed force buildups would affect his strategy, and what he could accomplish with specific alternate force levels. In my comments on this message, I took the opportunity to give General Wheeler my views once again on the total strategy involved. I emphasized that, while the recommended increase in forces was needed as soon as possible, it would not affect the situation immediately . . . and we did have an immediate problem. We needed to buck up the morale of the brave people of South Vietnam and change the pessimistic attitude that seemed to permeate the United States—and we needed to do both quickly. The only action that could be taken right away was to step up the air campaign. Westmoreland had both his forces and the South Vietnamese moving into the offensive as rapidly as possible. We needed to reinforce and supplement those actions *now*, with an increasingly strong offensive air action. I noted that we could mine Haiphong at any time, which would, of course, still be the single most important and damaging offensive action we could take. I called to mind that Westmoreland and I had earlier recommended feinting an amphibious landing against North Vietnam, and I recommended that present restrictions on this operation be lifted so it could be carried out as early as the weather and the current situation would permit. I further pointed out the ample evidence that the enemy was being supplied in quantity through Cambodia, asking how long we could tolerate this unmolested flow of war supplies.

I concluded my comments by stressing that with the power the United States had available we could have the enemy reeling by mid-summer, but to do so would require some hard decisions. After all this time we were still at the crossroads. We could either use our military power at full effectiveness, to include provision of the necessary in-country forces, or continue a campaign of gradualism and accept an even longer, more drawn-out contest. Or, as the last choice, we could retreat in defeat from Southeast Asia and leave our allies to face the Communists alone. The choices were not pleasant or easy, but they seemed obvious. We had made frequent, sincere and very reasonable efforts to negotiate, all to no avail. Now we needed to get tough in word and deed—the only policy the Communists understand.[3]

On 8 March, General Wheeler sent word to me and to General Westmoreland of a recent conversation he had had with the new Secretary of Defense, Clark Clifford. Secretary Clifford had made the point, first of all, that the Tet offensive had come as a great shock to the American public, and in his opinion the optimistic statements from various spokesmen supporting the administration's policy in South Vietnam had contributed to this. He had further indicated his concern over lessening public support for the war effort, pointing to the countless articles being published that contained erroneous accounts of the situation in Vietnam. In his view the public support that remained could not stand another blow such as the Tet offensive, and he considered that by playing down its effect we were apt to set up the public for an even bigger fall. Any future major enemy attacks over a substantial area of South Vietnam could create a credibility gap with both the American people and the news media, which would be extremely troublesome to him. In general, the new Secretary had been conspicuously negative and critical in his view of the military effort in Southeast Asia—and the bottom line was that we had best be apprised of it.

The reality of the 1968 Tet offensive was that Hanoi had taken a big gamble and had lost on the battlefield, but they had won a solid psychological victory in the United States. Any hope that the decision makers in Washington would ever begin to function with a *positive* attitude about the war had been very effectively dimmed. We were simply going to absorb a major enemy offensive without taking the obvious retaliatory action at hand. Our powerful air force and navy air resources were poised and ready. We could have flattened every war-making facility in North Vietnam. But the handwringers had center stage; the anti-war elements were in full cry. The most powerful country in the world did not have the willpower needed to meet the situation.

CHAPTER 24

MARCH 1968: THE DEBATE

THE RECENT TROOP-REQUIREMENTS exercise had touched off an intense reappraisal of where we stood and where we were going in the war, with divergent views aplenty. As part of this effort, the President had asked Secretary Clifford in late February to convene a group of senior advisers from the State and Defense Departments, CIA, and the White House to conduct a complete review of our involvement in Vietnam, reevaluating both our aims and the means by which we hoped to achieve them. The group consisted of former Defense Secretary McNamara; Gen. Maxwell Taylor, now serving as Special Military Advisor to the President; Undersecretary of Defense Paul Nitze; Secretary of the Treasury Henry H. Fowler; Undersecretary of State Katzenbach; Walt Rostow; CIA Director Richard Helms; Assistant Secretary of Defense for International Security Affairs Paul Warnke; and Philip C. Habib from William Bundy's office in the State Department.

General Westmoreland's request for additional troop deployments was the focus of the discussions for the first meeting, and, generally speaking, this was the main thrust of considerations by the committee, although the subjects of the air war and negotiations were also addressed. The preparation of the group's report to the

President, to include the supporting papers, was carried out not by the principals, but by four teams within the Office of International Security Affairs, which were headed by Mr. Warnke; Dr. Alain Enthoven, Assistant Secretary of Defense for Systems Analysis; Dr. Morton H. Halperin; and Richard C. Steadman. (It should be mentioned that each of these team leaders had already taken a strong stand against the bombing program.)

Lengthy inputs were provided to the group's deliberations by the CIA and Assistant Secretary Bundy's office in the State Department. General Taylor, in particular, provided an especially important contribution, for two reasons. First, in his capacity as the President's Special Military Advisor, he was able to feed his input directly to the President, as well as to the Clifford group. Second, his background as a past Chariman of the JCS and former Ambassador to Saigon gave particular pertinence to his analysis of the subject at hand.

In reviewing the objectives of U. S. policy in South Vietnam, General Taylor said, in part:

> We should consider changing the objective which we have been pursuing consistently since 1954 only for the most cogent reasons. There is clearly nothing to recommend trying to do more than what we are now doing at such great cost. To undertake to do less is to accept needlessly a serious defeat for which we would pay dearly in terms of our worldwide position of leadership, of the political stability of Southeast Asia, and of the credibility of pledges to friends and allies.

He further contended that the choice among the various available political alternatives would depend largely on what our decision was to be with regard to the reinforcements for General Westmoreland. He insisted, however, that the military situation in South Vietnam argued strongly against a new negotiating effort and any thought of reducing the bombing of the north. If it was decided to meet Westmoreland's request, the significance of that action should be underlined by sharply increased bombing levels (possibly to include the closing of Haiphong), preceded by a statement of our intentions as having been made necessary by the enemy offensive. In any case, Taylor believed that the United States would appear well advised to withdraw from the "San Antonio formula" in view of the heightened level of aggression conducted by North Vietnam.[1]

At the heart of the action, the four working teams in ISA were busy drafting various versions of the proposed memorandum for the President. Their intent, apparently, was to come up with specific recommendations on a course of action, and in so doing to either reconcile or exclude any widely divergent views that were incompatible with the thrust of those recommendations. (I would like to note that this is an extremely poor staff procedure and would be rejected by any good leader/manager. The decision maker, in this case the Commander in Chief, the President, should be provided with alternatives, accompanied by well-thought-out pros and cons to each, and not with a specific single recommendation on a course of action the staff has decided is best. Not unsurprisingly, General Taylor's memorandum on this issue followed the proper alternatives format.)

In any event, the final draft recommendations presented to the principals amounted to a major change in U. S. ground strategy based on a decision not to substantially increase U. S. forces as General Westmoreland and the JCS had desired. In lieu of Westmoreland's search-and-destroy strategy, adoption of a strategy of population protection was recommended. As for the air war, the recommendations were expressly against any escalation above the current levels, any reduction in the perimeters of the Hanoi/Haiphong Prohibited Areas, and any attempt at closing Haiphong harbor.

The Clifford group principals convened on 3 March to consider these recommendations but found little that could be readily accepted. Although there was a consensus that abandoning the initiative completely, as the draft memorandum seemed to imply, would be unwise, and that there was virtually no hope for near-term negotiations, the bombing issue once again proved the stumbling block, with opinions sharply divided along already well-drawn lines. In the end, the only decision taken at the meeting was to have the working group write an entirely new draft memorandum for the President, dealing primarily with the troop-numbers issue. It was to recommend only a modest increase, and to call for more emphasis on the contribution to the war effort by the South Vietnamese armed forces. Further, the memorandum was to propose a study of possible new strategic guidance, to recommend against any new initiative on negotiations, and to acknowledge the split over the bombing program. This new draft was completed the following day, circulated for comment, and eventually transmitted to the President, without change, by Secretary Clifford.

In this final form, the Clifford group memorandum included two papers on the controversial bombing issue. The first, written by the Joint Staff and submitted by General Wheeler, advocated reduction of the Hanoi/Haiphong Prohibited/Restricted perimeters, extension of naval operations, authority to use sea-based surface-to-air missiles against North Vietnamese MiGs, and, in the cover memo, action to close the port of Haiphong through mining or otherwise. To make the air campaign effective, Wheeler also recommended modification of existing regulations, chiefly the removal of those restrictions that had hampered the campaign to date. He pointed out, however, that since March, April, and part of May would be the bad weather season over North Vietnam, results could not be expected immediately. The second paper, submitted by ISA and drafted in Warnke's own office, took the expected position of turning back all of the JCS recommendations for expanding the air war, including mining the North Vietnamese harbors.

Ironically, neither of these two positions even considered the one that was eventually adopted, namely, restricting the bombing to the panhandle area of North Vietnam. Although it had apparently been a principal item of discussion at various levels, this option was for some reason not presented in the official paper. The suggestion has been made that Secretary Clifford personally advocated this idea to the President, but decided that by specifically recommending in the official memorandum restriction of the bombing to below the nineteenth or twentieth parallel, he would have called forth a full and formal criticism by the JCS.

Overall, March 1968 was most definitely a traumatic month for official Washington on all counts, especially for President Johnson. Among other things, he was still faced with the tough problem of how to handle public reaction to the recent Tet offensive and the dwindling public support for his war policies. Then on 10 March, the *New York Times* broke the story of General Westmoreland's 206,000-man troop request in banner headlines, understandably infuriating the President, who was concerned that such a security leak could dangerously compromise our military position. To make matters worse, the following day Secretary Rusk went before Senator Fulbright's Foreign Relations Committee for nationally televised hearings on U. S. war policy and was subjected to sharp questioning vis-à-vis the administration's position by virtually every member.

The final blow came on the thirteenth when it was learned that the President had just barely edged out his challenger, Eugene McCarthy, in the New Hampshire primary elections. McCarthy had based his campaign on a halt in the bombing and an end to the war, and in so doing had rallied sufficient support to make him a decidedly effective presidential challenger, at least in this instance. Moreover, when Sen. Robert F. Kennedy announced his presidential candidacy shortly thereafter, the handwriting was clearly on the wall that President Johnson now faced the prospect of a difficult battle for renomination within his own party. The unpopular Vietnam War, as McCarthy had shown, would almost certainly be the main issue.

To seek a clearer focus on that issue, the President called together in mid-March a small group of prominent men from outside the government, who were referred to as the Senior Informal Advisory Group. All experienced decision makers, they came to Washington on the eighteenth to be briefed on the latest developments in the war and to offer the President the benefit of their thinking. The group consisted of Arthur H. Dean, a New York lawyer who had been a Korean War negotiator; Dean Acheson, former President Harry Truman's Secretary of State; Gen. Matthew B. Ridgway, U. S. Army, the retiring Commander of the United Nations Forces in Korea; Gen. Maxwell Taylor; George Ball, former Under Secretary of State; Cyrus Vance, former Deputy Secretary of Defense; McGeorge Bundy, who had been a Special Assistant to the President; former Treasury Secretary C. Douglas Dillon; and Gen. Omar Bradley, U. S. Army (Ret.). With the exception of George Ball, these men had all taken a generally "hawkish" line in their previous advice to the President concerning his Vietnam War strategies.

After a dinner with various government officials, the group was briefed separately by Philip C. Habib, a member of the American negotiating team in Paris; Maj. Gen. William E. DePuy, U. S. Army, Special Assistant to the Joint Chiefs for counterinsurgency; and George Carver, a CIA analyst. The next morning they met in the White House to discuss what they had heard. According to the newspaper account quoted in the Pentagon Papers, the group arrived at a gloomy verdict: "Continued escalation of the war— intensified bombing of North Vietnam, and increased American troop strength in the South—would do no good. Forget about seeking a battlefield solution to the problem and instead intensify efforts to seek a political solution at the negotiating table."

Since that position was a decided reversal in thinking for most of the group, it is worthwhile to consider what General Taylor, who was one of the principals, has to say about the matter. In his opinion, some of the members had apparently arrived convinced in advance that the present policy should be changed. After debating the issue they met with the President and expressed their indiviudal views. Dean Acheson, Cyrus Vance and McGeorge Bundy took roughly the pessimistic position described above. Only former Ambassador Robert Murphy, and Justice Abe Fortas (whom Taylor mentions as also being present) joined Taylor in dissenting strongly from it. In between the two extremes the mood was generally for a change in strategy, although no definitive format for such change emerged. In Taylor's perception, the influence on the group of both the anti-war bias in the East Coast media and the Pentagon "doves" was obvious.[2]

In any event, the President was surprised by the new positions expressed by these trusted advisers of long-standing and was undoubtedly strongly impacted by their thinking in reaching his eventual decision not to expand the war, but to attempt a de-escalation.

In a dramatic culmination of almost two months of agonizing appraisal of our strategy in the war, President Johnson went on the air at 9:00 P.M. on 31 March to deliver one of the most important speeches of his career. He first reiterated the offer he had made public at San Antonio; namely, that the United States would stop the bombardment of North Vietnam when we were assured that it would lead promptly to productive discussions and that North Vietnam would not take military advantage of our restraint. He then announced that he had ordered our aircraft and our naval vessels to make no attacks on North Vietnam except in the area immediately north of the DMZ, where the continuing enemy buildup directly threatened allied forward positions and where the movements of enemy troops and supplies were clearly related to that threat. Even this very limited bombing of the north, he said, would come to an early end if our restraint were matched by restraint in Hanoi.

The President emphasized, further, that our objective in South Vietnam had never been to annihilate the enemy, but rather to bring about a recognition in Hanoi that its objective—taking over the south by force—could not be achieved. He reaffirmed his pledge that we were prepared to withdraw our forces from South Vietnam as the other side withdrew its forces to the north, stopped the infiltration, and the level of violence thus subsided. Finally, toward the end of his speech, Johnson made his most grave and unexpected pronouncement:

> With America's sons in the fields far away, with America's future under challenge right here at home, with our hopes and the world's hopes for peace in the balance every day, I do not believe that I should devote an hour or a day of my time to any personal partisan causes, or to any duties other than the awesome duties of this office—the Presidency of your country. Accordingly, I shall not seek, and I will not accept, the nomination of my party for another term as your President.

The President's remarks did not, of course, signal either the end of the bombing or, most certainly, the end of the war. But they did mark a major decision point, one that committed American policy irrevocably towards a negotiated, as opposed to a military, settlement of the war and that made significant concessions to that end.

I was fairly well isolated from all these discussions taking place in the month of March, and it was not until the thirty-first that we received word that combat air operations against North Vietnam north of twenty degrees north latitude would be discontinued, effective 8:00 A.M. on 1 April. We were further advised that the President would announce this decision publicly. In amplification, the Chairman JCS advised that, since the Tet offensive, support for the war by the American public and in Congress had decreased, and many of the strongest proponents for forceful action in Vietnam had either reversed their positions, moved to a neutral attitude, or were wavering. If this trend continued, public support of our objectives in Southeast Asia would be too frail to sustain the effort. The JCS advisory went on to point out that since the weather over the northern portion of North Vietnam would not be suitable for air operations during the next month or so anyway, it would be best from the military viewpoint to begin the cession immediately, if it were to be undertaken. The inference was that we might start up the bombing again if things did not work out the way the President hoped.

The long and short of it was that the President's advisers had led him into making concessions to the enemy in the hope of getting negotiations started. It was a forlorn hope, motivated at least partly by political conditions in our own country. Traditionally, as we should certainly have learned in Korea, Communists do not react in a forthcoming manner to concessions . . . they simply demand more. Increased pressure is the only thing they understand.

CHAPTER 25

THE AIR OFFENSIVE: EMASCULATED

J UST AFTER THE 31 March cessation of bombing north of latitude twenty degrees, our naval air forces made a heavy attack on transportation facilities near Thanh Hoa, an important communications/traffic center just south of the twenty-degree line. It was perhaps the most important target in the area then authorized for strikes, and, quite understandably, this heavy strike was ordered to stop the flow of material through this point southward. The attack was reported in a sensational story from UPI in Saigon, and since the President in his speech had avoided actually designating twenty degress latitude as the limiting line, saying only that the bombing would be confined to the panhandle, the anti-war element claimed he had acted in bad faith and had used misleading language. As a result of this partisan reaction, we were immediately told not to bomb north of nineteen degrees, which left Thanh Hoa immune from any further strikes and further reduced the effectiveness of what remained of the bombing program.

In early May, I noted to the JCS that the unilateral limitation of bombing over the greater part of North Vietnam was a major U. S. concession in return for which no matching restraint had yet been exercised by Hanoi. No decision had been reached regarding even the selection of a place for talks, nor had there been any evidence of intention by Hanoi to negotiate anything except complete cessation of the bombing and all other "acts of war" by the United States. On the contrary, since the bombing pause began, the enemy had taken every possible advantage of our restraint—supplies and personnel were being moved south in unprecedented volume. Any proposals for de-escalation by mutual withdrawal were clearly being rendered militarily unsound by this demonstrated duplicity of the enemy.

In mid-May, the JCS asked for my assessment of the capabilities of the U. S. and allied military forces at this point in time to achieve their objectives and to prevent the enemy from achieving his objectives in Southeast Asia. Briefly, I replied:

> As a result of the tremendous personnel losses inflicted on the enemy when he chose to come out in the open during the Tet offensive, followed by the successful offensive operations launched by the Vietnamese and Free World forces, we now have a stronger position on the ground in South Vietnam than before the Tet offensive. This is true notwithstanding the harassing attacks that the North Vietnamese and V. C. have undertaken for the past week. The enemy is hurting badly, both from our earlier bombing campaign in North Vietnam and from our successful operations in South Vietnam. In the near term we are militarily in a strong position—the relative balance of strength in the longer term will depend on the actions taken by both sides during the negotiating period.
>
> The position of strength we currently enjoy could not have been achieved without the air and naval campaign against northern North Vietnam. The enemy has responded to our unilateral limitation on these campaigns by increasing significantly his infiltration efforts and by stepping up his activities in South Vietnam. This reaction by Hanoi was to be expected in view of the Communists' penchant for a "fight while talk" strategy. Hanoi's reaction to the current bombing limitation gives further credence to

the view that the enemy will take every possible advantage of any restrictions which are imposed upon U. S./Free World military operations. If we accede further to Hanoi's demands without exacting comparable concessions, a deterioration in the overall U. S./Free World military situation in South Vietnam could develop in a gradual but steadily accelerating way. In the end we could lose at the conference table what the enemy could not take on the battlefield.

The aerial and naval bombardment of North Vietnam is the only strategic offensive weapon we have, not only for inhibiting infiltration but also for making North Vietnam pay a substantial price for their support of aggression in the South. The price for cessation of that bombardment must be a high one.

While the enemy does not have the means of achieving a military victory in South Vietnam, he does retain a dangerous capability to carry out attacks on a scale which could make the position of the U. S. delegation in Paris more difficult. We know that the enemy has reconstituted his forces and positioned them for further attacks in South Vietnam. His dispositions today could connote forthcoming attacks in the western highlands and in the northern I Corps area. Small successes on the part of the enemy could have major impact in Paris.

The process of infiltration, resupply and refitting makes time on the side of the enemy and against the United States. Hanoi needs time to strengthen its position while U. S. resolve and determination might be lessened or eroded by actions worldwide during the forthcoming summer. If the enemy succeeds in talking through the good weather period in North Vietnam without coming to terms, while avoiding resumption of bombing, he will have set the stage for protracting the war for another year.

In summary, the U. S./Free World military posture is good at this time. As we move into the months ahead, our now favorable situation could deteriorate on an accelerating basis if we withhold the use of our power and the enemy uses our forbearance to build his strength. This highlights the necessity of maintaining pressures upon the enemy during the negotiations and, after a limited reasonable period, to resume military operations throughout North Vietnam should the enemy not negotiate in good faith.

Earlier that spring the Republican party had gathered a task force of military experts to assess the situation in Southeast Asia. This distinguished group included Neil McElroy, former Secretary of Defense; Thomas Gates, former Secretary of Defense; Wilfred McNeil and Perkins McGuire, each a former Assistant Secretary of Defense; Adm. Arleigh Burke, U. S. Navy (Ret.), former Chief of Naval Operations; Gen. George Decker, U. S. Army (Ret.), former Chief of Staff of the Army; Adm. Harry D. Felt U. S. Navy (Ret.), former Commander in Chief Pacific; Gen. Alfred Gruenther, U. S. Army (Ret.), former Supreme Allied Commander in Europe; Craig Hosmer, member of Congress; James Pearson, Senator from Kansas; Adm. Arthur Radford, U. S. Navy (Ret.), former Chairman of the JCS; Gen. Bernard Schriever, U. S. Air Force (Ret.); Gen. Nathan Twining, U. S. Air Force (Ret.), former Chairman of the JCS; and Sen. John Tower of Texas. Their report, released on 18 April 1968 and entitled "The Failure of Gradualism in Vietnam," concluded in summary that the U. S. policy of measured escalation of combat had proved itself bankrupt in Vietnam. This policy, which they considered the brainchild of former Defense Secretary Robert McNamara, had not only failed, it had escalated the war unnecessarily.

The report further noted an urgent need to establish credibility with the world at large, indeed with our own people, that the United States did have the determination and the will to use its strength to restore and keep the peace. It also charged that the administration's new doctrines of flexible response and gradualism were dangerously unrealistic. It stressed that once this nation resorts to arms to stem aggression, force should be applied quickly and decisively to bring the conflict swiftly to an end. The longer a conflict is indulged, the greater the likelihood of escalation and expansion, and the greater the casualties and destruction. In other words, once committed to military action, we must not merely respond, we must achieve and maintain the initiative. Finally, the report was emphatic in recommending that our country announce at the highest level the resumption of a national security policy dictating that the size of our response to aggression would be as moderate or as potent as we considered appropriate to each situation, thus denying a potential enemy the assurance (as he appeared to have under the gradualism policy) that he would pay only a moderate and limited price in response to any aggression.

This was an excellent argument of the case for a strong, positive national will. Unfortunately, it did not have much effect on the administration then in office, and when the Republicans got into office they did not follow the advice of their party-mates very well either! The pressure of public opinion against further intensification of the war was too strong.

When the North Vietnamese finally condescended to enter into negotiations in Paris on 10 May 1968, the JCS requested periodic assessments of our military position in Southeast Asia. The assessments consistently pointed to a continuing military buildup by the North Vietnamese obviously aimed at taking every step possible to achieve a strong military posture that could be translated into a strong negotiating position. For example, in our 20 May assessment we noted massive infiltration from the north—75,000 to 85,000 enemy troops were moving southward. These were likely fillers and replacements for the heavy losses incurred during the Tet offensive, and information gleaned from prisoners of war indicated the troops were receiving only limited training prior to their movement south. There was also a very high rate of logistic activity. Captured documents suggested that the Communists intended to increase sharply the shipment of supplies into the northern provinces of South Vietnam, with the peak period slated to occur during June through August. Plans indicated, for instance, that one North Vietnamese truck company operating along the infiltration trails in Laos was to carry two tons of cargo per truck and travel 80 to 100 kilometers each night, twenty-six nights a month. Over 1,500 tons a month would be brought into the northern part of South Vietnam by this truck company alone. Further, transportation and supply facilities in North Vietnam were being repaired at an accelerating pace. The Paul Doumer Bridge—the big bridge at Hanoi—was being cleared and reconstruction was beginning, and the Haiphong railway-highway bridge was being returned to serviceable status. Efforts were also underway to provide electrical power, with every major power plant being rebuilt. In addition, enemy defenses were being extended southward, facilities repaired, and radars moved in, all in preparation for operating MiGs from airfields in the southern part of North Vietnam (but still north of nineteen degrees). Also noted were the wanton enemy attacks against nearly every provincial capital and many population centers in the south. Assassination tactics in and around Saigon and mass killings in Hue were clear evidence of the enemy's ruthless disregard for U. S. restraint, as was the fact that his logistical and offensive military actions in South Vietnam equalled or even surpassed in intensity actions observed at any time heretofore.

In my opinion, a news conference should have been called in Washington at this point to announce we had clear-cut evidence that the North Vietnamese were taking advantage of the negotiations, and since they were, we felt it necessary for protection of our forces in South Vietnam to resume air offensive actions against North Vietnam. With the good weather season at hand, this would have been an immediate and effective countermeasure to the enemy buildup and could have significantly altered the whole course of the war from that point forward. It would have enabled us, in my view, to win a military victory by the end of 1968. However, there was a horror in Washington of doing anything that even breathed of escalation and, of course, the North Vietnamese took advantage of this attitude.

On 12 June, I sent another assessment of the military position in Southeast Asia, stressing the fact that at this time we were experiencing extensive attacks in Saigon by both infiltrators and rockets from enemy troops in the vicinity. It was my contention that the mounting destruction in the city of Saigon and general disruption of the economy might have significant adverse effects on the South Vietnamese people and their government. I also noted that we had captured a Communist document indicating that the enemy wanted to create conditions favorable for the pacifist movements in the United States, thus forcing a drastic change in Vietnam policy.

Two days later, I advised the Chairman JCS of my increasing concern over the developing situation: allied casualties in South Vietnam continued to mount while the enemy was permitted uninhibited movement of men and supplies into the southern panhandle of North Vietnam, free from attacks. The fact that the enemy was able to increase his strength, improve his ability to inflict losses, and put pressure on our forces at points of his choosing clearly dictated the military urgency of resuming air-strike operations in the north. I strongly recommended that such action be taken.

By this time, Gen. Creighton W. Abrams, U. S. Army, had relieved General Westmoreland as COMUSMACV in South Vietnam. In response to my request for his assessment of the situation, his observation was that, despite my concerns, the continuing Viet Cong attacks on Saigon had thus far apparently served to turn South Vietnamese public opinion against the Viet Cong and to strengthen the resolve of both civil servants and the public in general to support the South Vietnamese government. Morale remained high . . . for the moment, at any rate. However, impatience was growing, and if the attacks continued over several months, General Abrams considered it possible that government stability would be threatened, as I feared. He noted that strong forces (twenty-seven U. S. and South Vietnamese battalions) had been shifted into the provincial area surrounding Saigon, and although this heavy concentration of troops cut down on what could be done in other areas, there were at least enough assets in the Saigon vicinity to defeat the enemy.

While the North Vietnamese were making this offensive thrust on the capital of South Vietnam, the fruitless negotiations droned on in Paris, with no real progress in sight. We were sitting back and allowing these bandits to do just as they pleased in South Vietnam without retaliating on their own country at a time when we had aircraft carriers and airfields full of planes that could have gone up and blasted Hanoi and Haiphong wide open, if we had just been given the "go" sign. It was the most asinine way to fight a war that could possibly be imagined!

In mid-July, Defense Secretary Clifford called a meeting in Saigon to discuss the current situation. I was in the midst of a trip to meet with various Chiefs of State throughout the Pacific, on a schedule I could not very well break. I therefore advised General Wheeler that my subordinate commanders would present our side of the air picture, with General Abrams presenting the ground war situation. In preparation for the meeting, I also sent a message to Wheeler, which examined the situation in South Vietnam as we viewed it:

> The time frame that I am addressing is the next six to eight weeks from the 16th of July 1968. Decisions critical to the successful prosecution of the war will be required during that period. Intelligence indicates that significant enemy activity could resume in early August. An assessment of all time indicators in the Saigon area points to late July as the earliest period to expect increased enemy activity.
>
> More than three months have elapsed since restrictions were imposed on the conduct of the air campaign in the North. There still has been no reciprocal move toward de-escalation by the North Vietnamese. Although the tempo of enemy activity in recent weeks has generally decreased throughout South Vietnam, it would be misleading to attribute this development to a responsiveness on Hanoi's part. The evidence is to the contrary. High personnel and logistic infiltration in recent months, coupled with low personnel losses in June, indicate that the enemy already has, or will shortly achieve, a capability to continue the "general offensive and general uprising" phase of the war.
>
> In the North, seaborne import statistics for the month of June reflect record highs in all categories. Deliveries of POL for the first half of 1968 show a 60 percent increase above the amount imported during the similar period of 1967. The number of dry cargo ships in Haiphong has reached a record high. Transportation facilities are being repaired or replaced by new construction on a priority basis. The enemy air defense posture has been improved and expanded. The overall picture is one of rapid recovery

by an enemy who only a few short months ago was hard pressed to maintain the momentum of his efforts to support the aggression in the South. The psychological lift of freedom from attack and the recovery and reconstruction which are evident to the population can only serve to fortify the will of the people of North Vietnam and give their leaders renewed confidence in the ultimate attainment of their objectives.

The rehabilitation and recovery achieved by North Vietnam since the 1 April bombing cessation are impressive. With the advent of the monsoon weather in November the enemy will have another three or four months to improve his defenses, his logistics base and lines of communication and to strengthen his war-making capability. He will, in effect, gain an additional respite until May of next year before the full weight of our air effort could be brought to bear effectively against the North Vietnamese heartland.

The sum and substance of the situation is that continuation of the present restraints in the absence of reciprocal moves by North Vietnam operates against us. Militarily it deprives us of our most important weapon to punish the enemy and to bring the war to the source of the support for continuing the war in the South. It compromises our resoluteness in the eyes of our allies and the South Vietnamese to fulfill our solemn commitments at whatever cost. It invites even greater U. S. and Free World casualties through the continued prolongation of the war in the South, through piecemeal application of our forces and resources that are available to the task. It prolongs the time until forces can be withdrawn and the larger fiscal outlays can be reduced.

It has been evident for some time that the enemy cannot achieve a military victory in the South. It is also unlikely that the war in the South can be terminated soon under conditions acceptable to ourselves and our allies so long as the enemy avoids confrontation, which he can do indefinitely. Consequently, there is little reason for North Vietnam to enter into meaningful negotiations as long as the enemy's campaign in the South can be waged under conditions which preclude his total defeat and the nerve center and mainspring of support in the North is immune to attack. The initiative is now in the enemy's hands.

While appreciative of the need for restraint in the light of the current negotiations, recognition should also be taken of the need for timely decisions directed toward conclusion of the war by military means. Accordingly, I recommend that the air campaign against North Vietnam be resumed. Those restrictions which limit the bombing to the area south of 20 degrees should be removed. This decision is time-sensitive if the advantages of the prevailing good weather are to be maximized. Postponement of a decision will prevent initiation of a concerted air and naval campaign against North Vietnam until spring of 1969. It will then require us to engage an enemy whose defenses have been reconstituted, whose resolve to continue the war will be strengthened, and whose war-making potential will have been substantially enhanced through Soviet and Chicom military and technical assistance. The consequences of such an engagement will surely be measured in higher casualties, greater costs, and potentially more dangerous risks of widening the conflict.

We received word on 30 July, subsequent to the meeting in Saigon, that there had been extensive talks in Washington on what action the United States should take if the enemy continued to pursue heavy attacks on Saigon and other major urban areas. Punitive measures were being discussed. Although I was on record as recommending offensive actions on a broad scale rather than limited punitive measures, the JCS asked for my position once again. This was just a formality, but it did generate the last message I sent on the air campaign. It went out on 31 July, the day I was relieved as Commander in Chief Pacific, incident to my statutory retirement from active naval service the following day.

Briefly, I said we were prepared to commence operations north of twenty degrees latitude as soon as authority was granted and against such targets as might be allocated. I further expressed the hope that any resumption of bombing in the north would not follow the same pattern as had been pursued for the past three years, but would, rather, be implemented as I had so often recommended heretofore. A decision of this magnitude, made during the peace talks, would give the American public and the men fighting the war assurance of our intent to win. I reiterated my conviction that resumption of full bombing, especially in the Hanoi/Haiphong area, was the only real key to getting the war over with as soon as possible. Adm. John S. McCain, U. S. Navy, who was to succeed me, went over the message with me and was in complete agreement with the thoughts expressed.

CHAPTER 26

AGGRESSION FROM A
SANCTUARY:
NOVEMBER 1968–MAY 1972

FROM AUGUST THROUGH October 1968, the air war continued as it had during the early summer months, limited to very restricted bombing in the panhandle of North Vietnam south of nineteen degrees latitude. Then on 1 November, President Johnson decided to cease all bombing of North Vietnam. It would be fair to say that this decision was the culmination of a frantic chase to get the North Vietnamese to negotiate. From 31 March, the time of President Johnson's speech, through the end of October, the United States had gradually moved further and further away from our announced objective when we introduced forces into South Vietnam. More and more one-sided concessions were made to the North Vietnamese in an attempt to get them to the negotiating table, and now we were talking about merely seeking an "honorable peace," with less and less being said about our obligations to our South Vietnamese ally.

We had completely forgotten the lessons learned in negotiating with the North Koreans—that the only way to negotiate with the

Communists successfully was to keep the military pressure on, not just before but during the negotiations. The U. S. negotiators in Paris, Averell Harriman and Cyrus Vance, had made no progress since our 31 March proposal. They just sat at the table and listened to the Communists direct their hate propaganda at the "American aggressors." There was absolutely no movement in the negotiations except ours . . . backwards.

Finally, our negotiators, instead of recommending a positive step forward—even if only to reintroduce some pressure by moving the bombing limit from the nineteenth parallel back up to the twentieth—became convinced that the only way to break the stalemate would be to take the ultimate step backward and end the bombing completely. Communist tactics were working. Harriman and Vance, apparently sincerely but clearly naively, thought they had reached a private understanding with the North Vietnamese to start substantive talks, providing we would call a halt to all bombing in North Vietnam. There was never a formal agreement, however, and when we did stop the bombing it was merely on the assumption that the other side would observe the "understandings." We needed only to look at history to know that every advantage would be taken of these so-called understandings. Did we truly believe the infamous leopard had changed his spots?

When the Nixon administration came into office in 1969, Henry Cabot Lodge, former Ambassador to South Vietnam, replaced Averell Harriman as our chief negotiator in Paris. The Communists were still adamant against making any positive moves towards peace, and rather than forcing their hand at that time, the primary strategy accepted by the new administration was called Vietnamization, a program designed to give the South Vietnamese sufficient modern arms to take care of themselves, providing they could muster the manpower needed to do so. Under this program, we turned over material at least as fast as they could use it and at the same time pulled out U. S. troops as rapidly as the South Vietnamese could take over with some assurance of guaranteeing the security of their country. In the meantime, the standdown of the air war against North Vietnam continued.

It is pertinent to note that during this period the new Secretary of Defense, Melvin Laird, held a view of the Vietnam War which differed considerably from that of President Nixon. Secretary Laird's chief objective was to get out of South Vietnam as quickly as possible—all other issues were secondary. It was he who coined the word "Vietnamization." He advanced the theory behind that word on every possible occasion, sold the idea to the public, and strove to let nothing get in the way of expeditious withdrawal from South Vietnam. On the other hand, although the President also wanted to Vietnamize the war, he wanted to do it in a way that was consistent with maintaining a favorable position for the South Vietnamese.

Much criticism has been voiced in our country to the effect that the Vietnamization process was not undertaken soon enough. It is important to realize, however, that when we moved into South Vietnam with troops in 1965, the South Vietnamese had a relatively small and a very young army, almost devoid of leadership (which had been supplied exclusively by the French military during their tenure in-country). Building an army to significant size and leadership from virtual scratch is a long, slow process, and when done in the midst of a war, it is even more difficult. The South Vietnamese armed forces were simply not a productive outfit when we started, but eventually they became effective and proficient in most of the needed capabilities. It was in actuality a rapid transition, pushed as hard as circumstances would permit. In fact, Vietnamization was quite successful. We had turned over vast quantities of equipment to the South Vietnamese and trained thousands of them to use it. The strength of their regular armed forces, as well as the paramilitary, increased quickly. In combination with an improved economy and better government control, it was actually the very success of Vietnamization that brought on the North Vietnamese invasion in early 1972.

A significant change in ground-force strategy also took place under the Nixon administration when, in April 1970, the President authorized an incursion into Cambodia to destroy North Vietnamese and Viet Cong base areas. At that time the Communists had been using the port of Sihanoukville (Kompong Som) extensively to bring in supplies for their forces in the southern part of South Vietnam. Moreover, Cambodia had routinely been used as an enemy sanctuary throughout the entire war. In any event, this operation was quite successful and resulted in a significant decrease in Communist military activities in the third and fourth corps areas of South Vietnam. However, the Cambodian foray also brought on a loud clamor against the Nixon administration from all the anti-war elements in the United States, which resulted, ultimately, in Congress passing an amendment to a special foreign assistance bill in December 1970 prohibiting the use of U. S. ground forces in Cambodia.

During 1971, no startling developments occurred on either the military or the negotiations front. Then, it became apparent that the North Vietnamese were planning a special effort sometime in the spring of 1972. By February of that year, twelve of their thirteen main-force divisions were deployed outside of North Vietnam. Two divisions were in Laos just opposite Military Region I in the northern section of South Vietnam, one division was in North Vietnam just north of the DMZ, three were in the southern part of Laos just opposite Military Region II of South Vietnam, and the remainder were in South Vietnam. In addition to the movement of ground troops, numerous surface-to-air missile sites had been set up just north of the DMZ, and many large artillery pieces (130mm guns) had also been positioned in that area so they could be fired across the DMZ into South Vietnam. Four new roads had been built leading through the DMZ into South Vietnam. With this combination of movement of forces, establishment of air defenses, positioning of artillery, construction of roads, and high logistics activity, it was clear the enemy was developing a military posture leading to heavy action in the south. Since two airfields had also been constructed between Dong Hoi and Vinh to complement the four already operational in the panhandle area, it was apparent that their air activity would be accelerated as well.

Despite all indications of a threatening North Vietnamese offensive into the south, in violation of the so-called agreements or understandings made when we ceased our bombing, the United States took no action to counter the buildup. Air power applied against the enemy accumulation of forces in Laos and southern North Vietnam could, of course, have severely blunted their forthcoming offensive; but we did nothing. The South Vietnamese on the other hand, observing the buildup that threatened their country, began to position forces to meet the anticipated attacks. By this time very few U. S. forces remained in-country, and the South Vietnamese knew they would have to do the ground fighting themselves, although U. S. air support was still available. They accelerated their recruit training program, cancelled all leaves, and expended considerable effort to position the militia so it could take part in the action. Their newest division, the Third Division, was deployed just south of the DMZ, reinforced with one brigade of South Vietnamese marines.

On 30 March 1972, under the cover of bad weather (very low ceilings and low visibility), the North Vietnamese initiated the offensive by moving a complete division directly across the DMZ, along with two regiments of tanks and large amounts of motorized artillery and anti-aircraft guns. This was the first time the North Vietnamese had attempted to operate in this mobile fashion, utilizing waves of tanks.

Generally speaking, the South Vietnamese acquitted themselves well in the battle that followed. The militia, the marines, and the regular army troops all performed in a competent fashion. As noted, the weather was bad for flying when the action started, but during April the weather improved and we were able to use our air power to help the South Vietnamese and cause the enemy very heavy casualties. Our B-52s, which could operate in any weather, were particularly effective. We, of course, were still operating only in South Vietnam. At the outset of this major invasion across the DMZ we did move some air force and navy forces from the west coast of the United States into Southeast Asia. B-52 squadrons were augmented in Guam and Thailand, and navy ships were deployed for gunfire support south of the DMZ.

It seems clear that the North Vietnamese had realized the Vietnamization program was progressively enhancing the strength of the South Vietnamese, and they undoubtedly calculated that this offensive would weaken and stall the effectiveness of the program before it got to the point where they could not handle the situation. They were also obviously aware that the war was increasingly unpopular in the United States and hoped to capitalize on the effect they could generate by an offensive.

This dramatic North Vietnamese military move, combined with the lack of any progress at the negotiating table, forced President Nixon to consider what action should be taken to salvage something from the rapidly deteriorating situation. At his direction there was a one-shot air strike at Hanoi and Haiphong in mid-April, which was intended to inflict damage on military installations and POL, and to demonstrate as well that the United States was willing to use its B-52 bomber force if necessary. This was followed by a series of warnings that North Vietnam would be running grave risks if it continued the offensive, but not surprisingly, the warnings were ignored. With the all-important assistance of our air support, however, the South Vietnamese were able to blunt and eventually contain the invading North Vietnamese forces.

In Paris, meanwhile, North Vietnam's negotiator Le Duc Tho, meeting with Dr. Henry Kissinger, displayed an almost unbelievable arrogance about the whole affair and merely reiterated his previously stated public position, which, in essence, virtually demanded complete surrender by the United States. The President apparently determined at this point that the time for reinstituting some kind of decisive military action had arrived.

CHAPTER 27

THE AIR WAR AGAINST NORTH VIETNAM: ON AGAIN, BUT LIMITED

O N 8 MAY 1972, President Nixon addressed the nation on television saying "Five weeks ago, on Easter weekend, the Communist armies of North Vietnam launched a massive invasion of South Vietnam—an invasion that was made possible by tanks, artillery, and other advanced offensive weapons supplied to Hanoi by the Soviet Union and other Communist nations." The President explained that on 20 April he had sent his National Security Advisor, Dr. Henry A. Kissinger, to Moscow for four days of meetings with Soviet General Secretary Leonid I. Brezhnev and other Soviet leaders, instructing him to emphasize our desire for a rapid solution to the war and our willingness to look at all possible approaches. The Soviet leaders had seemed interested in bringing the war to an end and had urged resumption of negotiations in Paris. Kissinger subsequently had met privately with Le Duc Tho on 2 May in Paris, at which time the North Vietnamese had flatly refused to consider any of the proposals offered and refused, furthermore, to put forth any of their own. Ambassador William J. Porter had also been directed to resume public peace negotiations on 27 April and on 4 May, in Paris. At those meetings the North Vietnamese had simply renewed their demands for surrender.

The President then continued his address by saying in amplification:

> Here is what over three years of public and private negotiations with Hanoi has come down to:
>
> The United States, with the full concurrence of our South Vietnamese allies, has offered the maximum of what any President could offer. We have offered a de-escalation of the fighting. We have offered a cease-fire with a deadline for withdrawal of all American forces. We have offered new elections which would be internally supervised with the Communists participating both in the supervisory body and in the elections themselves. President Thieu has offered to resign one month before the elections. We have offered an exchange of prisoners of war at a ratio of ten North Vietnamese prisoners for every one American prisoner they return.
>
> North Vietnam has met each of these offers with insolence and insult.
>
> They have flatly and arrogantly refused to negotiate an end to the war and bring peace.
>
> Their answer to every peace offer we have made has been to escalate the war.

President Nixon went on to announce that in view of the foregoing he had taken steps to bring the Vietnam War to an end by shutting off the flood of supplies that had long permitted Hanoi to carry on its war effort to the south. Specifically, he had ordered: (1) that all entrances to North Vietnamese ports be mined to prevent access to these ports as well as North Vietnamese naval operations from these ports, (2) that U. S. forces take appropriate measures within the internal and claimed territorial waters of North Vietnam to interdict the delivery of any supplies, and (3) that rail and all other communications be cut off to the maximum extent possible and that air and naval strikes against military targets in North Vietnam be reinstituted.

(Thus, the mining plan that had been in existence since the early 1960s, the same plan that had been recommended many, many times as a means of causing profound logistical difficulties in North Vietnam, was finally approved . . . one is tempted to say a decade too late!)

In deciding to take these actions (which was done on the recommendation of the JCS and Kissinger, but with the nonconcurrence of Defense Secretary Laird), the President had also directed that shipping in the open ocean be interdicted so coastal vessels would not attempt to run supplies into North Vietnam, and that bombing of Communist depots and supply lines be resumed. In exchange for terminating the harbor mining and the air war, he had demanded that the North Vietnamese and the Viet Cong agree to an immediate cease-fire under international supervision throughout all of Indochina, and that the Communists return all U. S. prisoners of war held in Indochina. He further indicated that if these conditions were met, the remaining 60,000 U. S. troops still stationed in South Vietnam would be withdrawn within four months.

President Nixon's 8 May pronouncement brought a strong reaction from his political opponents, as well as from the anti-war dissidents throughout the country. The following day scores of senators and congressmen stood up in Congress and criticized the new Vietnam War policy. Others denounced the move to newsmen. Senate Democrats in caucus adopted a resolution disapproving the escalation of the war. Offered by Sen. J. William Fulbright, Chairman of the Senate Foreign Relations Committee, it was approved by a vote of twenty-nine to fourteen. By an even greater margin, thirty-five to eight, the Senate Democrats further endorsed a proposal that all funds for the Vietnam War be cut off four months after North Vietnam returned American prisoners. Besides Fulbright, those opposing the President's policy included Majority Leader Mike Mansfield, and three current Democratic candidates for President—Sen. George S. McGovern, Hubert H. Humphrey, Jr., and Edmund S. Muskie. Senator Edward M. Kennedy was also in opposition, as were Senate Republicans Jacob K. Javits, Clifford P. Case and Charles H. Percy.

I neither can nor should go into detail on the conduct of the air war over North Vietnam after 8 May 1972, since I am not cognizant of all the official policies and directives. I do know that there were still some restrictions placed on our use of air power during that time, although not so great as the ones under which we were forced to operate in the earlier years. Furthermore, the overall effectiveness of our bombing program was greatly enhanced by this time through the use of the so-called "smart bombs" by our tactical aircraft, enabling us to make contained, precise target strikes.

Once again, however, the ongoing peace negotiations precipitated a decision on 23 October to halt all air and naval operations north of twenty degrees latitude. Up to that point the renewed bombing of North Vietnam had been quite productive. According to testimony by the Chairman of the JCS before the House Committee on Appropriations, key lines of communication had been interdicted and the important target systems supporting the land battle in the south had been damaged or destroyed (including supply depots, power plants and rail terminals). Moreover, shipping activity had virtually ceased due to the mining. As a matter of fact, since the mining, no foreign sea-going ship had either entered or left any of the harbors of North Vietnam, and the logistics flow south into the battle area was drastically reduced. Before the mining about two million tons of cargo per year had been received in the port of Haiphong. Now it had become necessary for the North Vietnamese to rearrange their lines of communication by increasing the load on the railroads and diverting ships into ports in China, primarily Fort Bayard. Supplies were being transported by rail and truck into North Vietnam, and at least one oil pipeline from China into the Hanoi area had been successfully built. The railroads and the roads in northern North Vietnam were being kept under heavy air attack, however, so Hanoi was having tremendous difficulty in getting enough supplies to keep going. The enemy's reserves were being used up at a rapid rate.

By the 23 October date, the situation in South Vietnam had generally stabilized, and the invaders were under heavy pressure. The South Vietnamese had been able to recapture Quang Tri and had established a line north of there, while in Military Region III, they had successfully concluded the battle for An Loc. The North Vietnamese had lost heavily in troops and material, and although they could mount few large-scale troop attacks, they were still carrying on heavy sapper activity, avoiding contact, refitting, and making an effort to strengthen their position.

In view of these circumstances, the enemy as usual took full advantage of this partial bombing standdown. There was a heavy resupply of war materials from both the U. S. S. R. and China. Steps were quickly taken to reconstruct the heavily damaged railroad system, and the North Vietnamese expanded storage areas, reconstituted the logistics system, and deployed large numbers of tanks, artillery and anti-aircraft toward South Vietnam. Their radar system was augmented, new MiG-21s were brought in to Gia Lam airfield, and four Komar-class missile boats were received from the Soviet Union. By 18 December the major lines of communication, particularly the railroads coming down from China, were serviceable. Coastal shipping north of twenty degrees had been resumed, and rail lines connecting Hanoi and Haiphong were reopened and transshipment points reactivated.

Again—unbelievably—we had relinquished the advantage of our superior air power in the hope we could get negotiations started, only to end up providing the same well-exploited sanctuary in the heartland of North Vietnam.

CHAPTER 28

THE DECEMBER 1972 BOMBING CAMPAIGN AGAINST NORTH VIETNAM

B Y MID-DECEMBER 1972, the situation in North Vietnam was unquestionably on the upswing, with both defenses and war-making capacity generally much improved. On the other hand, negotiations were at an impasse, with the Communists having recently pulled out one of their favorite tactics—reopening a number of old issues that the U. S. negotiators thought were already settled.

Official statements indicate that the historic decision to resume the bombing at this time was made in order to deny the North Vietnamese the sanctuary from which they were rebuilding their war-making potential and continuing their aggression. I would have to assume that an unannounced objective was to force the North Vietnamese to get serious at the negotiating table. In any case, it is my understanding that this decision was made by President Nixon in consultation with Adm. Tom Moorer, who by then was serving as Chairman of the JCS, again with the concurrence of Presidential Adviser Kissinger but against the recommendation of Secretary of Defense Laird (and probably most other officials of the National

Security Council as well). Whatever the counsel, the decision stirred up a great furor amongst the anti-war elements in Congress and in the public. It was, nonetheless, a courageous action, and probably the only move that would have assured the return of our prisoners of war and convinced North Vietnam of the necessity for purposeful negotiations.

Whatever else may be argued, the fact is that the eleven-day air campaign of December 1972 will go down in history as a testimonial to the efficiency of air power. "Linebacker II," as it was called, combined air force and navy air power in a skillfully coordinated effort, exemplifying the way air power should be used.

The air attacks started on 18 December and were brought to a halt on the twenty-ninth. This was a bad weather period over northern North Vietnam, with the area generally overcast to a ceiling of 3,000 to 6,000 feet, making visual bombing attacks impossible. It was decided, therefore, to use our best all-weather bombers, namely, the B-52s of the Strategic Air Command. All-weather tactical bombers, the F-111s of the air force and the navy's A-6s, were also used, but since these aircraft were available only in small numbers, they could not possibly have done the job alone. The strikes were carried out in accordance with a carefully designed plan generated by the JCS and the Field Commands (Commander in Chief Pacific and Commander in Chief Strategic Air Command). It had been worked out in detail beforehand and was precisely executed. During the entire eleven-day period there was only one twelve-hour break in the weather which permitted efficient use of our day-bombing capability, and it was most successfully utilized to strike many important targets with the smart bombs. An amazing amount of damage was done in that short time by extensive use of these new weapons. In considering the overall effectiveness of the operation, furthermore, it must be remembered that a thirty-six-hour standdown for the Christmas holiday was imposed in the middle of this period.

The Hanoi/Haiphong area was the obvious focus of the bombing effort. In the fields of logistics, communications, electric power, and air bases, most of the lucrative targets were centered within ten or fifteen miles of those two cities. Transportation-related targets and military supplies had high priority. Only valid military targets were attacked, and smart bombs were used on those close to heavily populated areas so as to minimize civilian casualties. Unmanned photo reconnaissance aircraft were used extensively to determine bomb damage. A brief assessment showed the following results: the entire railroad complex of North Vietnam was severely crippled—to include damage to 383 rail cars, fourteen steam locomotives, 191 storage warehouse buildings and two railroad bridges. The important railroad yard in downtown Hanoi was struck and badly damaged by laser-guided bombs. (This yard had been used by the North Vietnamese for years as a sanctuary, since they were able to bring railroad cars right into the "off limits" middle of Hanoi. We had only been allowed to attack it once or twice during the whole war, and then it was quickly repaired.) The railroad shops and the warehouse area were also hit with laser-guided bombs, all of which went directly into the target area. The railroad yard at Gia Lam, two miles across the river from Hanoi and jammed at the time with loaded rail cars, was hit hard and extensively damaged. The Haiphong railroad siding was fairly well broken up and interdicted almost completely. The Kinh No complex, where the railroad from Thai Nguyen and the northwest railroad come together to serve as the largest logistics grouping in North Vietnam, was well cleaned out. It was being used to assemble and redistribute cargo and contained many large warehouses packed with military supplies. The Yen Vien military complex and the Kep railroad yard were also hit heavily, and the Hanoi railroad-highway bridge over the Rapides Canal interdicted with one span dropped by a smart bomb.

In addition, nine major supply storage areas—seven in the Hanoi area and two near Haiphong—were struck with excellent results. Vehicle repair facilities (the North Vietnamese used trucks by the thousands) received considerable damage, as did the nine port and waterway targets on the strike list. Furthermore, the electric power grid of North Vietnam was sharply compromised by the combined effect of the Hanoi power plant being hit by smart bombs (all of which zeroed in on a very small area consisting of the generator room and the boiler house), the Hanoi transformer station being rendered inoperative, and the Viet Tri thermal power plant and two other big power plants (one at Uong Bi and one just north-west of Haiphong) all being successfully struck. The main control buildings of the Hanoi radio communications center (where the transmitters were located) were also damaged. Finally, ten airfields, mostly around the Hanoi area, were struck in order to ensure that aircraft operations from these fields would be interdicted, and a number of surface-to-air missile sites were put out of commission. Most importantly, all of this damage was done in eleven days of concentrated attacks. There was no respite for the North Vietnamese—the shock effect was tremendous.

During these strikes fifteen B-52s were lost, which caused a great uproar here at home when it became known. Our total aircraft losses were twenty air force and six navy planes, actually a little less than a two percent attrition of strike forces and well under the three percent anticipated when the operation was planned. Any losses are most assuredly regrettable, but these were not excessive. Further-more, in the last two or three days of the strikes, there was reliable photographic evidence that the enemy had used up most of his surface-to-air missiles and much of his anti-aircraft artillery. On these days our attacks were almost unopposed and, obviously, could have gone on much longer with very little loss. Apparently the North Vietnamese were attriting their missiles faster than they could assemble new ones and get them to the launchers, so toward the end of this period they were in an extremely weak air defense position. This is, of course, the expected result from a concentrated air campaign.

One of the indignant cries picked up in the press was that our air attacks were probably hitting the POW camps where our men were interred. Actually, we knew the precise location of these camps and great care was taken not to hit them. The fact that they were not damaged at all was confirmed not only by photo reconnaissance evidence but by the personal testimony of our returning POWs.

North Vietnamese reports that somewhere between 1,300 and 1,600 civilians had been killed in the course of this operation also brought on considerable criticism in the press. On the other hand, no one seemed to have been concerned at all over the fact that the North Vietnamese had killed 25,000 South Vietnamese civilians in the first weeks of the recent invasion across the DMZ. The news media's obvious double standard on the entire Vietnam War issue was seldom more flagrant!

As a result of the punishment inflicted during this bombing campaign, the North Vietnamese had a change of heart. For the first time in this war we had used our air power in a way that influenced their *will* to continue the aggression—we had convinced them that it was, in fact, becoming too costly. And so they began to negotiate in earnest. Sir Robert Thompson, a recognized expert in counterinsurgency warfare and head of the British Advisory Mission to Vietnam from 1961 to 1965 (whose opinions and advice had been sought by the United States many times during the Vietnam episode), saw it this way:

> In my view, on December 30, 1972, after eleven days of those B-52 attacks on the Hanoi area, you had won the war. It was all over! They had fired 1,242 SAMs; they had none left, and what would come in overland from China would be a mere trickle. They and their whole rear base at that point were at your mercy. They would have taken any terms. And that is why, of course, you actually got a peace agreement in January, which you had not been able to get in October.[1]

Unfortunately, we failed to press home our advantage of the moment. The great public clamor in this country against our strong offensive stand caused the President to be reluctant to give the North Vietnamese more of the same when they once again slowed up the negotiations. We did get our POWs back, and we were able to pull out of South Vietnam, but the terms of the peace settlement were much less than what could have been achieved had we threatened the North Vietnamese with a resumption of bombing on the scale used in those eleven days—or even given them an occasional taste of it again just to keep them honest at the negotiating table. Even more unfortunately, our "signals" were so clear that the North Vietnamese almost certainly *knew* we would not take this kind of step again. They were therefore able to negotiate an agreement on *their* terms and in accordance with *their* long-range goals.

In summary, I include a most articulate, graphic description of the staggering impact that this awesome display of our air power had on the enemy's will (our own lack of will to capitalize on it not withstanding), given by Rear Adm. James B. Stockdale—the same then-Commander Stockdale previously quoted. Stockdale had been a prisoner of the North Vietnamese for over seven years—an acknowledged, eminent leader in the POW community and, as he puts it, an expert of sorts on the reverse side of the air power coin. During the question-and-answer session at the conclusion of his address to the Armed Forces Staff College on 9 April 1975, he was asked, "Early in your presentation you alluded briefly to the effectiveness of the North Vietnamese in adapting to our interdiction efforts or air strikes over a sustained number of years. I wonder if you could comment further on this and perhaps your opinion of the misuse of air power as you may have seen it." His reply was explicit:

> I think the 22 members of this audience who spent years in Hanoi as POW's with me had similar perceptions as I on this subject—we're air power experts of a sort. After all, we've been through more air raids than any other Americans—hearing the street sounds before, during, and after—psyching out the attitudes and outlooks of our captors, interpreting their propaganda broadcasts, "feeling the pulse" of a country under siege as can be done, even from a cell. Don't scoff at "the pulse of a country." Maybe you can't put numbers on it as a systems analyst would hope, but through it one can sense a sort of corporate "will." If I learned nothing else in North Vietnam it is that Clausewitz is as right today as he was during the Napoleonic Wars. Targets destroyed, etc., may be used as an indirect measurement of military success, but true progress toward victory is, and I think always will be, simply a direct function of the degree to which enemy "will" is being subdued. Arms are effective only to the degree that they transmit a message of the ultimate futility of further resisting them. The essence of deterrence is to demonstrate a commitment that your adversary will find unprofitable, if not downright frightening, to challenge. If our escalation, our creeping

up the panhandle with graduated bombing raids, our bombing pauses, conveyed any message to the enemy, it was a lack of commitment. Furthermore, it provided a training ground for their political cadres to learn the rudiments of maintaining morale and production under intermittent fire. In Hanoi in late 1965 and early 1966, when the action was all down south, several of our interrogators (cadres) bragged about their "instruction tours" on the "hard stands," as they called them, near Dong Hoi and Vinh.

One of air power's biggest assets is its shock effect, its ability to create panic, particularly among the uninitiated and undisciplined. By the time our raids worked up to Hanoi, every civilian, who I imagine to be about as disciplined as our rank and file military troops, had probably undergone thorough indoctrination by these "missionaries" familiarized in the south. The siren rings in mid-morning, you get in your hole, the planes roll in, there is a lot of noise, a bridge is bombed, the all-clear is sounded, there are a few fires and the trucks will wheel past, there are likely a few casualties (usually at the AA batteries) and the ambulances are en route, everybody chop chops by the numbers to his work station, and that's all there is to it till afternoon when it will happen again. The mood the Communists tried to implant was that a city of a million people, dutifully motivated and selectively coerced when not, could continue such drills forever. It pains me to say so, but after years of wishful thinking I had about concluded that they could do so. There were few surprises, everything was programmed. The Americans were constrained by self-imposed rules that were public knowledge. The guards were wide-eyed and particularly hostile after the raid, but the city was back to normal within minutes. The street sounds picked up, patriotic music bleated from the speakers at every corner, the interrogators strutted about the prison yards defiantly. By nightfall an almost carnival atmosphere could be sensed. Songfests went off as scheduled in the guards' quarters and in the city parks. We could tell that some significant targets had pre-composed songs dedicated to them; at least their first introduction was blared from street corner speakers an hour or two after the raids on which they were destroyed.

So it was in the latter half of '66, '67 and '68 till the bombing stopped. These were the darkest days for the prisoners—when the brutality was of the sort you've read about.

A totally contrasting atmosphere swept the city on that December night in 1972 when the raids didn't last 10 minutes but went on and on—when the B-52 columns rolled in, and the big bombs impacted and kept on impacting in the distance—when the ground shook, and the plaster fell from the ceiling, and the prisoners cheered wildly, and the guards cowered in the lee of the walls, cheeks so ashen you could detect it even from the light from the fiery sky. Some of this light was from burning B-52s (I'm told that the losses were almost as predicted—low, but the important fact was that they kept coming). This was *commitment*. This was victory for the United States, and doomsday for North Vietnam, and we knew it and they knew it. By day, interrogators and guards would inquire about our needs solicitously. The streets were silent. The center of Hanoi was dead—even though like our prisons, thousands of yards from the drop zones. We knew the bombers knew where we were, and felt not only ecstatically happy, but confident. The Vietnamese didn't. Night after night the planes kept coming in—and night after night the SAM's streaking through the sky were fewer and fewer (the naval blockade worked). The *shock* was there—the *commitment* was there—and the *enemy's will was broken*. You could sense it in every Vietnamese face. They knew they lived through last night, but they also knew that if our forces moved their bomb line over a few thousand yards they wouldn't live through tonight. Our planes were transmitting the message of the ultimate futility of further resistance. That's what war is all about.

CHAPTER 29

WAS IT PEACE WITH HONOR?

THE PARIS PEACE Agreement of 27 January 1973, which we accepted and forced President Thieu to accept, was not a formula for peace. The aggressors were still in South Vietnam, and the terms of the agreement were unenforceable except by the *credible* threat of U. S. intervention. When subsequent events finally removed any North Vietnamese concern over the possiblity of such U. S. intervention, they were free to violate the treaty with impunity.

The terms of the agreement provided that both sides could hold the land they occupied at the time but could not add to the area under their control. Fighting was to cease and the two sides were to meet in negotiations to seek a permanent end to the war. In the meantime, neither side was to increase the size or strength of its military forces. The level of armaments possessed by both sides was to be completely frozen, and neither side was to introduce additional armament into South Vietnam except as such was expended in battle or worn out. The United States was permitted to supply the South Vietnamese with one-for-one replacements, and we committed ourselves to do just that. Both sides were required to report any armament replacements to the International Commission on Control and Supervision (ICCS), which was set up under the agreement, and to designate points of entry at which the ICCS would oversee all replacements coming in. The South Vietnamese immediately designated appropriate ICCS inspection points; the North Vietnamese refused to do so. The ICCS teams were to be deployed into those areas of South Vietnam that were controlled by North Vietnam as well as into the areas controlled by South Vietnam at the time of the cease-fire. However, the North Vietnamese never permitted deployment of these teams into their areas of control. Also, a National Council of Reconciliation and National Concord was to be formed whose sole duty was to prepare for elections, which would be held in each of the two areas with impartial international supervision. The South Vietnamese were willing to go through with the sequence laid out for holding these elections; the North Vietnamese refused to cooperate.

Finally—and most critically—at the time the peace agreement was effected, there were between 210,000 and 220,000 North Vietnamese troops in South Vietnam, in addition to perhaps 50,000 Viet Cong. These troops could remain. In contrast, the agreement gave the North Vietnamese what they had wanted more than anything else—*the complete withdrawal* of allied troops and air forces.

In announcing the peace agreement to the American people, President Nixon characterized it as "peace with honor." He went on to say:

> The most important thing was not to talk about peace, but to get peace and to get the right kind of peace; this we have done. Now that an honorable agreement has been achieved, let us be proud that America did not settle for a peace that would have betrayed our allies—that would have ended the war for us, but would have continued the war for the 50 million people of Indochina.

In a press conference the next day, Dr. Kissinger expounded:

> It is obvious that there is no dispute in the agreement between the parties that there is an entity called South Vietnam, and that the future unity of Vietnam, as it comes

about, will be decided by negotiation between North and South Vietnam; that it will not be achieved by military force; indeed, that the use of military force, with respect to bringing about unification, or any other form of coercion, is impermissible according to the terms of this agreement.

As a corollary to such pronouncements, press reports also noted that President Thieu was told by President Nixon that violations of the agreement by the North Vietnamese would not be permitted by the United States and that we would respond with full force against North Vietnam if such violations occurred, the inference being that our air power would be used again.

The ink was not dry on the agreement's pages before the North Vietnamese did, in fact, begin to violate every provision. They refused to deploy the teams that were to oversee the cease-fire. They refused to pay their prescribed share of the expenses of the ICCS. They broke off negotiations with the government of South Vietnam, including the political negotiations in Paris and the two-party Joint Military Commission talks in Saigon. Then in response to repeated calls for unconditional resumption of the negotiations, they laid on outrageous demands (such as the overthrow of the Thieu government) as a precondition for any renewed talks.

As further evidence of their contempt for the peace agreement, the Communists quickly started infiltrating additional troops into South Vietnam and went about improving their military logistics system, expanding stockpiles and introducing new weapons and armor into the south. The cease-fire itself was violated almost immediately, and the North Vietnamese steadily increased their military pressure, overrunning several areas that were clearly held by the South Vietnamese at the time of the cease-fire.

On the whole, however, the South Vietnamese managed the situation in their country quite adequately during 1973. Vietnamization continued to work well, and the army had fortunately withstood the North Vietnamese invasion of 1972 with moderate casualties, thanks to our massive air support. President Thieu's government was stable and in control. On the other hand, the North Vietnamese army had suffered so many casualties during 1972 that their forces in South Vietnam were relatively weak and in need of rebuilding, which, for the time being, was a point in favor of the South Vietnamese.

The early months of 1973 were difficult ones for the North Vietnamese in their country. Mining of the harbors had created a food crisis. The December bombing campaign had disrupted their transportation system, and they were short of military supplies. But we were already solving the food problem for them since, in accordance with the terms of the peace treaty, the U. S. navy was sweeping the mines. And, the Soviet Union and Communist China were taking care of the military equipment deficiencies with massive shipments, first by rail and truck from China and subsequently by ship through Haiphong. From that point on, military supplies and replacement personnel were moved into South Vietnam as rapidly as possible throughout the remainder of the year.

In reality, the most crucial developments relative to the situation in Vietnam during 1973 took place in the United States. Congressional opposition to any further military activity on our part in Southeast Asia steadily increased throughout the spring and early summer. Many attempts were made to add restrictive clauses to various appropriation bills until finally, on 26 June, Congress passed a supplemental appropriation bill that prohibited any U. S. military operations in or over Cambodia or Laos. President Nixon vetoed this bill, but by then testimony had begun before the Senate Watergate Committee, which would start the credibility of the Nixon administration on its steep and irrevocable downward slide. Undoubtedly sensing that already this had diminished his ability to sustain his veto through Congress, the President authorized House Minority Leader Gerald R. Ford on 29 June to inform the House that a bill cutting off all military action by U. S. forces in or over Laos, Cambodia, North and South Vietnam after 15 August would be acceptable. The compromise had been struck: in return for delaying prohibition of U. S. military action until mid-August, the Nixon administration had gone beyond the original congressional intent and added North and South Vietnam to the countries affected. In a sense, Watergate had claimed what may have been its first innocent victim—South Vietnam.

The legislative act that was forthcoming, which the President signed into law on 1 July 1973, read in part as follows:

Sec. 307. None of the funds herein appropriated under
this Act may be expended to support directly or indirectly
combat activities in or over Cambodia, Laos, North
Vietnam and South Vietnam or off the shores of Cambodia, Laos, North Vietnam and South Vietnam by
United States forces, and after August 15, 1973, no other
funds heretofore appropriated under any other Act may be
expended for such purpose.

Thus it was clear that the President would be forced to go back to
Congress for approval if he wanted to use our forces in Southeast
Asia after 15 August. It was equally obvious to friend and foe alike
that, given the mood of the Congress and the American people, such
approval would be most unlikely. It would therefore be next to
impossible to use our air power or our ground forces ever again in
support of South Vietnam. The peace treaty could no longer be
enforced—Hanoi now had a free hand. We had abandoned South
Vietnam.

Later that year, another congressional measure was taken,
which essentially sealed South Vietnam's fate. On 12 October, Congress passed the War Powers Resolution, by which the President's
traditional freedom of action with regard to the employment of the
armed forces was to be severely limited. Indicating that he believed
the resolution to be unconstitutional, the President vetoed the legislation on 24 October. By now, however, Watergate was becoming a
full-blown scandal, and the President's influence with Congress was
all but gone. It was not surprising, therefore, that Congress voted to
override the veto on 7 November and the bill became Public Law
93–148.

Since the impact of the War Powers Resolution goes far beyond
the effect on South Vietnam at the time of its passage, it is worthwhile to consider briefly the incredibly restrictive nature of its language. The important parts are quoted in Appendix H, but one key
paragraph reads as follows:

Sec. 2. (c) The constitutional powers of the President as
Commander-in-Chief to introduce United States Armed
Forces into hostilities, or into situations where imminent
involvement in hostilities is clearly indicated by the cir-

cumstances, are exercised only pursuant to (1) a declaration
of war, (2) specific statutory authorization, or (3) a national
emergency created by attack upon the United States, its
territories or possessions, or its armed forces.

The legislation goes on to proscribe that even then the President
must withdraw such forces in sixty days unless Congress declares
war or gives him authorization to do otherwise. Furthermore, it
specifies that Congress may, by a concurrent resolution, direct the
President to withdraw forces from action at *any* time, if they have
not given him such authorization.

As a personal aside, I must comment that if the War Powers
Resolution is strictly enforced it will be impossible to use our military forces without the approval of Congress, and this would appear
to mean that the world, including a potential enemy, will be informed of our intentions in advance. The strategic element of surprise will thus be lost, with the ultimate result that our casualties
will skyrocket. And, while the Congress debates, any situation that
requires armed intervention in the first place is bound to deteriorate.
In the end, the all-important deterrent effect of our armed strength
will be drastically reduced. It is my view that this little-known and
less-understood legislation should be subjected to public scrutiny
and tested for its constitutionality before we are called upon to test it
in the arena of serious world conflict.

During 1974, Congress continued its assault on what was left of
our support for South Vietnam by cutting funds for the procurement of military supplies for that beleagured country. The fiscal
year 1975 (starting 1 July 1974) military procurement bill made a
relatively modest request of 1.6 billion dollars for South Vietnam,
but it was reduced by one-third. The ultimate result was a signficant
decrease in South Vietnamese military capability. By mid-1974,
they were already experiencing shortages of ammunition, fuel and
repair parts for all equipment, which seriously affected the fighting
capacity of their armed forces—and it was going to get much worse.
By 9 August, when Watergate pressures finally forced President
Nixon to resign and Gerald Ford became President, the anti-war
element was in full control in Congress and continued to systematically choke off supplies to South Vietnam.

While Watergate held center stage in Washington, the North Vietnamese continued their buildup of strength in South Vietnam in flagrant violation of the agreement. In January of 1975, the State Department issued a special report noting that the North Vietnamese had infiltrated over 170,000 troops into South Vietnam, building up their army from about 220,000 to 300,000. They had tripled the strength of their armor in South Vietnam by sending in over 400 new tanks and armored personnel carriers, and had increased their artillery and anti-aircraft weapons significantly. In addition, their military logistics system had been improved, armament stockpiles expanded, and a new pipeline built to provide fuel for their extensive armor and troop-carrier vehicles. It was obvious the enemy was gearing up for a major offensive. On the other hand, we had reneged on our commitment and were not even supplying the South Vietnamese with the one-for-one replacements for armaments lost.

In February, President Thieu sent the President of the South Vietnamese Senate, the Honorable Tran Van Lam, and some of his colleagues to Washington in an attempt to convince the administration and the U. S. Congress of the seriousness of the situation in South Vietnam. President Ford issued a note of greetings to the visitors and wished them success in their visit, but their mission was, in fact, something less than successful. Senator Mansfield of Montana, the Majority Leader, and Sen. Hugh Scott of Pennsylvania, the Minority Leader, both reportedly refused to see the delegation. Ironically, President Ford was, at this time, pleading with Congress for $300 million in aid for South Vietnam, but Congress was being markedly uncooperative. The mood at the seat of our government must have been quite clear to the members of the delegation, and it would be fair to assume that when they returned to Saigon they warned President Thieu not to expect any further support from the U. S. Congress.

By 1 March, the South Vietnamese situation with respect to acute shortages of fuel, ammunition and equipment made it obvious that President Thieu would be forced to give up some territory in order to reduce his long lines of communication. It would also be necessary to concentrate his forces to conserve fuel and ammunition as well as to reduce their exposure against the overwhelming odds in the northern part of South Vietnam. Several days later when the North Vietnamese did in fact start a heavy offensive, Thieu directed a withdrawal of South Vietnamese forces from the highlands around Pleiku and Ban Me Thout, and a withdrawal in Military Region I back toward Da Nang.

Unquestionably, the withdrawal was not well planned, and it was certainly badly executed. However, a retreat is a most difficult military maneuver, requiring careful planning, thorough organization, and disciplined execution. It also requires superior mobility. (The United States has had some well-executed retreats, notably the fallback of the U. S. marines from the Chosin Reservoir. We have also had some near routs that we would rather not talk about.)

In any event, one of the unique problems the South Vietnamese experienced in their attempted withdrawals was that their families were in the areas they were defending, and when a retreat was ordered, there was immediate concern that the families move with the withdrawing forces. Further, a majority of the populace not involved with the military was also fleeing before the Communists. Thus the roads were immediately jammed, and the troops were unable to move in any organized way. A breakdown of organization and discipline followed, which was quickly capitalized on by the enemy. News of the retreat from the highlands quickly spread in Military Region I, and refugees streamed down the roads from Quang Tri and Hue toward Da Nang, catching up some of South Vietnam's best fighting units, the airborne division and a marine division, in the panicking hoards. Again, an orderly evacuation was not possible.

The North Vietnamese, well supplied with armor and mechanized equipment, rapidly overran the retreating troops in Military Region I and reached Da Nang so swiftly that it fell without a fight. The same maneuver was repeated throughout the country so that the South Vietnamese-held territory was rapidly reduced to a perimeter around Saigon, and that was soon threatened with imminent attack. Saigon fell with tragic speed, and the whole sad story of South Vietnam's fight for freedom was concluded.

CHAPTER 30

How Did It Happen . . .
Will It Again?

THE VIETNAM EPISODE was one of the most controversial eras of U. S. history. I have attempted to set forth and analyze the chronology of our initial option for commitment, of the major decision points in its deepening vortex, and of our frantic, pathetic retreat from that commitment in the end. I do not suggest that mine has been a complete and thorough review—that would require a team of unbiased historians with access to all the data and to each of the decision makers involved. This has been a review from the unique position of personal association. The conclusions I draw from it are equally personal. Both inevitably inject me into the controversy surrounding this era—and rightfully so, as I was a part of it.

In thinking about conclusions, I wish I could offer something brilliantly new and startling on the subject of lessons learned, which would make us sit up and take notice. And we need to do just that, for I fear we are already well on the way to our distressing, if quite human, national tendency to bury yesterday's mistakes under today's obsessions, not stopping even to mark the grave in our rush to do so. My conclusions, however, are essentially the same as those drawn by others whose personal vantage point and viewpoint approximate mine. For the purposes of this discussion, I have presented my own judgments on "how it happened" in the context of several key intermeshed areas of concern.

First, I began this book by stating I intended to demonstrate the case for air power and its viability as one—*one*, not the only—potent tool in the exercise of international power diplomacy through military action. This chronology of facts and events pertaining to the almost unbelievable misuse of that tool proves the case beyond the need for my philosophizing. Even remembering my barely contained frustration at the time, I found myself shaking my head in disbelief as I set down this record of "on again, off again" tinkering with the coercive force implicit in the proper application of air power. If I am harsh in my judgment of those civilian, political decision makers who chose out of flagrant arrogance or naive wishful thinking to ignore the sound, time-vindicated principles of military strategy in their direction of the Vietnam air war, I must also look to the role of those of us who knew better. The JCS argued throughout against the restrained approach of gradualism in our bombing strategy, insisting that only a most dramatic, forceful and *consistent* application of air power would accomplish our intended objectives. It was, and is, the Joint Chiefs legal right to carry that argument directly to the President. Even though they may have been discouraged from doing so during this period, my opinion in retrospect is that perhaps they did not exercise this right to a sufficient extent. As for myself, the reader by now is aware that my arguments on the subject were presented voluminously and with nagging frequency. (On the latter point, I also found myself wondering as I set down this chronology why on earth Washington did not give in to my recommendations if only to silence Sharp's squeaky wheel!) But was that enough? Again in retrospect I am inclined to think I should perhaps have injected myself, early on and more than once, into the Washington arena with *personal* briefings of the sort I gave to Secretary McNamara at Saigon in mid-1967. In any event, there is more than enough responsibility to go around for each to take his share.

How did we come to the point where "flagrant arrogance or naive wishful thinking" could put us in the position of making such a

costly error in strategy? Of the many reasons that suggest themselves, I choose to emphasize one that seems to me to strike at a root
cause. We are a nation of innovators. We are continually looking for
new ways to do things, and our efforts are usually quite successful.
Our "carrot and stick" strategy (more carrot than stick!) was an
attempt to adopt a new, more cost-effective, more humane strategy
of convincing an enemy that aggression does not pay. A fine goal,
perhaps, but in this case the innovators were supremely self-
confident and intransigent. Convinced they were on the right
course, they turned out tons of studies in justification thereof and
were scornful of sound military advice. They also willfully ignored
unmistakable signals that the tough Communist enemy was completely unconvinced by gradualism and equivocation. The older,
wiser voice of history must be heeded when war becomes necessary.
The application of military, war-making power is an ugly thing—
stark, harsh and demanding—and it cannot be made nicer by pussy-
footing around with it.

On a wider screen, I view with chilling concern the weaknesses
which this laid open with respect to the American public's will to
support U. S. foreign policy objectives. We went into this era on a
positive note with the altruistic intention to do what was necessary
to help South Vietnam remain free and hopefully non-Communist,
believing that unless we did so virtually all of Southeast Asia would
fall under Communist domination. We also recognized that the rest
of the world would regard the Vietnam conflict as a test of the U. S.
ability to aid a nation victimized by Communist "Wars of National
Liberation." The stakes were high and we knew it. We have always
been blessed with public support for our armed forces in any war we
got into for good and apparent reasons, providing we prosecuted the
war in the approved American manner, i.e., to proceed towards
victory posthaste and all-out. Americans traditionally have not put
much stock in the no-win approach. For example, we became disenchanted with the Korean War when we settled for less than clear-cut
victory. But in this war Americans not only accomodated to the
no-win approach, they acquiesced to defeat.

What happened? Was our will eroded solely because those
"good and apparent reasons" were not emphatically delineated by

our political leadership? Or was it because we were subjected to a skillfully waged subversive propaganda campaign, aided and abetted by the media's bombardment of sensationalism, rumors and half-truths about the Vietnam affair—a campaign that destroyed our national unity? Or has there been a fundamental change in the attitude of Americans toward world affairs, marked by a lack of national will to continue our role of Free World leadership? When we accepted defeat after losing 55,000 American dead and another 300,000 wounded, with 150 billion dollars spent on a lost cause, we seemed to be clearly saying to the world that what we had ultimately lost was our concern for the responsibilities, indeed the honor, that goes with a leadership role. If this is true, I fear for the peace of the world.

My concern about what I perceive happened to the politico-military relationship during the Vietnam era is equally pressing. What I am pointing to in this case goes far beyond the criticism—which I strongly share—that civilian politico decision makers have no business ignoring or overriding the counsel of experienced military professionals in presuming to direct the day-to-day conduct of military strategy and tactics from their desks in Washington, D. C. I am decrying the supposition—shown nowhere more vividly than in the mishandling of the air war—that somehow military strategy and tactics can be orchestrated to satisfy all manner of political limitations. It is a supposition as incredible as it is illogical and dangerous. The aims or objectives of an international political strategy may quite reasonably and legitimately be limited, as were ours in Vietnam, but the actual application of military force required to achieve those aims cannot and *must not* be tactically limited. Our civilian leadership has the awesome task of deciding when the United States should resort to armed force to gain its objectives, limited or otherwise. Once the decision has been made to wage war, that leadership must permit the war to be engaged expeditiously and full bore, not halfway. The marine who steps on a land mine that was not interdicted at the enemy's supply port does not die halfway. And the pilot hit by a surface-to-air missile whose site he was not permitted to bomb does not fall halfway out of the sky or spend seven years as a limited prisoner of war.

Finally, I reiterate the point I have made consistently throughout this book concerning our abject failure to learn our lessons in how, and when, to negotiate with the Communists. In deference to redundancy, I ask the reader to take another look at Chapter XV and then ponder with me the answers to these questions. How could our leadership have been aware of our negotiating mistakes in Korea and still have proceeded along the tack we took in negotiating an eventual, if inglorious, end to the Vietnam affair? How could we have called time and time again for negotiations with an enemy whose military position was still unquestionably favorable to him—or sat in humiliating stalemate week after month at the negotiating table— and not, at the very least, have played the one quick-response ace we had in the hole, our coercive air power? From the day our troops were first landed in South Vietnam, we began a feverish drive to get peace negotiations started. Did we really believe the enemy would not take these premature proposals as a demonstration of a lack of will to prosecute the war to victory for our cause? And how did the American people take these peace overtures? Never before had the United States pleaded for peace before a conflict was well on the way to successful conclusion, but the President did so, publicly, barely two months after our first troops landed in Vietnam. It should surprise no one that the American people wondered what was going on in Washington when we still had 550,000 troops fighting in Vietnam three years later. In the end, we not only did not play our ace in the hole (except once in December 1972, and then we all but apologized for doing so), we did not even try to bluff. We simply turned it and the rest of our hole cards face up on the table and told the enemy we would not use them. And that, according to Hoyle or Alexander Solzhenitsyn or Admiral Turner Joy, is no way to win a high-stakes pot from the Communists.

Most wars have in common the fact that they were won by one side or the other. This war is the exception. For the real tragedy of Vietnam is that this war was not won by the other side, by Hanoi or Moscow or Peiping. It was lost in Washington, D. C. There and there alone lies the answer to our final question—will it happen again?

APPENDIX A

*Memorandum for the President
from the Secretary of Defense
8 November 1961*

The basic issue framed by the Taylor Report is whether the
U. S. shall:

a. Commit itself to the clear objective of preventing the fall of
South Vietnam to Communism, and

b. Support this commitment by necessary immediate military
actions and preparations for possible later actions.

The Joint Chiefs, Mr. Gilpatric, and I have reached the following conclusions:

1. The fall of South Vietnam to Communism would lead to the
fairly rapid extension of Communist control, or complete accommo-
dation to Communism, in the rest of mainland Southeast Asia and in
Indonesia. The strategic implications worldwide, particularly in the
Orient, would be extremely serious.

2. The chances are against, probably sharply against, preventing that fall by any measures short of the introduction of U.S. forces
on a substantial scale. We accept General Taylor's judgment that the
various measures proposed by him short of this are useful but will
not in themselves do the job of restoring confidence and setting
Diem on the way to winning his fight.

3. The introduction of a U.S. force of the magnitude of an
initial 8,000 men in a flood relief context will be of great help to

273

Diem. However, it will not convince the other side (whether the shots are called from Moscow, Peiping, or Hanoi) that we mean business. Moreover, it probably will not tip the scales decisively. We would be almost certain to get increasingly mired down in an inconclusive struggle.

4. The other side can be convinced we mean business only if we accompany the initial force introduction by a clear commitment to the full objective stated above, accompanied by a warning through some channel to Hanoi that continued support of the Viet Cong will lead to punitive retaliation against North Vietnam.

5. If we act in this way, the ultimate possible extent of our military commitment must be faced. The struggle may be prolonged and Hanoi and Peiping may intervene overtly. In view of the logistic difficulties faced by the other side, I believe we can assume that the maximum U.S. forces required on the ground in Southeast Asia will not exceed 6 divisions, or about 205,000 men (CINCPAC Plan 32–59, Phase IV). Our military posture is, or, with the addition of more National Guard or regular Army divisions, can be made, adequate to furnish these forces without serious interference with our present Berlin plans.

6. To accept the stated objective is of course a most serious decision. Military force is not the only element of what must be a most carefully coordinated set of actions. Success will depend on factors many of which are not within our control—notably the conduct of Diem himself and other leaders in the area. Laos will remain a major problem. The domestic political implications of accepting the objective are also grave, although it is our feeling that the country will respond better to a firm initial position than to courses of action that lead us in only gradually, and that in the meantime are sure to involve casualties. The overall effect on Moscow and Peiping will need careful weighing and may well be mixed; however, permitting South Vietnam to fall can only strengthen and encourage them greatly.

7. In sum:
    a. We do not believe major units of U.S. forces should be introduced in South Vietnam unless we are willing to

make an affirmative decision on the issue stated at the start of this memorandum.

b. We are inclined to recommend that we do commit the U.S. to the clear objective of preventing the fall of South Vietnam to Communism and that we support this commitment by the necessary military actions.

c. If such a commitment is agreed upon, we support the recommendations of General Taylor as the first steps toward its fulfillment.

Sgd: Robert S. McNamara

APPENDIX B

26 October 1966 Message from
CINCPAC to the Joint Chiefs of Staff

The purpose of this message is to establish clearly the critical importance of the air operations against North Vietnam to our military efforts in South Vietnam and to identify the grave risks involved should these operations either be suspended or their scope significantly reduced before North Vietnam actually ceases infiltration of men and material into South Vietnam and the DMZ. Self-imposed controls on the use of air power against North Vietnam have had an adverse impact upon the effectiveness of air power in reducing the capability of North Vietnam to direct and support the insurgency in South Vietnam. These operations, nevertheless, have had a significant impact on the military capabilities of the North Vietnamese Army and the V. C.

Indeed the amount of disruption and enemy material destroyed has been of such magnitude as to represent probable balance of power which to date has denied the enemy a capability for seizing significant portions of the first and second corps areas in South Vietnam. The enemy has been unable to move concentrations of requisite military force to South Vietnam to accomplish such a task without incurring unacceptable losses from air attack. The tactics of the enemy, the nature of the terrain in South Vietnam, and the concealment which it affords all dictate that we must not withhold our air power until he closes with us in close ground combat. We must begin disruption, harassment and attrition of the enemy forces as far back as we can find and attack them, thus degrading his capability qualitatively and quantitatively before he reaches the battlefield. Otherwise, his full capability must be met on the battlefield in a mode of combat which is certain to increase our casualties by appreciable and unnecessary numbers.

The risks described above are of immediate and pressing concern in connection with the North Vietnamese concentrations now known to be in and near the DMZ. This is an area where the enemy is adept at moving and concealing large forces, and from which he can attack with little warning. The military security of our numerically smaller forces in this area depends in great measure on the ability of our air power to deny the enemy freedom to move and concentrate in positions from which he can attack with great advantage. A standdown of air operations against enemy forces in or within supporting distance of the DMZ for even the shortest period of time would create the gravest of risks to the security of friendly forces in the area. The enemy would be accorded a greater freedom of movement for his men and supplies. We cannot afford to risk creation of a sanctuary of this nature close to our own forces.

Our air campaign in the North is a major military activity wherein we have the initiative and control over the intensity of combat. In South Vietnam the enemy can engage or disengage on the ground almost at will; thus, in a sense, pacing the ground war to his advantage. Such is not the case in the air over his homeland where he must make a concession if he is to gain any relief from the pressures being applied against him. It must be quite apparent to him that decisions which can increase his losses at home will not be of his own making. We cannot afford to relinquish these initiatives except under conditions clearly indicative of success in our overall objectives.

There are very serious military risks attached to any form of a partial standdown, either in terms of reducing the targeting base or in restricting air operations to smaller geographic areas. As soon as such reductions became apparent in the past the enemy has reacted quickly by readjusting his air defenses and our attrition has increased proportionately. It is essential that we avoid any voluntary simplification or reduction of his air defense problems.

In fact, it is becoming critically apparent from current attrition trends that a broader target base in North Vietnam is urgently needed. Our primary objective in the air campaign against North Vietnam is to make it as difficult and costly as possible for the North Vietnamese to continue effective support of the V. C. and to cause Hanoi to cease controlling and directing the insurgency in South Vietnam. To achieve this objective a steady increase in the pressure applied to the enemy is necessary to cause him to reconsider his support of the aggression. The most recent increase in pressure was applied through the systematic destruction of the POL system. Inaugurated in early July, the program has resulted in the destruction, greatly reduced capacity, or abandonment of all major POL targets authorized for attack. In recent weeks our pressure on the enemy has not continued to increase. In fact, it has decreased. Our air power is not being used to its maximum effectiveness. Many lucrative targets and target systems should be attacked to increase the pressure applied to the enemy. This is not the time for relaxation of pressure. A broadened target base designed to lead Hanoi to expect attacks anywhere at anytime, against any type of military target or activity that supports their aims is essential. The targets and freedom of action proposed by the JCS for Rolling Thunder 52 are a first step towards this broadened target base. Implementation of Rolling Thunder 52 will again increase the pressure on North Vietnam, although not using our air power to its maximum effectiveness. It is time now to tell Hanoi that no military target, no activity that helps sustain the North Vietnamese effort to prosecute the war, is free from attack.

In summary, air operations in North Vietnam have not yet reduced North Vietnamese support of the insurgency in South Vietnam to the level desired. Hanoi has not been brought to the negotiating table. However, air operations in North Vietnam have prevented the enemy from supporting his forces sufficiently to mount any major offensive or to seize and hold any vital areas in South Vietnam.

The North Vietnam air campaign is the one action that brings the war home to North Vietnam. It disrupts the daily life in North Vietnam. It causes multiple and increasing management and logistic problems. It prevents the enemy from conducting aggression from the comfort of a sanctuary. Any continued relaxation of pressure in our air campaign against North Vietnam will provide the enemy with the incentive to sustain and increase his support of the aggression in South Vietnam. Our allies in South Vietnam will consider the U.S. irresolute in its determination to force the Hanoi government to stop supporting the insurgency. The Communists will be encouraged to increase their disruptive effort throughout Southeast Asia. Our alternative is to convince Hanoi that its best hope is the negotiating table. A broadened target base is essential to achieve this end. The JCS proposed Rolling Thunder 52 is a first step toward a broadened target base. It is recommended that RT-52 be implemented now, with additional broadening of target base authorized at the earliest to clearly signal our intent to Hanoi.

APPENDIX C

*14 January 1967 Message from
CINCPAC to the Joint Chiefs of Staff*

During 1966 we deployed into South Vietnam a balanced and effective military force for the conduct of the war. Our successful spoiling operations forced the enemy to revert to defensive employment of his main force units. These operations have been instrumental in our successful efforts to prevent a military takeover of South Vietnam by the Communists. Nevertheless, a capable and resourceful enemy is continuing to engage in overt warfare in South Vietnam. He is being supported by major infiltration through Laos and there is strong evidence that enemy logistical support is also coming through Cambodia. Subversion and insurgency in Thailand, though still limited in scope, is being actively pursued. At the same time, the enemy maintains the capability to deploy substantial additional regular forces to South Vietnam.

Our strategy for the conduct of the war for Vietnam embraces three interdependent undertakings, which together constitute an integrated concept for the conduct of the war. These undertakings are: (a) to take the war to the enemy in North Vietnam by unremitting but selective application of United States air and naval power, (b) to seek out and destroy Communist forces and infrastructure in South Vietnam by offensive military operations, and (c) to extend the secure areas of South Vietnam by coordinated civil and military operations and assist the government of South Vietnam in building an independent, viable, non-Communist society. (Author's note: These three elements of our strategy were continually outlined to the JCS and others in Washington to try to get an understanding that all three of these operations were necessary for success.)

Our Rolling Thunder operations have a twofold objective—to apply steadily increasing pressure against North Vietnam in order to cause Hanoi to cease its aggression in South Vietnam while making continued support of the Viet Cong insurgency as difficult and costly as possible. Our tasks to accomplish this objective are as follows: (a) reduce or deny external assistance to North Vietnam, (b) disrupt and destroy in depth those resources that contribute most to the support of the aggression, (c) harass, disrupt and impede movement of men and materials to Laos and South Vietnam. Little has been accomplished in preventing external assistance to North Vietnam. With the exception of the POL strikes, the key port of Haiphong, through which 85 percent of North Vietnam's imports flow, has been out of bounds. Some progress has been made in destroying those resources which contribute most to the support of the aggression. However, the amount is minor in comparison to what could have been accomplished. As an example, of the 104 targets located in the northeast section of North Vietnam, only 20 were hit in 1966. The interdiction task has received the primary emphasis. In the final analysis it must be concluded that in 1966 our Rolling Thunder campaign did not apply adequate and steady pressure against the enemy. Imposed restrictions have resulted in inefficient use of our air power.

We have reviewed in detail our Rolling Thunder operations, including the objective, the results, and future courses of action. We conclude that: first, our basic objectives and tasks remain valid as set forth above; and second, effective operations in support of these tasks, together with continued successful operations in South Vietnam, offer the greatest prospect of bringing the war to an end on terms advantageous to the U. S. and its allies. I will submit a second message containing a concept which emphasizes attacks against target systems as opposed to individual strikes against only a small part of any given capability. The concept will stress increased pressure through a steady application of air power against key target systems. It is aimed at targets of primary importance to the enemy and is designed to disrupt and destroy in depth those resources which contribute most to the support of the aggression.

The results desired are not necessarily the total destruction of any given system, but rather a broad destruction, within defined limits, that will have important indirect economic and psychological as well as direct military effects. We have full initiative and control over the intensity of combat in our air campaign against North Vietnam. We cannot afford to relinquish this initiative. In South Vietnam we have been able to take the initiative against enemy main force units. However, the enemy can disengage many of these units almost at will by returning to his sanctuaries in Laos, Cambodia and North Vietnam where ground forces cannot search him out, thus pacing the ground war to his advantage.

An effective complementary effort to our Rolling Thunder operations has been naval gunfire directed against coastal waterborne logistics traffic. These operations should be authorized in the DMZ and extended northward from the current limits imposed. The extension northward would compound the enemy logistics problem by forcing him to transport additional materials over already overtaxed land lines of communication.

During 1967 our operations will be designed to defeat the Viet Cong-North Vietnamese main force units, destroy the enemy's base areas and resources and drive him into the sparsely populated areas where food is scarce. Concurrently we will strive to locate, interdict and destroy the enemy's ground and water lines of communication in South Vietnam. The course upon which we have embarked in South Vietnam is a sound one. It would be an oversimplification to suggest that the enemy has reverted to tactical guerrilla action as his primary mode of operation. He realizes that he cannot defeat and eject U. S.-Free World military forces by large unit operations and that he is vulnerable, particularly when concentrated, to our air, artillery and tactical mobility. He is practical enough to attempt to operate in any mode; i.e., phase two or three or a combination thereof, at times and places where circumstances indicate to him a good probability of success. It would be erroneous to conclude that the V. C.-NVA main forces are no longer dangerous, that their unit integrity has been destroyed or that their logistical capability has fallen below that needed to continue the war. It is far more likely that he is avoiding major contact, using his sanctuaries, fighting defensively when forced to do so, and attempting to rebuild and reinforce for operations at an opportune time. Tactical guerrilla warfare probably will be intensified without fragmenting main force units or discarding plans for their buildup and use. He probably will attempt to keep up his present rate of infiltration in order to counter our buildup and replace his losses. He remains a dangerous enemy whose strategy hinges on prolonging the war and outlasting our determination to see the job done.

Revolutionary development is just getting under way and its continued growth will be a slow and painstaking process. We must press on vigorously to strengthen revolutionary development and assist the government of South Vietnam in this important undertaking. Although the Army of South Vietnam has the primary mission of supporting revolutionary development, U. S. forces will reinforce their efforts by direct support. The South Vietnamese units are being redeployed and retrained to support revolutionary development programs, but the reorientation of the South Vietnamese Army will not be easily accomplished.

There is another element of the enemy's basic strategy which warrants consideration. The enemy propaganda campaign is aimed at increasing both domestic and international pressure on the U. S. Government to get out of Vietnam or to settle on terms favorable to the enemy. A specific goal appears to be to prevent our bombing of the profitable targets which lie in or near highly populated areas in North Vietnam. The United States should turn the tables on North Vietnam and develop a hard-hitting psychological campaign of our own. There is no doubt but for our efforts and sacrifices, South Vietnam would have collapsed militarily and politically to Communist control, and Laos, Cambodia and Thailand would be faced directly by a similar fate. Although the length of this conflict is not yet predictable, the course upon which we have embarked successfully to bring it to an end is a necessary and a sound one.

We face a complex situation which will demand constant review of our tactics, adequacy of our forces, and effectiveness of our operations against the enemy. In my opinion, the most important requirement for success is a demonstrated determination to stick to our guns. Our goal for 1967 is to increase the prospects for an early end to the conflict in South Vietnam which is satisfactory to the United States, to the Republic of Vietnam and to those nations which are providing Free World military assistance forces. To achieve this goal at the earliest possible time, we must step up the air war against North Vietnam, thus imposing a steadily increasing cost on Hanoi for their aggression.

APPENDIX D

Remarks by CINCPAC at a Briefing
for the Secretary of Defense,
the Undersecretary of State and Others in Saigon
On 5 July 1967

This presentation will review the air campaign against North Vietnam and describe the changing situation which is emerging in the northeast sector as a result of the increased tempo and weight of strike effort in that area.

Prior to discussing the significant changes, a brief review of Rolling Thunder operations will help us to focus more clearly on why changes are occurring. Since January 1966 I have recommended an air campaign based on attacks on target systems to accomplish the three basic tasks of Rolling Thunder. In November of 1966 a complete target package which included significant targets of various target systems was authorized. Regrettably, from the standpoint of impact on the enemy, some of those targets were cancelled before we could apply a real weight of effort. You will remember that the POL system was authorized for strike in June of 1966. But the enemy had been forewarned of this attack and had dispersed, camouflaged and hardened these supplies. He prevented us from accomplishing the job as effectively as it could have been done if we had achieved surprise. In January of 1967 the total target array was refined into six basic systems. The objective was the progressive and concurrent disruption of these systems to assure that each was made ineffective. In February targets from several systems, including important power targets, were authorized. Weather slowed us down and reduced the potential impact. In April 1967, Rolling Thunder 55 authorized strikes against portions of all six target systems. The weather was good enough to maintain a substantial level of operations in the northeast quadrant, and nine of the ten assigned JCS targets were hit prior to 1 May, five of them more than once.

The frequency of the strikes for the first time was approaching that necessary to carry out our target systems concept. This level of effort increased in May when an additional ten important targets were authorized. The weather continued to improve with the result that nineteen strikes were conducted against these new targets prior to 23 May. All had been struck at least once. For the first time since the war began we were able to keep the heat on the vital northeast quadrant. Over a five-week period starting in late April, the level of stress against the Hanoi government was greater than during the entire previous Rolling Thunder program. Our air resources were being applied in a systematic, cohesive program.

On 23 May we were told not to operate within 10 miles of Hanoi. Strikes against important targets were interrupted. Frequent presence in and over Hanoi was denied. The importance of the northeast quadrant to Hanoi is reflected by their air defense effort. Over 60 percent of the AA order of battle is in Route Package 6. Practically all of the MiG activity has been confined to Route Packages 5 and 6. Of 1,433 SAM sightings from 1 January through 30 June 1967, 1,111 or 77 percent have been in Route Package 6. It is this area that the enemy considers he *must* defend. This is his *base support area* for the war in South Vietnam.

Our increased level of effort in the northeast has not been at the expense of our reconnaissance throughout the remainder of North Vietnam, nor at the expense of the concentrated interdiction effort in Laos and Route Package 1. Our air operations have been complemented by naval operations south of 20 degrees north. Coupled with the mining of key river mouths, these operations have been effective in the interdiction program against waterborne logistic craft. During April, May and June, 620 waterborne logistic craft were destroyed or damaged, and 826 targets ashore were hit by naval gunfire.

As we studied and refined our target systems concept it was recognized that more attention to the many important non-JCS targets was required, and that these must be integrated with the JCS targets. As a result, a Rolling Thunder target list has been developed which concentrates on Route Package 6. Targets in the area are broken down by target system and placed in four categories. In each category the targets are rated in importance and given a priority for strike and for reconnaissance. The chart shown here provides a perspective of numbers of targets of value in Route Package 6. This is an ever-changing list. Targets move from one category to another as new intelligence is uncovered or their value changes. We expect it to grow in size. It is an important management tool for planning and directing a sound program of strike operations, particularly with regard to time-phasing of attacks and re-attacks on whole system complexes. Because of its importance, a machine runout is made weekly. It is the basic target list throughout the command and is kept current by inputs from the field and by the Component Commanders, as well as CINCPAC.

With that brief summary of where we have been and what we are doing, I will now highlight what, in my judgment, indicates a significant trend. We are experiencing marked changes. These changes are having important effects on the efficiency of our operations and are degrading the North Vietnamese capability to support the war.

First, there is a change in the way the MiGs are employed. They are not challenging us in air-to-air combat now. They are not forcing us to jettison bombs because of their presence. Their air order of battle has been reduced 50 percent. Three of their airfields have been denied to them for effective use. When they did challenge us, 30 of their aircraft were destroyed in five weeks. This is only 12 less than were destroyed during the whole previous campaign. Attacks against the three airfields further reduced the MiG inventory.

Another change is in the use and effectiveness of their surface-to-air missiles. There is increasing evidence of launches without effective guidance. In some cases there is no apparent target. There have been occasional barrage-type firings. They are reluctant to fire during good visibility for fear of attack on the site. Although 3,800 combat sorties were flown in June in Route Package 6, there have been but two aircraft lost to SAMs. Multiple firings against single flights have failed to bring down aircraft or, in most cases, even inflict damage. The effectiveness and pattern of AAA fire is also changing. Since mid-May ground fire is frequently less intense and less effective than normal in several important target areas. The northeast rail line is an excellent example. Last summer we lost 43 aircraft in this area on 1,557 combat sorties. Since late April of this year through June, the losses have been 12 aircraft on 2,371 combat sorties. We judge that our improved weapon systems coupled with an increased and continuing weight of effort is responsible for this changed environment. Simply put, when we operate in force in an area over a period of time, enemy defenses are beaten down and their effectiveness falls off markedly.

The decrease in effectiveness of the MiG, the SA-2 and AAA has resulted in the lower aircraft loss rate. For the first six months of 1967 we have lost 5.2 aircraft in Route Package 6 per 1,000 combat sorties. During the last six months of 1966 the rate was 10.0. This chart indicates a further trend that is most significant. The number of attack sorties has risen from 660 in March to 2,243 in June. Loss rates for this period held fairly constant at about one percent through May, then dropped sharply to one-third of one percent in June. Thus far in July the loss rate is up slightly but it's too early to indicate a trend.

The preceding significant changes are largely a result of our changed posture. Just in recent months the CBU-24 (a cluster bomb) has been available in sufficient numbers to have an impact on North Vietnamese defenses. The effectiveness of this weapon has exceeded our expectations. Pilots are enthusiastic over its results against gun emplacements. Hanoi is busily engaged in revetting gun positions in an attempt to gain some protection from this weapon. Other new weapons—Walleye and the Mark-36 Destructor—are changes which will greatly affect our operations. The Walleye has already proven its accuracy, making it possible for the first time to use a small, precise attack with minimum collateral damage. The Destructor Mark-36 has just become operational. Its characteristics provide us with a new dimension for sustained interdiction of land and water lines of communication. The individual effectiveness of the CBU-24, the Walleye and the Mark-36 is impressive. As a family of weapons they are even more impressive.

Equally as significant as the new weapons is our changed ECM posture. Only in recent months have we reached the point where strike aircraft in adequate numbers were equipped with an integral capability to counter the SA-2. As a result improved tactics have been possible which are effectively degrading the AAA threat, while at the same time improving effectiveness of attacks. On the other hand, improvement of our standoff jamming is needed urgently to help degrade the enemy's early warning and GCI defenses. The Navy, in particular, is weak in this vital protective role.

There is another aspect to the changing situation in North Vietnam—the ever-mounting problems facing the Hanoi government. The drawdown on manpower has greatly decreased his food production. Considerable amounts of food now have to be imported. Imports, including food, are causing congestion on the docks, in warehouses, wherever there is space in the Haiphong sanctuary. Ship offloading time is increasing. Large hatch cargo ships averaged 19 days offloading time in March, 47 days in June, and it appears that the trend will continue in July. Their transportation system is not recuperating. Of 3,500 trucks destroyed in the past year, it is estimated 2,000 have not been replaced. The same is true of rail rolling stock. For the first time the northeast rail line has been interdicted at at least one point with a frequency that is meaningful—during late April and May, 20 days, and during the month of June, 17 days.

In my judgment the trend of the war in the north has changed in our favor. This change was gradual until late April. Since that time the rate of change has increased. Our continued presence in Route Package 6 is having a marked effect on the North Vietnamese. We established the momentum in late April and May when 20 JCS targets were struck in Route Package 6 in five weeks compared with 22 in all of 1966. We are attempting to retain our momentum by continued presence in the northeast quadrant, but we are hampered by the prohibited and restricted areas around Hanoi and Haiphong, the primary areas where our presence would have the most powerful effect on the North Vietnamese government.

Earlier in this briefing I summarized for you the number of priority targets carried in Annex Alpha of our Rolling Thunder operations orders. The number is large. The job yet to be done is significant. The majority of those targets which have not been struck are not authorized—59 percent of the military complex targets, all of the remaining power targets, nearly 70 percent of the transportation targets, all of the air defense targets, and all but two of the remaining 15 war-supporting industrial targets. With regard to POL, although only 20 percent require authority, the remainder are pretty well dispersed and hardened, but worthwhile should actions be authorized which would reduce the current import of POL by sea.

If we took the various systems individually there would be a definite order of priority. Transportation, for example, would head the list, and the port targets are considered the most important of the transportation targets. We do not believe, however, that the impact against the North Vietnamese will be as significant should we concentrate on one target system as it would be to strike elements of each system. Diversified strikes compound his management problems. Attack against all systems prevents establishing patterns. We should avoid a preoccupation with interdiction and infiltration to the degree that too little consideration is given to the overall objective of making Hanoi cease its support of the aggression. The best way to convince Ho Chi Minh to stop his aggression against the South is to impress upon him the consequences to North Vietnam if he does not desist. This is another reason for striking all target systems. It is another reason for not diverting the modest effort now devoted to the northern quadrant in an attempt to further interdict the infiltration routes in the South.

Certainly it is important that we continue our efforts to reduce the infiltration of men and material into South Vietnam. The barrier project, with its new weapons and tactics, will present new obstacles to infiltration. It should be recognized, however, that an increase in the strike effort in the southern route packages will result in a relatively small return per sortie. Only in the north can we be assured of maximum returns per sortie expended on interdiction. It has been estimated that only 55 tons per day, or 18,000 metric tons per year, are required to support operations in South Vietnam. Even if this were tripled to over 50,000 metric tons a year, it is insignificant when compared with the nearly 2 million metric tons estimated entering North Vietnam through the ports, rail lines and roads of Route Package 6. This large amount of tonnage provides many high-value targets, whereas the limited amount going into South Vietnam requires a relatively high sortie rate against fleeting and dispersed targets with only limited returns per sortie. Disruption of key segments of the transportation system in the northeast quadrant creates bottlenecks and blockages compounding the enemy's problems and providing additional targets of value. Interdiction in the northeast cuts directly into the capability of North Vietnam, not only to support the aggression, but also to support itself. Interdicting the imports into North Vietnam, combined with strikes against other vital target systems, particularly the rather limited but important industrial base, is the best way to raise the plateau of pain to a sufficient level to affect the North Vietnamese will to resist.

It is difficult to estimate the level to which imports may be lowered. It should be pointed out, however, the degree to which we have been successful to date. Imports through the port system provide an excellent example. A current JCS study shows a theoretical maritime port capacity of 6,000 metric tons per day. The current utilization rates based on actual ship count is about 3,700 metric tons per day. Judging from the ship offloading times previously mentioned, this is probably the current peak capacity. Port capacity has been affected by various means—interdiction effort against the Haiphong/Hanoi railroad system, strikes against power and harassment by other strikes in the area. Continued interdiction of the lines of communication will cause further degradation of port capacity. There is evidence that the Haiphong area is being used as a sanctuary for the storage of material. Precise attacks against warehouses and storage yards would be the most direct means of preventing this safe storage. Mining the ports, of course, remains the most effective way to reduce maritime imports.

The rail lines from China provide a similar example. Theoretical capacities are 5,200 metric tons per day, whereas actual usage is considerably less. Our heavy strike effort will further limit imports by this means. The continued direct and indirect effort against imports through Route Package 6 will have dire effects on the North Vietnamese economy, and inevitably on the amount of goods infiltrated into South Vietnam. It is my contention that this is where the pain must be inflicted against the North Vietnamese.

I am not going into details on other target systems. A complete listing of targets by system has been attached as an appendix to your copy of this discussion. I will say that a single target should not necessarily be evaluated on its particular worth. Many targets taken separately are relatively unimportant in comparison with others. However, as a part of a group of targets, or as part of a target system, a single target is important. This was clearly demonstrated in the attacks against the power system. Another obvious example is the air defense system, which, like the power system, is closely interconnected. But it is also true with eight nonrelated targets. The effect of destroying several or many relatively low value targets assures presence in the area with its associated harassment, and the cumulative effects provide a high degree of destruction to the system as a whole.

APPENDIX E

CINCPAC Message to the Joint Chiefs of Staff
of 25 September 1967
Outlining an Optimum Air Campaign

The general concept for the air campaign against North Vietnam was stated in a message to the JCS on the 22nd of January 1966, and on the 18th of January 1967. The concept remains valid. The basic objective is restated as follows:

To apply increased pressure against North Vietnam as an element of an overall strategy to cause North Vietnam to cease supporting and directing insurgencies in Southeast Asia and to cease its aggression in South Vietnam.

Three basic tasks have been assigned to achieve this objective: (a) Deny external assistance to North Vietnam, (b) destroy in depth those resources within North Vietnam that contribute to the aggression, and (c) harass, disrupt and impede the movement of men and materials into South Vietnam and Laos.

The subtasks derived in support of these basic tasks are: deny all external assistance by sea and by land, destroy war-supporting industries and resources, isolate Hanoi and Haiphong from the rest of Vietnam, isolate Haiphong itself, and interdiction of men and supplies into South Vietnam and Laos.

The most effective and efficient means of denying external assistance to North Vietnam by sea is by mining the three deep-water ports of Haiphong, Cam Pha, and Hon Gai. Relatively few mining sorties would be required to accomplish this task. Without sea imports, which constitute about 80 percent of total imports, North Vietnam would be unable to continue the war for a protracted period. It is recognized that there are special international problems associated with deep-water mining. Denying entry of war supplies into North Vietnam is a far superior way to impede the war effort than any subsequent action that can be taken to interdict the movement of supplies west and south. A more costly and less effective method of interdicting sea imports is to strike major port facilities in North Vietnam, but this also generates international problems, since there are always ships alongside the all-important Haiphong docks. Thus, accomplishment of most of the subtasks hinge on the closure or destruction of the port of Haiphong. If we closed the port of Haiphong, then isolation of Haiphong from Hanoi would be unnecessary, and thus forces would become available for application against other subtasks.

The current interdiction plan for the northeast and northwest sectors provides for the disruption of traffic flow and interdiction of the main and secondary rail and road lines of communication. This can be an effective denial of external assistance by land. The objective here would be to reduce the flow to an absolute minimum by destroying the transportation vehicles and by destroying the elements of the lines of communication. In order to apply optimum air power in this area the Chicom buffer zone should be reduced to 15 miles and authority granted to conduct unrestricted attacks against the northeast and northwest rail lines.

Destruction of war-supporting industries and resources should be conducted in a way to destroy them in the shortest possible time, and then we would have to mount strikes to prevent these targets from regenerating. Most of these important targets are contained within the current Hanoi and Haiphong prohibited areas which should be removed.

A drastic reduction in the movement of supplies through Hanoi and from Haiphong southward is desired. For maximum effect, interdiction strikes along all major LOC's to the center of both cities is required. Until authority is granted to close the port of Haiphong, it will be necessary to interdict the flow of supplies out of Haiphong as completely as possible. In order to reduce the dispersal of these supplies to Hanoi and southward, interdiction and seeding of LOC's would be conducted in a pattern which would, to the extent feasible, isolate the Haiphong complex. The flow of supplies should be interdicted as close to the docks as possible. However, it is not possible to completely isolate Haiphong by this method.

This concept requires maximum effort against the most critical targets in North Vietnam during the period of good weather. When weather in the North precludes visual operations, increased effort would be applied in the southern route packages and in Laos. Then with the advent of good weather in the spring of 1968, an all-out campaign would be resumed with increased emphasis on the denial of external assistance and further isolation of the Hanoi and Haiphong complexes. The objective would be to convince the enemy that further aggression in the south is too costly to continue.

Implementation of the concept does not lend itself to advance static allocation of sorties by route package. Weather factors, degree of destruction of target systems, the effectiveness of the interdiction of lines of communication, and generation of new targets preclude a preplanned or a fixed allocation of a specific number of sorties by route package. Operational flexibility in the use of air power is required in order to apply strike and armed reconnaissance effort when and where it is needed. Primary strike effort should be applied against authorized fixed targets as functionally related to the denial of external assistance, the destruction of war-making capabilities, and the isolation of the Hanoi/Haiphong complexes. All targets will require repeated restrikes and will be restruck as necessary.

The prohibited areas around Hanoi and Haiphong provide the enemy with recognized sanctuaries within which he is allowed freedom of movement of men and supplies. Key targets authorized in the past within these areas have frequently been authorized only for single strikes or for strikes under further restrictive conditions. This does not permit the optimum application of our air power or optimum results against these targets.

I recommend that the concept be approved and restrictions be removed on the 1st of November 1967, or earlier. CINCPAC should be delegated the authority to conduct strikes and restrikes, mining and seeding operations as necessary against all targets in North Vietnam, as required to pursue this concept.

APPENDIX F

CINCPAC Message to the Joint Chiefs of Staff
of November 1967

Recognizing that mounting pressure to halt the bombing campaign is being heard through many elements of the world press by the so-called peace movements, among certain neutral nations, and from all Communist nations, the following assessment of the impact of the bombing cessation has been prepared:

Cessation as used herein is not the same as brief holiday stand-downs.

As a general statement, cessation would lead to the military, economic and psychological recovery of the enemy and would be a resounding political victory for North Vietnam. A unilateral U. S. cessation of bombing would give the North Vietnamese the major victory that they have been unable to achieve on the battlefield. Study of available data concerning the air and ground campaigns for the last two years, and in particular the effect of the air campaign against North Vietnam, leads to the following detailed assessment:

(a) Economic — First, Hanoi would soon rebuild its transportation system, its power grid, its war-related industries, and its POL storage facilities. The receipt and distribution of increased quantities of material aid from the Communist world would be greatly facilitated. Second, major interdicted LOCs would be restored to full use in a matter of weeks. The degree of success achieved thus far in isolating Haiphong, presently impeding the distribution of imports out to the rest of the country, will have been to no avail. A daily average of about 4,400 short tons per day would continue to flow into this port from the sea and be distributed throughout the country in support of the war effort. The rail line to Vinh, which has been either completely inoperable or useful only for short-haul operations, would be restored to full capacity. Capabilities for resupplying Communist forces in the South would be expanded and North Vietnam would resupply and reinforce its divisions in South Vietnam at will. During the four-day Tet Holiday stand-down, North Vietnam moved an estimated 25,000 tons of material below 18 degrees north. A bombing respite would make every day a "Tet holiday" and allow war materials to be transported unhindered to the South. Tonnages would increase because heavier and more sophisticated weapons would be introduced to counter those of the Free World forces. It is estimated that over 200 heavy artillery weapons, 150 heavy rocket launchers, 300 AAA guns with caliber up to 100 millimeter, and adequate surface-to-air missile coverage would be placed from the Mu Gia Pass southward. With material aid free to flow into North Vietnam unhindered by air strikes, most industries, power plants and fuel oil storage areas could be restored in a relatively short period. Restoration of 14 of North Vietnam's 23 key power plants would take an estimated six months, thus, putting back into operation the 80 percent of electrical generating capacity destroyed to date. Major fuel oil storage facilities would be rehabilitated as materials and technical assistance became available. Reconstruction and refurbishing of the economy would have a rejuvenating effect on the leadership and North Vietnamese people. It would be as though they had achieved much of their purpose and were pursuing their advantage to consolidate their gains.

With the restoration of transportation systems, manpower will become available for redirection in the war effort. The constant bombing pressure caused the enemy to transfer nearly a million workers to full-time and part-time war-related activities, such as civil defense and repair of lines of communication. This manpower pool, in addition to some of the 142,000 personnel in the air defenses of

North Vietnam, would become available as needed for reconstruction activities or military duty in Laos or South Vietnam.

In the agricultural sector a bombing cessation would be increasingly beneficial to North Vietnam, as armed recce harassment ended and fertilizers, insecticides, and manpower gradually became more plentiful.

(b) Military — North Vietnam could, and probably would, immediately increase its capabilities in the I Corps tactical zone for tactical operations and artillery fire from north of the DMZ. As supplies became stockpiled just north of the DMZ, more supplies could be sent through Laos to the central provinces of South Vietnam. Within six months the enemy's capabilities in II and III Corps zones would be increased, particularly in artillery support. The morale and health of infiltrating troops would improve as their time en route became shortened, and transportation was allowed to proceed unhindered by our air attacks within North Vietnam, and tactical air efforts in Laos became degraded. An expanded enemy artillery capability, coupled with a U. S. bombing standdown, would dictate re-evaluation of our current strong point obstacle system. Bombardment of defensive strong points and a less effective surveillance of the barrier would result. With the stronger enemy posture resulting from force improvements and major increases in personnel and materials, our casualties would multiply. A four division increase in enemy strength would not be unreasonable to expect.

North Vietnam's air and air defense forces would be regrouped and reorganized. Most North Vietnamese fighter aircraft now out of country would return as major airfields were restored to serviceability. Bases in the North Vietnam panhandle which have long been abandoned due to U. S. air action would be reactivated and others would be built to provide air and helo support for Communist ground troops near the DMZ. Bombing attacks against Da Nang and other Free World bases in South Vietnam would become a threat.

(c) Psychological — The bombing cessation would lead to a false hope in the world that the conflict was about to be settled. North

Vietnam would probably continue to evade a settlement and use the respite to gain a marked military advantage in the South. The U. S. would thus face a difficult decision. A resumption of the bombing would be damaging morally and psychologically to the U. S. image throughout the world and at home. On the other hand, if the U. S. did not resume the bombing, lack of military success, or worse yet, military setbacks in the South would not be acceptable to the American public. Hanoi, the nations of the Communist world and anti-war sympathizers in the Free World would gain tremendously in a sense of the strengthening of morale and resolve. With renewed feelings of confidence, Communist propaganda lines likely would change from present demands that "all acts of war against North Vietnam should cease" to the now less emphasized requirement for "unconditional withdrawal of all foreign troops." In effect, the Communist psychological campaign would gain in force and persuasiveness once the U. S. actions had been interpreted as a lack of resolve.

(d) Political — A bombing cessation would most probably be interpreted as a weakening of U. S. resolve and initial failure on the part of the U. S. to achieve its objectives. It would appear that we had withdrawn into "fortress" South Vietnam in the hopes that the North Vietnamese would not try to win against us militarily in the South. To Hanoi our bombing cessation would act to reinforce the belief that its course of action has been correct. North Vietnam could be expected to assail in an intensified campaign U. S. objectives, policies, and presence in Vietnam.

In recent weeks of anti-war demonstrations Ho Chi Minh's position on acceptance of his four points has solidified even more firmly. To the Asian community a bombing cessation would signal not an effort toward peace, but the beginning of failure of a powerful nation opposed by a small Communist state.

Lack of success in Southeast Asia on the part of the United States and the Free World enhances the prestige of Communist China and serves to weaken the resolve of the remainder of our Asian allies, who want to "ride with the winner." In our desire for an early end to the fighting we must not throw away one of our principal military advantages for shortening the war.

APPENDIX G

CINCPAC Message to JCS, January 1968
1967 Progress Report
(Partial Quote)

Air attacks were authorized and executed by target systems for the first time in 1967 although the attacks were limited to specific targets within each system. The campaign against the power system resulted in reduction of power generating capability to approximately 15 percent of original capacity. Successful strikes against the Thai Nguyen iron and steel plant and the Haiphong cement plant resulted in practically total destruction of these two installations. North Vietnamese adjustments to these losses have had to be made by relying on additional imports from China and the U. S. S. R. or the Eastern European countries. The requirement for additional imports reduces available shipping space for war-supporting supplies and adds to the congestion at the ports. Interruptions of raw material supplies and the requirements to turn to less efficient means of power generation has degraded overall production.

The overall effect of our effort to reduce external assistance has resulted not only in destruction and damage to the transportation systems and goods being transported thereon, but has created management, distribution and manpower problems. In addition, the attacks have created a bottleneck at Haiphong where inability effectively to move goods inland from the port has resulted in congestion on the docks and a slowdown in off-loading ships as they arrive. By October, road and rail interdictions had reduced the transportation clearance capacity at Haiphong to about 2,700 short tons per day. An average of 4,400 short tons per day had arrived at Haiphong during the year.

Although men and material needed for the level of combat now prevailing in South Vietnam continued to flow despite our attacks on the LOCs, we have made it very costly to the enemy in terms of material, manpower, management and distribution. Air attacks destroyed or damaged more than 5,000 motor vehicles, about 2,500 railroad rolling stock, and more than 11,000 watercraft. Through external assistance the enemy has been able to replace or rehabilitate many of the items damaged or destroyed and transport inventories are at roughly the same level they were at the beginning of the year.

The primary effect of our efforts to impede movement of the enemy has been to force Hanoi to engage from 500,000 to 600,000 civilians in full-time and part-time war-related activities, in particular for air defense and repair of the lines of communication. This diversion of manpower from other pursuits, particularly from the agricultural sector, has caused a drawdown on manpower. The estimated lower food production yields, coupled with an increase in food imports in 1967 (some six times that of 1966), indicate that agriculture is having great difficulty in adjusting to this changed composition of the work force. The cost and difficulties of the war to Hanoi have sharply increased, and only through the willingness of other Communist countries to provide maximum replacement of goods and material has North Vietnam managed to sustain its war effort.

In South Vietnam we have been able to detect impending major offensives and to mount spoiling attacks to knock them off balance and force them to fight defensively. It is estimated that the enemy strategy continued to reflect an effort to draw allied forces into remote areas, especially those areas adjacent to border sanctuaries, thereby enabling local and guerrilla forces to harass and impede the nation-building effort in South Vietnam. The enemy has also shown a willingness to engage our forces in sustained combat. Recent large deployments from North Vietnam indicate that the enemy may be seeking a spectacular win in South Vietnam in the near future.

Despite a general feeling of optimism regarding the progress reflected to date, we must not overlook the fact that the enemy has demonstrated a willingness to accept the situation as it exists and continues to attack, harass and terrorize in many areas of the countryside. The V. C. infrastructure in January of 1968 peristed as a significant influence over portions of the population. The infiltration from the North continued at a high rate, estimated to be over 6,000 personnel per month. The enemy has been importing artillery, rockets and mortars at a marked increase in intensity in both quality and caliber. He is now using 120 millimeter mortars, 122 millimeter rockets, and 130 millimeter field guns.

Careful exploitation of the enemy's vulnerabilities and application of U. S. and Vietnamese superior firepower and mobility should make it possible for us to expect that we would gain increasingly in 1968.

There were a number of programs started during 1967 which were designed for overall improvement in the Vietnamese armed forces. The M-16 rifle was issued to the airborne battalions and to selected infantry and ranger units since U. S. forces had been completely equipped with the M-16 rifle. There was much effort put into stressing day patrols and night ambushes for the Vietnamese units and their intelligence gathering capability was increased.

The Royal Thai Army Volunteer Regiment came into South Vietnam in September of 1967, and during the whole year the Republic of Korea forces consisted of two army divisions and a marine brigade and performed in an outstanding manner. The Australian and New Zealand task force conducted operations throughout 1967. The task force in December came to a full three battalions in strength and the New Zealanders also deployed a second rifle company.

The overall munitions picture improved considerably in 1967 with modern ammunition from production satisfying approximately 95 percent of the stated requirements, whereas before that time we were using stocks held over from the Korean War. Increased availability of ammunition permitted increases in stockage objectives and monthly expenditures also increased. During that year we also received supplies of the television-guided Walleye bomb and the Mark-36 Destructor, which converted 500-pound bombs to influence mines.

During 1968 we will intensify combat operations in South Vietnam since we have increased combat strength and the Vietnamese armed forces and Free World forces are expected to increase in capability during 1968 so that in-country operations would intensify.

The air and naval campaign against North Vietnam continues to be the one element of our strategy where we are on the offensive. We must continue to press this advantage. There is no doubt that our past efforts have hurt the enemy and continued support of the war in South Vietnam is causing him severe hardship. To increase the effectiveness of the war, our air and naval forces need additional operational latitude. With such additional authority the air and naval campaign against North Vietnam can be designed and executed to bring about a more rapid deterioration of the enemy's economy and total war-supporting structure. When this curtailment of the enemy's effort is achieved by drains on his resources, the ultimate result should be reduction of the insurgency and aggression in South Vietnam to a level where effective internal political and military actions can achieve and maintain stability.

APPENDIX H

The War Powers Resolution
Public Law 93—148, 93rd Congress
7 November 1973
Pertinent Extracts

Sec. 2. (a) It is the purpose of this joint resolution to fulfill the intent of the framers of the Constitution of the United States and insure that the collective judgment of both the Congress and the President will apply to the introduction of United States Armed Forces into hostilities, or into situations where imminent involvement in hostilities is clearly indicated by the circumstances, and to the continued use of such forces in hostilities or in such situations.

Sec. 2. (c) The constitutional powers of the President as Commander-in-Chief to introduce United States Armed Forces into hostilities, or into situations where imminent involvement in hostilities is clearly indicated by the circumstances, are exercised only pursuant to (1) a declaration of war, (2) specific statutory authorization, or (3) a national emergency created by attack upon the United States, its territories or possessions, or its armed forces.

Sec. 3. The President in every possible instance shall consult with Congress before introducing United States Armed Forces into hostilities or into situations where imminent involvement in hostilities is clearly indicated by the circumstances, and after every such introduction shall consult regularly with the Congress until United States Armed Forces are no longer engaged in hostilities or have been removed from such situations.

Sec. 4. (a) In the absence of a declaration of war, in any case in which United States Armed Forces are introduced—

(1) into hostilities or into situations where imminent involvement in hostilities is clearly indicated by the circumstances;

(2) into the territory, airspace or waters of a foreign nation, while equipped for combat, except for deployments which relate solely to supply replacement, repair, or training of such forces; or

(3) in numbers which substantially enlarge United States Armed Forces equipped for combat already located in a foreign nation;

the President shall submit within 48 hours to the Speaker of the House of Representatives and to the President pro tempore of the Senate a report, in writing, setting forth—

(A) the circumstances necessitating the introduction of United States Armed Forces;

(B) the constitutional and legislative authority under which such introduction took place; and

(C) the estimated scope and duration of the hostilities or involvement.

(b) The President shall provide such other information as the Congress may request in the fulfillment of its constitutional responsibilities with respect to committing the Nation to war and to the use of United States Armed Forces abroad.

(c) Whenever United States Armed Forces are introduced into hostilities or into any situation described in subsection (a) of this section, the President shall, so long as such armed forces continue to be engaged in such hostilities or situation, report to the Congress periodically on the status of such hostilities or situation as well as on the scope and duration of such hostilities or situation, but in no event shall he report to the Congress less often than once every six months.

NOTES

CHAPTER II
How Did the United States Get Involved?

[1]U. S., Department of Defense, "United States-Vietnam Relations 1945–1967," IV, B.1, p. 145. (Hereinafter cited as the Pentagon Papers.) (New Delhi [Galbraith] message 9941 for the President, 21 November 1961)

CHAPTER III
The Situation in South Vietnam Deteriorates

[1]Pentagon Papers, IV, C.1, p. 47.

CHAPTER IV
The Tonkin Gulf Incidents

[1]CINCPAC message to JCS, 17 August 1964.

CHAPTER V
U. S. Involvement: Should It Deepen?

[1]Pentagon Papers, IV, C.2, p. ii.
[2]*Ibid.*, C. 3, pp. 45–46.
[3]Memorandum to the President from McGeorge Bundy, re: "The Situation in Vietnam," 7 February 1965.
[4]CINCPAC message to JCS, 17 February 1965.

CHAPTER VI
Rolling Thunder: On The Beginning

[1]Pentagon Papers, IV, C. 3, p. 66 (Saigon 2889 to SECSTATE, 8 March 1965).
[2]*Ibid.*, pp. 70–71.
[3]*Ibid.*, C.5, p. 125.
[4]*Ibid.*, C.3, pp. 91–92.
[5]*Ibid.*, p. 109.
[6]*Ibid.*, p. 97.

CHAPTER VII
A Halt to Bombing

[1]Pentagon Papers, IV, C.3, p. 112 (SECDEF 001900 of 11 May 1965).

CHAPTER VIII
The Concept of the Creeping Approach

[1]Pentagon Papers, IV, C.3, pp. 133–34.
[2]*Ibid.*, C.5, p. 94 (JCS Memorandum 457–65 to Secretary of Defense).
[3]*Ibid.*, C.7a, p. 8.
[4]*Ibid.*, C.1a, pp. 15–16 (Memorandum for the President, "Evaluation of the Program of Bombing North Vietnam," 30 July 1965).

CHAPTER IX
Bombing Suspended, Retreat from Reality

[1]Pentagon Papers, IV, C.7a, p. 21.
[2]*Ibid.*, p. 23.
[3]CINCPAC message to JCS, 12 January 1966

CHAPTER X
Off Again, On Again Pressures:
American Casualties Mount

[1]Pentagon Papers, IV, C.7a, p. 166.
[2]*Ibid.*, pp. 166–67.
[3]*Ibid.*
[4]CINCPAC message to Chairman of the JCS, 24 December 1966.

CHAPTER XI
Vigorous Action: Why Not?

[1]Pentagon Papers, IV, C.7b, p. 3.
[2]*Ibid.*, C.7a, pp. 179–80.
[3]*Ibid.*, C.7b, p. 1.

CHAPTER XIII
Naval Operations

[1]CINCPAC message to JCS, 1 February 1967.

CHAPTER XIV
The Tet Pause and the Guam Conference

[1]Pentagon Papers, IV, C.7b, p. 12.

CHAPTER XV
When We Negotiate: Keep the Pressure On

[1]Pentagon Papers, IV, C.7b, p. 13.
[2]CINCPAC message to JCS, 6 February 1967.

CHAPTER XVII
Strategy Debate in Washington

[1]Pentagon Papers, IV, C.7b, p. 25 (William Bundy Memorandum to Undersecretary of State, 1 May 1967).
[2]*Ibid.*, p. 29 (McGeorge Bundy letter to President Johnson, received 4 May 1967).
[3]*Ibid.*, (Chairman JCS Memo to the President, 5 May 1967).
[4]*Ibid.*, p. 33 (W. W. Rostow Memorandum, "U. S. Strategy in Vietnam," 6 May 1967).
[5]*Ibid.*, p. 50.
[6]*Ibid.*, p. 53.
[7]*Ibid.*, p. 54 (Robert S. McNamara Memorandum for the President, 20 May 1967, transmitting JCS Memorandum 286–67).
[8]*Ibid.*, (Chairman's Memorandum for the Secretary of Defense, "Alternative Courses of Action," 24 May 1967).
[9]*Ibid.*, p. 56 (JCS Memorandum 307–67, 1 June 1967).

CHAPTER XIX
The Stennis Hearings

[1]Pentagon Papers, IV, C.7b, p. 90.
[2]U. S., Congress, Senate, Preparedness Investigating Subcommittee of the Committee on Armed Services, hearings on the air war in Vietnam, 90th Congress, 1st sess., 9–10 August 1967, part I, p. 2.
[3]Pentagon Papers, IV, C.7b, p. 91.
[4]Ibid., pp. 93–98.
[5]Ibid., p. 98.
[6]Ibid., p. 99.
[7]Ibid., p. 101.

CHAPTER XX
Another Attempt to Negotiate . . . Restrictions Anew

[1]Pentagon Papers, IV, C.7b, p. 105.
[2]Ibid., p. 111 (JCS Memorandum for the Secretary of Defense, 17 October 1967).
[3]Ibid., p. 112.

CHAPTER XXI
Pressure to De-escalate

[1]Pentagon Papers, IV, C.7b, p. 116 (SEACABIN study report, 22 November 1967).
[2]Ibid., p. 126 (Paul C. Warnke Memorandum for the Secretary of Defense, 3 January 1968).

CHAPTER XXII
More Peace Feelers

[1]Pentagon Papers, IV, C.7b, p. 143 (Testimony of Secretary of Defense [designate] Clark M. Clifford before the Senate Committee on Armed Services, 25 January 1968).

CHAPTER XXIII
The Tet Offensive Erodes U. S. Peace Efforts

[1]Gen. William C. Westmoreland, *A Soldier Reports* (New York: Doubleday & Co., Inc., 1976), p. 332.

[2]Gen. Maxwell Taylor, *Swords and Plowshares* (New York: W. W. Norton & Co., Inc., 1972), p. 384.
[3]CINCPAC message to Chairman of the JCS, 3 March 1968.

CHAPTER XXIV
March 1968: The Debate

[1]Pentagon Papers, IV, C.7b, pp. 165–66.
[2]Gen. Maxwell Taylor, *Swords and Plowshares* (New York: W. W. Norton & Co., Inc., 1972), p. 391.

CHAPTER XXVIII
The December 1972 Bombing Campaign against North Vietnam

[1]W. Scott Thompson and Donald D. Frizzel, eds., *The Lessons of Vietnam* (New York: Crane, Russak & Co., Inc., 1967), p. 105.

INDEX

313

air strikes and mining, 3, 246
Dec. 1972, orders heavy air
strikes, 251
Jan. 1973, announces peace with
honor, 260
June 1973, Watergate problem,
262–64
Nolting, Ambassador Frederick E.,
15, 21
North Vietnamese invasion of 1972,
243–44

O'Brien, USS, 139
Oriskany, USS, 97

Paris Agreement of 1973, 259–63
Pearson, Sen. James B., 230
Pentagon Papers, 129–30
Percy, Sen. Charles H., 247
Philippines, Republic of, 16, 32
Phoumi Nosavan, 15
Phuc Loi, 143
Phuc Yen airfield, 49, 79, 102
·attacks on, 202
CINCPAC requests to attack,
163, 201–2
sanctuary area, 102
Phu Qui, 65
Pleiku, 56, 89, 91, 266
Poland, 3, 12
Policy, U. S. on Vietnam War. See
also Negotiations, attempts at;
Strategy, U. S. military
commitment of U. S. forces, 7,
16, 19, 39
to combat, 70–71
congressional action shapes,
262–64
criticism of,
by author, 1–4, 33–34, 70,
267–71
by JCS, 33, 120, 174
evolution from World War II to
1961, 5–19

national objectives, 19, 25, 28
in NSAM of Nov. 1963, 29;
NSAM 288, 31–32;
NSAM 328, 70–71
in Southeast Asia Resolution,
45–46
reviewed/studied, 51, 59–60,
171–72
recommendations concerning. See
CINCPAC; Joint Chiefs of
Staff. See also Ball, George
W.; McCone, John A.;
McNamara, Robert S.; Ros-
tow, Dr. Walt W.; Taylor,
Gen. Maxwell D.
redirected by President Johnson,
225
POL strikes, 109, 113, 116–19
Porter, Ambassador William J., 245
Port Wallut, 143
Press, leaks to, 117, 223
Prisoners of war (POWs), 1, 4, 247,
252, 254–58, 270

Quang Khe, 63, 64, 143
Quang Tri, 248, 266
Quat, Premier Phan Huy, 81, 84
Qui Nhon, 59, 91

Raborn, Vice Adm. William F.,
74–75
Radford, Adm. Arthur W., 230
Ranger, USS, 57
Republican Party, study group re-
port, 230–31
Restricted Areas. See China, Com-
munist, buffer zone;
Demilitarized Zone; Haiphong;
Hanoi
Ridgway, Gen. Matthew B., 223
Rolling Thunder operation: Nos.
1–4, 63; No. 5, 64; No. 6, 65;
No. 7, 67; No. 8, 69; Nos.
9–12, 77; No. 17, 85; No. 21,
102; No. 48, 111; No. 49, 111;